Early Daoist Hagiographies
早期上清仙傳

The Hsu-Tang Library of Classical Chinese Literature

Made possible by a generous gift from Hsin-Mei Agnes Hsu-Tang 徐心眉 and Oscar L. Tang 唐騮千, the Hsu-Tang Library presents authoritative, eminently readable translations of classical Chinese literature, ranging across three millennia and the entire Sinitic world.

Series Editors
Wiebke Denecke 魏樸和, *Founding Editor-in-Chief*
Lucas Klein 柯夏智, *Associate Editor*

Editorial Board
Cheng Yu-yu 鄭毓瑜
Wilt L. Idema 伊維德
Victor H. Mair 梅維恆
Michael Puett 普鳴
Xi Chuan 西川
Pauline Yu 余寶琳

Early Daoist Hagiographies
早期上清仙傳

The Revelations of Yang Xi and the *Inner Tradition of Han Emperor Wu*
楊羲所受啟示與《漢武帝內傳》

Translated by
J. E. E. Pettit and Matthew V. Wells
裴 玄 錚 與 馬 修 譯

Contents

Acknowledgments vii
Introduction viii

Traditions of Lord Pei, the Perfected Being of Pure Numinosity
清靈真人裴君傳
    Compiled by his disciple Deng Yunzi 鄧雲子 3

Traditions of Lord Su, Upper Chamberlain of the Mysterious
Continent 玄洲上卿蘇君傳
    Compiled by Zhou Jitong 周季通 67

Inner Tradition of Lord Wang, Perfected Being of Pure Vacuity
清虛真人王君內傳
    Compiled by his disciple Wei Huacun 魏華存,
        Lady of the Southern Sacred Peak 79

Inner Tradition of the Lady of the Southern Sacred Peak,
Primal Lord of Purple Vacuity 紫虛元君南嶽夫人內傳 101

Traditions of the Perfected Director of Destinies, Grand Prime Perfected
Being and Upper Chamberlain of the Eastern Sacred Peak
太元真人東嶽上卿司命真君傳
    Compiled by his disciple the Middle Marquis Transcendent
        Being Li Dao 李道, styled Anlin 安林 111

Inner Tradition of Han Emperor Wu 漢武帝內傳 149

Appendix: List of Titles from the Daoist Canon of the Zhengtong Era 241
Bibliography 245

OXFORD
UNIVERSITY PRESS

Oxford University Press is a department of the University of Oxford.
It furthers the University's objective of excellence in research, scholarship,
and education by publishing worldwide. Oxford is a registered trade mark of
Oxford University Press in the UK and in certain other countries.

Published in the United States of America by Oxford University Press
198 Madison Avenue, New York, NY 10016, United States of America.

© Oxford University Press 2026

All rights reserved. No part of this publication may be reproduced, stored in a retrieval system, or transmitted, in any form or by any means, without the prior permission in writing of Oxford University Press, or as expressly permitted by law, by license or under terms agreed with the appropriate reprographics rights organization. Inquiries concerning reproduction outside the scope of the above should be sent to the Rights Department, Oxford University Press, at the address above.

You must not circulate this work in any other form and you must impose this same condition on any acquirer.

Library of Congress Control Number is on file at the Library of Congress.

ISBN 978-0-19-758000-4

Printed by Sheridan Books, Inc., United States of America.

The manufacturer's authorised representative in the EU for product safety is Oxford University Press España S.A. of El Parque Empresarial San Fernando de Henares, Avenida de Castilla, 2 – 28830 Madrid (www.oup.es/en or product.safety@oup.com). OUP España S.A. also acts as importer into Spain of products made by the manufacturer.

Acknowledgments

First and foremost, the authors owe a debt of gratitude to Dr. Chao-jan Chang of Fu-jen University (Taipei), who introduced us to each other in 2014 and continued to advise us as we worked on this project. As our work progressed, we received guidance from many colleagues, whose insights improved these translations. We want to especially thank Terry Kleeman and Paul Kroll, who went above and beyond in offering their time and energy by reading significant portions of the manuscript. We are also grateful to Stephen Bokenkamp, Joshua Capitanio, Stephen Durrant, Stephan Kory, Manling Luo, Gil Raz, Thomas Smith, Michael Stanley-Baker, Dominic Steavu, and Liying Xu for their feedback on early drafts. We also wish to thank Robert Campany, Tyler Feezell, Shu-wei Hsieh, Naoki Hirose, Michael Ing, Xiaojing Miao, Michael Naprastek, Norifumi Sakai, Pierce Salguero, Anna Shields, and Tobias Zuern for comments and feedback along the way. And we are grateful for the editors of the Hsu-Tang series for their insights and careful editing of the final manuscript. All errors, oversights, and omissions remain our own. Finally, we would like to thank our partners, children, and pets for their never-ending support and love: Emily Yuhua Chang, Margaret McGladrey, Kaya Pettit, Leo Pettit, Myra Pettit, Alfie, Heike, and Mae.

Introduction

Many writers in medieval China, from approximately the third through tenth century, knew a great deal about the Daoist religion, not only because of the ubiquity of Daoist texts and practices during the period, but also because some of China's most famous literati were themselves Daoist initiates. Traces of Daoist practice are omnipresent in the imagery and themes of such writers, including China's most famous poet, Li Bai 李白 (701–762). Li developed a deep interest in Daoism in his teenage years, and at the age of twenty described his initiation as follows:

In heaven's capital city of white jade	天上白玉京
Are a twelve-story tower and five city walls.	十二樓五城
Transcendent beings rub my forehead,	仙人扶我頂
As I with knotted hair accept Long Life.[1]	結髮受長生

Here the poet imagines himself atop a tall tower in a heavenly city, the Jade Capital, named after a mountain by the same name, where heavenly beings known as transcendents stand over him. The speaker, referring to the hairstyle of a man who has come of age at twenty, then receives "long life," which also happens to be the name of one of the first esoteric texts that a Daoist would receive upon initiation, the *Register of Long Life* (*Changsheng lu* 長生籙).

Poems like Li Bai's are not reliable eyewitness accounts of rituals in medieval China, but these literary projections are valuable for understanding how writers imagined Daoist realms and their inhabitants. The images and themes of these literary works reflect rituals common among medieval Daoists, and Li's real-life experience with Daoism may have enhanced his poetic vision. Furthermore, Li's use of Daoist imagery resonates with many of his biographical details, including his travels to many mountains with connections to Daoism (such as Mt. Emei), his study of Daoist scriptures at Mt. Daitian, and his participation in Daoist fasts and ceremonies at Mt. Ziyun.

Beyond the genre of poetry, Daoist scriptures also served as sources of inspiration for narrative works, such as marvel tales (chuanqi 傳奇) and

---

1 Peng Dingqiu 1960, 1751.

novels, such as *Journey to the West* (*Xiyouji* 西遊記) and *Canonizations of the Gods* (*Fengshen yanyi* 封神演義).

This book presents five hagiographies written by fourth-century Supreme Purity (Shangqing 上清) Daoists, along with an early sixth-century narrative of the failed effort of Han Emperor Wu 漢武帝 (156–87 BCE) to achieve immortality. Taken together, these texts present one example of how Daoist ritual texts found expression in the production of popular literary forms in medieval China. The first five hagiographies were composed between 363 and 370 by the spiritual advisor Yang Xi 楊羲 (330–386), who was employed by his aristocratic patron Xu Mi 許謐 (303–376). Yang claimed that during nightly seances, gods called perfected beings (zhenren 真人) descended into his oratory at Mt. Mao (Maoshan 茅山) in southern China to reveal these narratives. The texts detail the trials human practitioners faced centuries earlier when they reached godhood through a repertoire of Daoist techniques. These accounts were cast in the voice of the gods' disciples, who had in turn become perfected beings by practicing the techniques learned from their masters. All these divine beings, Yang claimed, now lived and worked in a high stratum of heaven called Supreme Purity. Furthermore, the initial readers of the texts, Yang's clients Xu Mi and his family members, were thought to be destined to be reborn into the Supreme Purity heavens after death. This body of material came to be known collectively as the Supreme Purity. The five hagiographies at the beginning of this volume formed a key record of Supreme Purity practice. They include the *Traditions of Lord Pei, the Perfected Being of Pure Numinosity* (*Qingling zhenren Peijun zhuan* 清靈真人裴君傳), the *Traditions of Lord Su, Upper Chamberlain of the Mysterious Continent* (*Xuanzhou shangqing Sujun zhuan* 玄洲上卿蘇君傳), the *Inner Tradition of Lord Wang, Perfected Being of Pure Vacuity* (*Qingxu zhenren Wang jun neizhuan* 清虛真人王君內傳), the *Inner Tradition of the Lady of the Southern Sacred Peak, Primal Lord of Purple Vacuity* (*Zixu yuanjun nanyue furen neizhuan* 紫虛元君南嶽夫人內傳), and the *Traditions of the Perfected Director of Destinies, Grand Prime Perfected Being and Upper Chamberlain of the Eastern Sacred Peak* (*Taiyuan zhenren dongyue shangqing siming zhenjun zhuan* 太元真人東嶽上卿司命真君傳).

The Supreme Purity hagiographies were soon adapted into the popular medieval tale featured toward the end of this book, the *Inner Tradition of Han Emperor Wu* (*Han Wudi neizhuan* 漢武帝內傳). This story had begun circulating by the early to middle sixth century.[2] The author recounts the events of a night in 110 BCE when the Queen Mother of the West (Xiwangmu

---

2   The text is mentioned in *Essential Techniques for Commoners* (*Qimin yaoshu* 齊民要術). Bray 2015.

西王母) visited Emperor Wu, who had requested Daoist scriptures from the goddess to attain longevity. Though the emperor received the texts, he could not quell his carnal desires and murderous mind. The story ends with the emperor's palace in flames and a haunted graveyard where he was laid to rest, thus serving as a cautionary tale for others hoping to attain long life as a Daoist god or goddess. The story of Han Emperor Wu's divine encounter circulated among readers in Tang, Song, and Ming China. The narrative layers and psychological complexity of the *Inner Tradition of Han Emperor Wu* make it an important specimen of early narrative writing in China. Yet because its author borrowed and heavily adapted from Supreme Purity hagiographies, it is also one of the best early examples of how Daoist religious literature was understood and depicted in popular literature.

The translations of the following six texts thus give readers of Chinese literature key tools to explore the place of Daoist narratives in elite and popular literature in premodern China. There is already a considerable body of research on the literature of early China, largely focused on the classics, philosophical masters, historiography, and early poetry. Much of this research has examined elite literature in terms of its relationship to classical Confucian texts or as political allegory. Consideration of Daoist texts has often been limited to highlighting resonances with well-known Warring States (ca. 475–221 BCE) texts such as *Laozi* 老子 (also known as *Daode jing* 道德經) and *Zhuangzi* 莊子. But the imprint of Daoist religious traditions on Chinese literary history is quite vast, as evidenced by Daoist imagery in Tang poetry and the intersections between elite religious writing and popular daybooks.[3] Interest in religious Daoism extended beyond philosophical texts. Ritual texts such as the hagiographies translated in this volume were widely read and circulated in the late imperial era. The adaptation of these narratives into popular literature, such as the *Inner Tradition of Han Emperor Wu*, demonstrates the need for close attention to how the religious Daoist texts emerging after the Han dynasty informed the literary imagination of medieval and late imperial writers.

Historical and Cultural Context

The early medieval era was a time of immense social, economic, and cultural changes occurring between the end of the Han empire (220 CE) and the establishment of the Sui and Tang empires (581 and 618, respectively). The period began with the establishment of three independent kingdoms that emerged after the collapse of the Han political order, the kingdoms of Wei, Shu, and Wu. By the turn of the fourth century, these kingdoms had been absorbed by the Jin empire, which ultimately reconquered much of

---

3 Schafer 1981–1983; Schafer 1984; Kroll 1997; Harper 2017.

the territory that had been held by the Han. Political intrigue, civil war, and conflict with pastoral peoples who had settled in Han territory during the preceding centuries led to the collapse of the Jin state north of the Huai River in the early fourth century.

Elites fleeing the conflict established a revived Jin court at Jiankang 建康 (modern Nanjing) in the southeast, which became known as the Eastern Jin dynasty (317–420). The city of Jiankang became the capital of several successive empires in southern China until its destruction by the Sui in the sixth century. In the north, the Yellow River plains region would see the rise and fall of numerous smaller states during the so-called Sixteen Kingdoms period (ca. 304–439) and several large empires such as the Northern Wei (386–535) and Sui empires. These northern and southern dynasties saw new forms of political organization, demographic shifts, military and technological advancement, and the Sinicization of indigenous populations that were increasingly brought under centralized imperial rule.

While marked by warfare and change, the early medieval era was also one of extraordinary innovations in literature, the arts, and culture. As local elites acquired new power in the context of weakened centralized states, the literature and art of the period began to reflect concerns beyond court life. Lines of local patronage became increasingly important for political and social advancement. New styles of poetry emerged, defined by both formal features and content, tied to famous individuals or coteries of elite literati. Historical writing flourished, particularly the new genres of biography and local history. Geographical treatises focused less on the universal geography of large centralized states and more on regional sites.[4] The diffusion of writing and decline of traditional commentary on classical texts led to the increasing popularity of philosophical and political treatises, essays on literary theory, and quasi-historical writing such as strange tales (zhiguai 志怪) and accounts of filial children. Individual painters became well known in elite circles and calligraphy became a mature artform, flourishing with new styles.

Yang's hagiographies present several opportunities to deepen our understanding of the cultural history of this critical period. First, the texts reflect the development of communities of Daoist practitioners, who circulated new and authoritative texts that superseded Warring States and Han canonical literature. The hagiographies are valuable evidence for the practices of these early medieval religious communities, practices such as taboos, rituals, and the social lives of Daoist adepts. Second, these hagiographies preserve teachings that served as didactic material for the community of believers. They demonstrated to readers how one receives and uses

---

4 Felt 2021, 33–35.

scriptures, and they provided a template for the qualities of character and practice that marked one for success. In addition to outlining the contours of religious belief, they also attest to historical figures and events in ways that were sometimes reimagined or at odds with the accounts of imperially sanctioned historical texts. They thus testify to how different authors and audiences appropriated and deployed historical evidence and narrative, and the many ways that Chinese intellectuals of the period understood their political and social worlds. Third, these texts also provide us with innovative ways to approach early historiography and biographical writing of the period. Like the biographies found in standard histories, these materials have long since been divorced from their previous contexts and reinterpreted in forms suited to a new, broader audience. Thus, these narratives allow us to understand the editorial needs for and audience demands on such texts in a broader context during a period that witnessed extraordinary social, cultural, and literary changes.

Early Medieval Daoism

During this turbulent and innovative period, Daoist religious technologies emerged as practices that brought solace and peace to individuals and resulted in social cohesion and harmony. The Dao 道, literally "Way" or "Path," is often used to describe the total universe. It is what enveloped all creation before it came into being and will be all that remains once the world implodes upon itself in the great cosmic cycle of life. While there are many kinds of practices espoused by Daoist writers, nearly all of them share the goal of "returning to the Dao." This meant that a person should seek to reintegrate with the Dao and return to the cosmic beginning of the universe. Some Daoists even claimed that by returning to the Dao, they would reemerge in the universe when the Dao started its new cosmic cycle.

This notion of the Dao as the great cosmic framework enveloping our world, as well as the practices that help an individual connect to the Dao, had existed many centuries before Yang Xi's revelations. Descriptions of the Dao were articulated as far back as the fifth century BCE in books such as *Laozi* and *Zhuangzi*. *Laozi* was supposedly the product of Laozi, the "Old Master," identified by Sima Qian 司馬遷 (146–86 BCE) as a Zhou archivist. *Laozi* is a short collection of 81 stanzas in roughly 5,000 characters. *Zhuangzi*, an extremely influential text in Chinese literature, presents several important ideas taken up in later traditions, including those of the perfected person and the sage who lives life according to his understanding of the greater cosmic order. Both texts are broadly concerned with the ideas of nonaction (wu wei 無爲) and being natural or "self-so" (zi ran 自然), themes later taken up by the early medieval exegetes Wang Bi 王弼 (226–249) and Guo Xiang 郭象 (252–312). In the early Han dynasty,

Huang-Lao syncretists fused the figure of Laozi to the Yellow Emperor, Han cosmology, legalism, and early folklore to create a cosmological political order for the new empire. The *Master of Huainan* (*Huainanzi* 淮南子), by Liu An 劉安 (ca. 179–122), is often considered representative of this movement. However, as is clear from the first century writings of Wang Chong 王充 (27–97), "Daoism"—by incorporating transcendent beings, pacing the heavens, searching for immortality, and mountain rituals from Han-era masters of esoterica (fangshi 方士)—had coopted Liu An and his followers into a constellation of ideas and practices that foreshadowed the messianic movements of the second century.

Transcendent beings had for centuries been objects of reverence by both the imperial court and the general population. In the first and second centuries, local cults emerged that focused on individuals who had attained immortality or exhibited other miraculous abilities.[5] These practitioners were understood within the Qin and Han tradition of masters of esoterica—purveyors of marvelous methods to achieve longevity and immortality. Whereas classical practitioners and their methods were closely associated with the imperial court, by the early medieval era these techniques were popularized and theorized by a broader circle of literati, such as Ge Hong 葛洪 (283–343). His work on macrobiotics and alchemical techniques for immortality demonstrates both the popularity of the subject and the transmission of these techniques within lineages of practitioners.

By the second century CE, Daoists began to imagine the Dao as a deified, transformative force in human history, acting through avatars such as Laozi and others.[6] In 142 CE, Zhang Daoling 張道陵 (ca. 34–146) claimed to have been visited by the deified Laozi. Zhang's successors and followers, who became known as the Celestial Masters (Tianshi dao 天師道), established a theocratic state in Hanzhong 漢中 (present-day Sichuan Province), which fell to Cao Cao in 215. They subsequently scattered throughout eastern and southern China and spread Daoism to new communities. These messianic movements infused religion with political overtones. Leaders of these new Daoist institutions asserted the existence of a celestial bureaucracy that oversaw all human activity. One's actions were reported to these gods, and years were added or subtracted from one's lifespan on Earth according to one's virtues or transgressions. Initiation into a Daoist group meant that one would eventually serve in these celestial bureaucracies. A Daoist practitioner did not die, but underwent a transformation to be reborn as a god or goddess, with a position in the heavenly bureaucracy. The lack of early sources means we have only a vague understanding of the duties that

---

5   Raz 2012b, 39.
6   Bokenkamp 1997, 13.

each heavenly position entailed. In most cases, they are simply bureaucratic titles modeled after the political language of the imperial court. Daoist techniques, which ranged from meditative practices to ingesting medicinal brews and the so-called bedroom arts, all provided different paths toward this transformation from a human into a god.

One feature of medieval Daoism is that practitioners imagined that the entire macrocosm of the universe existed as a microcosm within the human body. An adept could travel vast distances by turning his gaze inward, and sometimes the name of a celestial palace simultaneously refers to a place in the heavens, a location within the human body, and a locale in subterranean realms. A practitioner could employ such an inner vision to communicate with a vast range of gods and goddesses occupying all corners of the universe. Unlike the deities of many other religious traditions, Daoist gods all were once human practitioners themselves. Throughout the translations in this book, readers will see gods tell stories about their own initiation and training in the Daoist arts. Even the Queen Mother of the West, a powerful goddess in the Daoist pantheon, will address in the final translation how she once studied with the Celestial King of Primordial Commencement (Yuanshi tianwang 元始天王) eons ago. Although Daoists view the pantheon of gods as hierarchical, with certain beings occupying positions of lofty importance, these positions of divine prestige were, at least in theory, attainable for the zealous and steadfast Daoist practitioner.

The Supreme Purity texts of the mid-fourth century encapsulate these cultural and religious trends. The aristocratic Xu 許 family who received the revelations lived in Jurong 句容 near Jiankang, the capital of the Eastern Jin. Through familial ties, they were proximate to traditions devoted to becoming gods through such practices as macrobiotics, alchemy, talismans, sacred texts, ritual, and visualization techniques. Xu Mai 許邁 (300–348), the eldest of the Xu family, was a disciple of Bao Jing 鮑靚 (ca. 260–330), Ge Hong's father-in-law, and was also a disciple of a Celestial Masters libationer. Some sources claim that he was an acquaintance of the eminent author of strange tale literature, Guo Pu 郭璞 (276–324), and knew the foremost calligrapher of the period, Wang Xizhi 王羲之 (ca. 321–379).[7] The Xu family were also enmeshed in patron-client relationships typical of their era, particularly with their patronage of two mediums who communicated to divine beings on their behalf. The first, Hua Qiao 華僑 (ca. 363), had previously transmitted the *Inner Tradition of the Perfected Purple Yang* (*Ziyang zhenren neizhuan* 紫陽真人內傳, *DZ* 303) of the deity Zhou

---

7 Espesset 2011, 1147.

Yishan 周義山 (also known as Zhou Jitong 周季通) before being dismissed and replaced by Yang Xi in 363.⁸

Very little is known about the life of Yang Xi himself. Like the Xu family, he too may have hailed from Jurong. Prior to being hired by Xu Mi, Yang appears to have traveled in communities of practitioners who exchanged esoteric texts and techniques.⁹ It should be noted that calling Yang the "author" of these texts only partly captures his presumed role in their composition. Yang's manuscripts were seen as supernatural reflections of the heavenly realms he accessed through nightly seances. To Yang's patrons and to later readers, these were revelations transmitted from the gods themselves; not only did Yang record his revelations in ecstatic verse, he also recorded the date of each revelation as well as the deity who revealed it. In the turbulent cultural milieu of the period, such revelations inspired enormous interest on the part of the literati class. The marvelous calligraphy, otherworldly quality of the poetry, recasting of earlier traditions of alchemy and visualization, and incorporation of gods into the new religious and literary contexts of the period would have appealed to the literati of southeast China during the fifth and sixth centuries.

Inner Traditions and the Literature of Early China

The translations of the following six texts give readers of Chinese literature key tools to explore the place of Daoist narratives in elite and popular literature in premodern China. The Supreme Purity hagiographies lie at the intersection of multiple cultural and literary trends of the early medieval period, chief among them developments in the genre of biography. While a rich tradition of biographical writing developed during the first century BCE following the completion of Sima Qian's monumental historical classic *Records of the Historian* (*Shiji* 史記), there was no specific Chinese equivalent to hagiography, which emerged in second century Europe. Most biographical texts, even those of divine beings, were labeled as *zhuan* 傳, which we translate as "tradition," but which can be understood in different contexts to mean memoir, biography, transmission, or commentary. As individual texts, *zhuan* were often veritable anthologies, merging biographical details with other materials, such as memorials, decrees, letters, poems,

---

8   Throughout this Introduction and the translations, we will refer to this and other texts from the Daoist canon by the text numbers assigned in Schipper and Verellen 2004, 1392–1440, hereafter referred to as *DZ*. A full list of the *DZ* titles used in this book is featured as an appendix.

9   In 350 he received the *Most High Prolegomena to the Five Numinous-Treasure Talismans* (*Lingbao wufu xu* 靈寶五符序, *DZ* 388) from Wei Huacun's eldest son, Liu Pu 劉璞. Espesset 2011, 1147.

prose, eulogies, and speeches by or about the subject into a life-narrative that served didactic purposes. When arranged together as an anthology, they were referred to as "arrayed traditions" (lie zhuan 列傳).

Beginning at the end of the first century BCE, these traditions were collected into anthologies organized around specific groups of people. One type of collection was traditions of transcendent beings (xian zhuan 仙傳). The two most well-known examples of such collections in early Chinese literary history are undoubtedly *Traditions of Arrayed Transcendents* (*Liexian zhuan* 列仙傳), often attributed to Liu Xiang 劉向 (77–6 BCE), and Ge Hong's *Traditions of Divine Transcendents* (*Shenxian zhuan* 神仙傳). These collections were didactic insofar as they purported to provide a case-by-case record of the quest for transcendence, longevity, and immortality in ways that could be understood and even be persuasive to readers of the period.[10] However, unlike the Supreme Purity biographies translated in this volume, neither collection reflects a single tradition of techniques or point of view on the topic of longevity; rather, they record a diverse range of individuals and methods spanning centuries, united only by the underlying assertion that transcendence and immortality are achievable.

There are two other forms of biographical writing that were also influential to Yang Xi's work: the "independent tradition" (biezhuan 別傳) and the "inner tradition" (neizhuan 內傳), which both proliferated during the Eastern Han (25–220) and early medieval periods. According to the "Bibliographic Treatise" ("Jingji zhi" 經籍志) of the *History of the Sui* (*Suishu* 隋書), independent traditions accounted for nearly a quarter of all the historical texts written before the early seventh century. Most of this material was concerned with prominent local figures, rather than officials at the central imperial court. These biographies were produced within the context of large, aristocratic families. Unlike earlier biographies, which were often collected together as arrayed traditions, independent traditions circulated individually to attract the patronage of powerful local elites. Their popularity reflects the growing interest among aristocratic clans in biographical narratives about elite individuals who possessed unique talents and qualities of character.

Only nine texts are designated as inner traditions in the "Bibliographic Treatise" of the *History of the Sui*, and all of them are concerned with prominent figures in Han and early medieval Daoism, such as Zhang Daoling and the legendary disciple of Laozi, Yinxi 尹喜. Five of the six hagiographies translated in this volume are also listed in the "Bibliographic Treatise" as inner traditions: those of Director of Destinies Mao Ying 茅盈 (Lord Mao 茅君), Wang Zideng 王子登 (Lord Wang), Pei Xuanren (Lord Pei), Wei

10 Campany 2002, 90–103.

Huacun, and Han Emperor Wu. The term "inner tradition" first appears in the context of Han period historiography, though in an unsystematic manner. The word "inner" (nei 內) could be used to refer to the core teachings of an author, while also having connotations of privacy or what is not made public. So "inner tradition" may have initially referred to texts that relied on a limited range of sources and were not widely circulated.[11] By the early medieval period, however, the term "inner" was increasingly associated with writing on esoteric topics. For example, Ge Hong referred to his writings on methods for longevity and transcendence as his *Inner Chapters* (neipian 內篇), in contrast to his *Outer Chapters* (waipian 外篇), which focused on political and social matters. In a similar fashion, the inner tradition in Daoism came to refer to esoteric biographies, such as those produced by Daoist mediums like Yang Xi or biographies that circulated within communities of Daoist practitioners, and connoted content beyond the concerns of both traditional historiography and earlier collected biographies of transcendent beings intended for a broader audience.[12]

Authors of inner traditions used the genre to provide a historiographic frame for texts, anecdotes, techniques, and other materials that were not well known, were esoteric, or were intended for a small community of readers. They drew upon earlier sources and often claimed to be a more comprehensive revelation that clarified earlier material. Figures from Warring States or Han texts who over time had become emblematic of specific practices of achieving longevity were incorporated into the narratives of later adepts and became one way in which authors consciously responded to and sublimated earlier techniques into new traditions, integrating the subject into a new textual and community context.[13] Thus we find Master Red Pine (Chi Songzi 赤松子), a divine official in charge of the rain in *Traditions of Arrayed Transcendents*, appearing to Lord Pei as a powerful Supreme Purity deity. This reimagined material subsequently circulated within the space of the initiated. However, unlike other forms of biography, which often wove together anecdotes, direct speech, and excerpts of writing from the subject, early readers interpreted Yang's work as a kind of divinely revealed autobiography dictated to human disciples. The primary appeal of these texts lay in their usefulness as collections of material that were divinely inspired and reinterpreted in the form of life narratives for new audiences. As biographies, they also served a commentarial function, demonstrating how one receives and uses scriptures through encounters with divine beings, while also providing models for esoteric practices of

---

11 Lagerwey 1975, x.
12 Pettit and Wells 2020, 8.
13 Pettit and Chang 2020, 29–54.

meditation, herbal and mineral drugs, and templates for the qualities of character and practice that marked one for success.

Yang Xi's inner traditions and the textual corpus of the Supreme Purity lineage initially circulated among a select group of Daoist initiates. When the Supreme Purity lineage enjoyed royal patronage during the Tang dynasty, however, these readers were often part of or had an intimate relationship with the highest levels of society. There is evidence that the hagiographies translated in this volume were incorporated into public records. Lady Wei, for example, was commemorated in the eighth century in a stele inscription written by the eminent statesman and calligrapher Yan Zhenqing 顏真卿 (709–785) at Linchuan 臨川 (in present-day Jiangxi), a text that has been translated and studied by Edward Schafer.[14] Several of the texts were also listed in medieval bibliographies, such as the *History of the Sui*, which was completed around 636. All of these hagiographies are featured in imperially sanctioned Song collectanea such as the *Seven Slips from a Cloudy Bookbag* (*Yunji qiqian* 雲笈七籤, DZ 1032), *Imperial Reader of the Taiping Era* (*Taiping yulan* 太平御覽), and *Extensive Records of the Taiping Era* (*Taiping guangji* 太平廣記). The inner tradition of Lord Pei, which is the longest of Yang Xi's extant hagiographies, was quite influential among later Daoist readers and writers, as seen from early imperial retellings of the text such as *Illustrations of the Flight of Most High Jade Dawn to the Sun and the Moon of Streaming Regalia and Knotted Spangles* (*Taishang yuchen yuyi jielin ben riyuetu* 太上玉晨鬱儀結璘奔日月圖, DZ 435), an illustrated version of Pei's inner tradition.

However, the most significant literary adaptation of Yang's hagiographies is found in the *Inner Tradition of Han Emperor Wu*. Unlike Yang's texts, which circulated among Daoist initiates, the *Inner Tradition of Han Emperor Wu* was a literary work well-known among a wider range of medieval readers. In his introduction to his French translation, Kristofer Schipper (1934–2021) collected much of the evidence that this story, while largely unknown today, was well known in the early medieval and Tang era. For example, the late Tang poet Li Shangyin 李商隱 (813–858) stated, "The Inner Tradition of the Han Emperor Wu exists perfectly; do not tell me that no one knows anything about it" 漢皇內傳分明在，莫道人間總不知.[15]

A century earlier, Li Bai wrote a poem testifying that he was familiar with the book and associated its contents with the history of King Mu of

---

14 Schafer 1977b.
15 In "Poem on the Bi-Jade City" ("Bicheng shi" 碧城詩) (Peng Dingqiu 1960, 6169).

An illustration of Lord Pei establishing communications with the heavens. Photo taken of *DZ* 435 from the edition housed in the Bibliothèque nationale de France (Richelieu). Photo by J. E. E. Pettit.

Zhou 周穆王, the sovereign who visited the Queen Mother on her mountain in the western regions:

> King Mu aspired to distant lands,
> and all powerful was the sovereign of the Han.
> Their hearts overflowed with limitless passions.
> How could a hero restrain his aspirations?
> One feasted with the Queen Mother of the West on the shores of the Western sea;
> The other, in the Northern pavilion, was greeted by the Lady of the Upper Prime.[16]

Still other poets of the Tang dynasty, such as Han Yu 韓愈 (768–824) and Li Qi 李頎 (fl. 742) also show familiarity with this text and produced literary works based upon it.[17] The *Inner Tradition of Han Emperor Wu* has been copiously borrowed from, and the book, at least in large excerpts, has been reproduced many times in literary encyclopedias. We can thus see the influence of Yang's hagiographies and the *Inner Tradition of Han Emperor Wu* on early Chinese historiography, public documents, poetry, and literary collections.

Literary Conventions

There are many literary tropes and features shared between the inner traditions written by Yang and the *Inner Tradition of Han Emperor Wu*. All of the texts revolve around interactions between human adepts and deities, both male and female. Interaction with divine beings and receiving from them texts and esoteric instruction are central to the adept's journey toward transcendence and apotheosis. Most of the texts include an elaborate description of a central heavenly being descending from the skies along with an entourage of servants and officials. Upon arriving, there is an exchange in which the god identifies himself as a guide and teacher to the adept. Such encounters are accompanied by the transmission of esoteric scriptures, which signals that the adept has taken the first step toward transcending the human body.

During these conversations the god often articulates the combination of mental qualities and previous deeds qualifying the adept to receive

---

16 "Ancient Airs" ("Gufeng" 古風), 43 (Peng Dingqiu 1960, 1677).
17 In Han Yu's writings, we find a short prose piece that contains elements of our story. See "A Miscellany on Reading Dongfang Shuo zashi" ("Du Dongfang Shuo zashi" 讀東方朔雜事 (Qu Shouyuan and Chang Sichun 1996, 924). In Li Qi's poetry, one poem titled "Song of the Queen Mother of the West" ("Wangmu ge" 王母歌) seems based entirely on the *Inner Tradition of Han Emperor Wu* (Peng Dingqiu 1960, 1349).

scriptures. The early efforts of adepts are diverse, but include seclusion and reading *Laozi* (Director of Destinies Lord Mao), seclusion and ritual practice (Lady Wei, Lady of the Southern Sacred Peak), and performing state rituals to please deities (Emperor Wu). All of the adepts, however, are sincere in their early efforts to "have a mind" (youxin 有心), a term used in contemporary Buddhism to refer to a sentient being's ability to discern and discriminate phenomena despite being in a world of attachments and desires. In these Daoist texts, the phrase emphasizes a person's diligence in striving toward a deep state of concentration and dedication to the Daoist path, no matter their life circumstances. Lady Wei, for example, was forced into marriage, and Emperor Wu had to run an empire, but the gods and goddesses applaud how they always "focused their thoughts" (yongsi 用思) and "longed" (huai 懷) to attain the Dao.

Yang and the author of the *Inner Tradition of Han Emperor Wu* also use the term "cinnabar" (dan 丹) to modify different nouns, sometimes describing the zealous intents of the adepts. Common compounds include "fervent mind" (danxin 丹心), "fervent spirit" (danshen 丹神), "heartfelt longing" (danhuai 丹懷), "heartfelt pain" (danku 丹苦), and "heartfelt sincerity" (dancheng 丹誠). At other times, *dan* describes the elixirs that adepts concocted in terms such as "elixir chamber" (danfang 丹房).

Central to the process of transcendence is the trope of receiving texts from the gods. In Yang's hagiographies, texts are rewards for achievement, signs of divine patronage, a guide to a higher circle of knowledge, the result of extensive practice, or a combination of these. The biographies of Lord Pei and Lord Wang contain extensive lists of texts transmitted to the adept, while Yang's other hagiographies list these texts in the course of the narrative. So central is textual transmission in Daoism that Li Bai describes it in the poem that opens this Introduction, and the Song dynasty *Seven Slips from a Cloudy Bookbag* devotes an entire section (fascicle 4) to the subject. The author of the *Inner Tradition of Han Emperor Wu* plays with this trope by turning divine texts into yet another object of Emperor Wu's ambition. Knowing well the power of textual transmission, the emperor begs, bullies, and finagles his way into receiving important Supreme Purity texts, even sparking an argument about the emperor's eligibility among the goddesses who provide them.

Other features in Yang's hagiographies are not found in the *Inner Tradition of Han Emperor Wu*. Most of Yang's narratives include details about the family background and upbringing of the adepts. Many of these families occupied a peripheral or liminal position in society: Lord Mao's family was from an insignificant branch of the Ji clan, Lord Pei grew up on the northwestern frontier, and Lord Wang's family was Sogdian. As children or young adults, most of the Supreme Purity adepts encountered resistance or pushback from their families for their desire to become Daoist adepts. Both Lord Wang and Lady Wei were forced into arranged marriages preventing them from pursuing their true calling as an ascetic. Lord Mao was even physically beaten by his father, who saw his life as a recluse as an unfilial act. All of the adepts in Yang's inner traditions feel the tension of human responsibilities, either as a wife (Lady Wei), a local official (Lord Pei), a husband (Lord Wang), or a son (Lord Mao), and a turning point in the narratives comes when they break free from the constraints of human society to devote their full attention to Daoist practice.[18]

Yang's inner traditions also include details about Daoist practice that enabled adepts to become gods and goddesses. Most of the adepts practiced in places called chambers (shi 室), oratories (jingshi 靜室), or hermitages (jingshe 精舍). This focus on meditation indoors resonates with Yang's other revelations featured in *Declarations of the Perfected* (*Zhen'gao* 真誥, DZ 1016), in which he tries to convince his patrons to build a compound at Mt. Mao to engage in similar arts.[19] All of these texts culminate in the arrival of divine masters who impart esoteric books to adepts. In Yang's inner traditions, bestowal of texts is coupled with the adept receiving a new name and heavenly posts. Scriptures are not simply containers of knowledge, but also symbols of office. Many adepts (Pei, Mao, Wang) are also described as engaging in celestial travel and roaming the universe as Daoist gods prior to assumption of their celestial duties.

History of the Inner Traditions and Its Editions

Whereas some religions like Christianity and Islam have fixed scriptures, Daoist texts have always been in a state of flux. Scriptures have been altered, adapted, and revised, and one title might designate two completely different texts. Even during Yang Xi's tenure as the Xu family's spiritual advisor, information about the life and the texts associated with a god or goddess was released and circulated in a piecemeal fashion. Typically, Yang would assert these details in short pronouncements, and the details would be collated in an inner tradition and later spun into a scripture. All three kinds of texts share information and build upon one another in creative ways.

There are no extant manuscripts that survive from Yang's time as an advisor. We do, however, have evidence from a few different late-fifth-century collections compiled by Gu Huan 顧歡 (425–479) and Tao Hongjing 陶弘景 (456–536) that give us a sense of how these different manuscripts

---

18 Conversely, this is the reason that Emperor Wu ends up as a failure in his story, for he cannot break free from the fleshly desires and attachments of being emperor.
19 Yoshikawa Tadao 1987; Tuzuki Akiko 1995; Pettit 2013b.

circulated a century after Yang's death.[20] The most useful collection to study the circulation of these texts is Tao's *Declarations of the Perfected*, in which he writes at length about his collection and evaluation of Yang's manuscripts. He often notes in the commentary which inner traditions existed before and during Yang Xi's time writing for the Xu family. Tao also includes details about other medieval writers, such as Wang Lingqi 王靈期 (fl. 404), who used information from the inner traditions to fabricate new scriptures.

While there are a few Tang dynasty versions of the inner traditions (see *Traditions of the Perfected Director of Destinies, Grand Prime Perfected Being and Upper Chamberlain of the Eastern Sacred Peak*, the traditions of Lord Mao, below), most of these are abridged versions of the text. The earliest and most complete versions of these hagiographies are included in the late-tenth-century *Seven Slips from a Cloudy Bookbag*. This collection of Daoist texts grew out of Song imperial efforts to create a Daoist canon. Song Taizong (939–997) ordered a compilation of Daoist writings during his reign, and in 990 appointed various officials to the task of collating the collected material. In 1010, Taizong's third son and successor, Emperor Zhenzong (968–1022), ordered a new recension of this collection to be overseen by Wang Qinruo 王欽若 (962–1025). The catalog for this collection, titled *Comprehensive Register of Precious Literature* (*Baowen tonglu* 寶文統錄) was presented to the emperor in 1016.[21] The collation and recopying of the texts took three more years and was overseen by Zhang Junfang 張君房 (ca. 960–1040), who supplemented the initial catalog with additional texts drawn from collections in Jiangsu, Zhejiang, and Fujian.[22] Seven copies of this final canon, titled *Precious Canon of the Heavenly Palace of the Great Song* (*Da Song tiangong baozang* 大宋天宮寶藏), were presented to the emperor in 1019.

Zhang subsequently selected texts out of this material and compiled them into a second collection, which he called the *Seven Slips from a Cloudy Bookbag*. He presented this collection to the court as a tribute to Emperor Zhenzong so that the emperor could "peruse it in the second watch of the night" 乙夜之覽.[23] Of the 122 fascicles, biographies comprise fifteen (103–117), though biographical narratives can be found throughout the collection. For example, our text for the Lady Wei biography is drawn from fascicle 4 in which Lady Wei's hagiography is embedded within a treatise concerning the transmission of scriptures.

20 Pettit and Chang 2020, 101–120.
21 Boltz 2011, 292.
22 *DZ* 1032, 1.2b.
23 *DZ* 1032, 1.2b.

The earliest extant edition of the *Seven Slips from a Cloudy Bookbag* is found in the Ming dynasty (1368–1644) *Daoist Canon of the Zhengtong Era* (*Zhengtong daozang* 正統道藏), compiled in 1445 under the first reign of Ming Emperor Yingzong (1427–1464). We used this edition as our base text. Other editions provided us with useful notes and textual variants. In particular, we have consulted the edition published by Zhonghua shuju (fourth edition, 2012) and edited by Li Yongcheng 李永晟. This edition uses the *Daoist Canon of the Zhengtong Era*, collated by Shanghai Commercial Press in the early twentieth century as its base text. Li and the editors compared this text to two other primary editions for variants: the Ming period *Seven Slips from a Cloudy Bookbag*, collated by Zhang Xuan 張萱 (ca. 1558–1641) and preserved in the first edition of the *Collected Works of the Fourfold Classification* (*Sibu congkan* 四部叢刊, 1919–1922), and those parts of the *Seven Slips from a Cloudy Bookbag* found in the Qing period *Collected Essentials of the Daoist Canon* (*Daozang jiyao* 道藏輯要), collated by Peng Dingqiu 彭定求 (1645–1719).[24]

Unlike Yang's hagiographies, which exist in fragments, the *Inner Tradition of Han Emperor Wu* has multiple extant versions. Kristofer Schipper has compiled the various versions where late imperial bibliographers have studied the text.[25] As noted above, the "Bibliographic Treatise" in the *History of the Sui* lists the *Inner Tradition of Han Emperor Wu* in three fascicles, but does not name an author.[26] The bibliographies of the tenth-century *Old History of the Tang* (*Jiu Tangshu* 舊唐書) and the Song dynasty *New History of the Tang* (*Xin Tangshu* 新唐書) also list the text, but not as an *Inner Tradition* and only in two fascicles.[27] By the Song dynasty, the name of the historiographer Ban Gu 班固 (32–92) appears as the author of this book. This attribution never garnered support from critics and appears to be based on a confusion of the work with a text titled *Tales of Han Emperor Wu* (*Han Wudi gushi* 漢武帝故事), also wrongly attributed to Ban Gu. More recent scholarship has linked the development of this inner tradition with other similar stories in circulation.[28]

---

24 See the "Foreword" ("Qianyan" 前言) to Li Yongcheng 2012 for a thorough discussion of the editing process of this edition of the text.
25 For a list of the relevant late imperial studies, see Schipper 1965, 4 n. 5.
26 Wei Zheng 1973, 979.
27 The *Old History of the Tang*, "Treatise on Classics and Texts" ("Jingji zhi" 經籍志), fascicle 46, lists the *Tradition of Han Emperor Wu* in two fascicles (Liu Xu 1975, 2004). The *New History of the Tang*, "Treatise on Art and Texts" ("Yiwen zhi" 藝文志), records a text with the same title in two fascicles (Ouyang Xiu 1975, 1519), as well as a text titled *Tales of Han Emperor Wu* 漢武帝故事 (Ouyang Xiu 1975, 1473). The relationship between these texts and the *Inner Tradition* listed in the *History of the Sui* is unclear.
28 Smith 1992; Liu Yuan-ju 2000.

Our translation uses the version included in the *Daoist Canon* as its base text. This text has thirty-one folios and contains no internal division into chapters or paragraphs.²⁹ This recension is more complete, twice as long as the story first included in *Extensive Records of the Taiping Era* and was subsequently included in many later literary collections. Another version, equally very abridged, is preserved in *Further Conversations* (*Xutan zhu* 續談助), by Chao Zaizhi 晁載之 (late 11th c.). Apart from a few scattered passages in encyclopedias (especially the *Imperial Reader of the Taiping Era*), most early versions exist in the *Daoist Canon*.³⁰ Moreover, an apocryphal text (weishu 緯書) traditionally considered a work of the Han dynasty annotated by Zheng Xuan 鄭玄 (127–200), the *Book of Documents: Periods for Imperial Verification* (*Shangshu diyanqi* 尚書帝驗期), which is now lost, but which was cited in the *Imperial Reader of the Taiping Era*, contained a long passage of the *Inner Tradition of Han Emperor Wu*.³¹ The most well-known critical edition of this text belongs to Qian Xizuo 錢熙祚 (1801–1844) in the 1844 *Collection from the Mt. Shou Pavilion* (*Shoushan ge congshu* 守山閣叢書).³² It is based on the version of the *Daoist Canon*, completed and corrected with the aid of the versions of *Extensive Records of the Taiping Era*, as well as other citations in *Further Conversations*. This latter edition is the base text that Schipper and Smith use in their translations, as discussed below.

Previous Translations

With the exception of the *Inner Tradition of Han Emperor Wu*, none of the texts in this volume have been translated into a modern language in their entirety. Various sections of these narratives (and their source materials) have been studied and partially translated by earlier scholars, and we have

---

29 The *Daoist Canon* version is missing a section at the beginning that can be found in *Extensive Records of the Taiping Era* (Li Fang 2003, 13). This passage foretells the birth of Emperor Wu with two dreams by his predecessor, Han Emperor Jing (Liu Qi 劉啟, 188–141 BCE): one of a red boar that descends from the clouds and goes straight into the Pavilion of Sublime Fragrance, the other a dream of a divine woman who offers Wu's mother the sun to eat.

30 See *Numinous Treasure Great Rites of the Book of Universal Salvation* (*Lingbao wuliang duren shangjing dafa* 靈寶無量度人上經大法, DZ 219) 21.1a–7b; *Continuation of the Comprehensive Mirror of the Transcendents Who Embodied the Dao through the Ages* (*Lishi zhenxian tidao tongjian houji* 歷世真仙體道通鑑後集, DZ 298), 1.13a–18b; *Records of the Assembled Transcendents of the Fortified Walled City* (*Yongcheng jixian lu* 墉城集仙錄, DZ 783), 1.13a–18b; *Introductory Treatises to the True Forms of the Five Sacred Peaks* (*Wuyue zhenxing xulun* 五嶽真形序論, DZ 1281), 1a–8a.

31 Li Fang 1967, 3081 (661.1a–2b).

32 The *Collection from the Mt. Shou Pavilion* is reproduced in the *Compendium of Collected Works* (*Congshu jicheng* 叢書集成) (Wang Yunwu 1935, 3436).

relied on this body of research to guide our own translation. Chief among these earlier studies is the research of Robert F. Campany, who has extensively studied the social and cultural world in which these texts circulated and were understood.[33] Another guidepost in translating these texts was Isabelle Robinet's work on Supreme Purity Daoism. Most notably, Part B of volume 2 of *La Révélation du Shangqing dans l'histoire du Taoisme* (1984), in which Robinet studies the interplay of various recensions of these texts, was instrumental in helping us to recover the meaning of these hagiographies. Robinet's close attention to how the titles and content of the inner traditions resonate with the extant Supreme Purity scriptures and ritual manuals was most important in this regard.[34]

Previous translations of parts of the *Traditions of Lord Pei* include Gil Raz's study of the second of Zhi Ziyuan's divine formulas, Monica Esposito's analysis of the techniques for visualizing the sun and moon deities, and our analysis of the text's structure.[35] Chang Chao-jan's analysis of Lord Pei's Five Numen method was also extremely useful in understanding the relationships between the ritual techniques described in this hagiography and those in other extant scriptures.[36] Portions of the *Traditions of Lord Su* have been previously translated by Jonathan Pettit and Chang Chao-jan in their study *A Library of Clouds: The Scripture of the Immaculate Numen and the Rewriting of Daoist Texts* (2020).[37] The hagiography of the deity Zhou Yishan, the *Inner Tradition of the Perfected Purple Yang*, which tells the story of Su Lin 蘇林 from Zhou's point of view, overlaps with the *Tradition of Lord Su* in significant ways. This text has been translated by James Miller (2008) and Manfred Porkert (1979).[38] Dominic Steavu's study of Lord Wang and the *Writ of the Three Sovereigns* (*Sanhuang wen* 三皇文) addresses many of the problematic issues with Lord Wang's identity and his relationship to other deities and texts in the Supreme Purity scriptures.[39] Edward Schafer translated and annotated a stele by Yan Zhenqing 颜真卿 (709–785 CE) inscribed with an abbreviated hagiography of Wei Huacun based on Tang-period sources.[40] An ambitious dissertation by Xie Conghui (1999) reconstructs the Wei Huacun hagiography from extant fragments and versions of the text.

---

33 Campany 2002, 326–328, 549; Campany 2014, 58 n. 68.
34 Robinet 1984, 2.365–405; see also Strickmann 1981, 62–66; Kroll 2003; Bokenkamp 1996; Bokenkamp 2007; Chang Chao-jan 2008.
35 See Raz 2008, 101–102; Esposito 2004, 355–356; Pettit and Wells 2020, 8–21.
36 See Chang Chao-jan 2012, 113–115.
37 See Pettit and Chang 2020, 29–54.
38 Miller 2008; Porkert 1979.
39 Steavu 2009, 130–138.
40 Schafer 1977b, 129–137.

There are five variants of the Mao Ying hagiography that have been at least partially translated into Western languages. In addition to the hagiography collected by Ge Hong and translated by Robert Campany mentioned above, there is the translation by Alan J. Berkowitz of the Mao Ying hagiography found in the *Record of Occultists* (*Xuanpin lu* 玄品錄, *DZ* 781), written ca. 1350, in Donald Lopez's edited volume *Religions of China in Practice* (1996).[41] Suzanne E. Cahill has translated the account of Mao Ying written by Du Guangting 杜光庭 (850–933 CE) in his *Records of the Assembled Transcendents of the Fortified Walled City* (*Yongcheng jixian lu* 墉城集仙錄, *DZ* 783). Her translation appears in her *Transcendence and Divine Passion* (1993), which Cahill describes as closely following the hagiography of Mao Ying found in fascicle 5 of the *Monograph on Mt. Mao* (*Maoshan zhi* 茅山志, *DZ* 304), compiled in the early 1300s by Liu Dabin 劉大彬, the forty-fifth Supreme Purity patriarch.[42] Kristopher Schipper provides a useful breakdown of where the *Inner Tradition of Han Emperor Wu* borrows liberally from the hagiography of Mao Ying in his *L'Empereur Wou des Han dans la légende taoïste* (1965).[43] Thomas Smith (1992) furthers this analysis and provides a summary of Mao Ying's encounter with the Queen Mother of the West.[44]

Unlike Yang Xi's hagiographies, which have been translated only in pieces, we are fortunate to have two full translations of the *Inner Tradition of Han Emperor Wu*, one into French by Kristofer Schipper and another into English by Thomas E. Smith. Both Schipper and Smith use the 1844 version of the text collated by Qian Xizuo, which is slightly longer as it includes more information at the beginning of the story about the emperor's life prior to meeting the Queen Mother of the West. We chose the version included in the *Daoist Canon* (*DZ* 292) to give readers access to a different version of the text. In many places, we refer to Schipper's and Smith's different versions, especially in places where they have developed a different translation strategy. Our translation of the Yang Xi material at the beginning of this book often gave us a distinct perspective on how best to render the story of Han Emperor Wu into English.

Conventions of the Translation

Throughout this book, we have rendered titles, place names, and most Daoist images in English translation rather than as transliterations or loose

---

41 Berkowitz 1996, 446–470.
42 Cahill 1993, 183–186.
43 Schipper 1965, 16–17.
44 Smith 1992, 197–199.

transliterations, what Edward Schafer once called the "uncooked and indigestible lumps in the Sinological puddings."[45] In accordance with the editorial guidance for the Hsu-Tang series, we use transliterated pinyin names for earthly cities and mountains, for example, Jurong 句容 and Mt. Mao 茅山. But for fantastic places imagined to exist in heavenly or otherworldly locations, we translate place names such as Ziwei gong 紫微宮 as Purple Tenuity Palace rather than as Ziwei Palace or Ziwei gong. In our translation we do not italicize basic Chinese and Daoist concepts well known to students of Daoist sources (terms such as yin-yang, Dao, qi), as these terms are widely understood among English speakers. Another key term is *zhi* 芝, which we translate as mushroom. Elsewhere translated as polypore, fungus, excrescence, cryptogam, or plant—*zhi* (mushrooms) are plants with divine energies that Daoist hermits and alchemists sought to locate and ingest.[46]

With translations of Daoist words, we follow the conventions most commonly used by historians of Daoism, even where we find recent translations more appealing.[47] We translate the term *cun* 存 as "visualize" rather than "actualize," even though the latter term conveys more accurately the way practitioners manifested divine beings in their immediate presence. We feel visualization is a more accessible and broadly used concept. The only major break from previous studies is our translation of Shangqing as Supreme Purity rather than Upper Clarity, Upper Purity, or Supreme Clarity, as *qing* 清 is a word that contrasts with "sullied" (hui 穢) and *shang* means merely high, not the highest, as there are even higher levels of heaven, such as Jade Purity (Yuqing 玉清).

For translations of medieval terms, we have relied heavily on Paul Kroll's *Student's Dictionary of Classical and Medieval Chinese* (2015), which features not only literary words, but also esoteric Daoist terms, some of which have their locus classicus in the texts we translate. In instances where clusters of words have overlapping translations, we have tried to be consistent in maintaining the same translations across the different texts. For example, *chi* 赤 is rendered "red," *zhu* 朱 as "vermillion" and *jiang* 絳 as "scarlet." We avoid marking any graphic variants that do not affect the basic meaning in Chinese or its English translation. Examples include *zai* 災 for *zai* 灾, *wu* 無 for *wu* 无, *qi* 炁 for *qi* 氣. We have marked true variant characters found in other texts in the endnotes at the end of each chapter.

---

45 Schafer 1954, 251.
46 Campany 2002, 27–29; Stanley-Baker 2013, 169–175.
47 An example is *zhenren* 真人, for which we follow the prevailing English translation of "perfected being," though we are tempted to use "true being" (see Andersen 2019, 53–63).

We have not made a critical edition of these texts, but rather have translated just one recension. We also followed the Hsu-Tang series editors' recommendation to use Hucker's *Dictionary of Official Titles in Imperial China* (1985), but when necessary have also consulted Michael Loewe and Michael Rogers for more obscure official titles from the Han and early medieval periods.[48] For measure words, with their rough English equivalents, we follow the translations of Endymion Wilkinson in *Chinese History: A Manual*: "mile" for *li* 里, "foot" for *chi* 尺, "inch" for *cun* 寸, and so forth.

Throughout the notes of this translation, we refer to texts from the *Daoist Canon of the Zhengtong Era* (hereafter referred to as "*DZ*") by the text numbers assigned to them in Schipper and Verellen. This provides a succinct and accurate way to indicate intertextual references to the Daoist canon without repeating the lengthy and sometimes confusing titles of the texts. A full list of the *DZ* titles used in this book is featured as an appendix. We have followed the English translations of titles suggested by Schipper and Verellen with minor changes. Page numbers are given for traditional pagination, with the right side of a folio labeled "a" and the left side as "b."

Synopses of Texts in This Volume

Below we present a summary of the hagiographies in this volume to guide the reader. In arranging the texts, we place our translation of Yang Xi's inner traditions first to introduce the reader to the literary conventions of the Daoist hagiographies prior to their adaptation in the *Inner Tradition of Han Emperor Wu*. We lead with the hagiography of Lord Pei because it was first mentioned during Hua Qiao's tenure as the spiritual advisor of the Xu family. It likely was adapted rather than composed by Yang Xi. The remainder of the hagiographies we place in chronological order, based on when the gods or goddess appeared to Yang Xi.

Traditions of Lord Pei, the Perfected Being of Pure Numinosity

Pei Xuanren, or Lord Pei, was one of the two gods who bestowed revelations on Hua Qiao in the late 350s or early 360s, when Hua claimed that he had made contact with two spiritual beings who served as his informants, the other being Zhou Yishan. A fifth-century postface to Zhou's hagiography, the *Inner Tradition of the Perfected Purple Yang*, indicates that Lord Pei had begun dictating his hagiography to Hua Qiao before Xu Mi fired the medium. This makes it likely that existing parts of the hagiography were revised and adapted by Yang Xi after he became the Xu family's new medium in 363. Lord Pei remained part of the group of gods who

---

48 Loewe 2000; Rogers 1968.

continued to appear to Yang Xi.[49] According to Tao Hongjing, the entire fifth fascicle of revelations in the *Declarations of the Perfected* were from Lord Pei.

This hagiography begins with Lord Pei's pilgrimage to a Buddhist monastery on the northwestern frontier of China. During this pilgrimage, Pei meets a master of meditative and pharmacological arts, Zhi Ziyuan 支子元, who details five esoteric rituals thought to enable Pei to extend his life by hundreds of years. Most of these techniques were meditative exercises to be conducted in a private chamber. Pei practices these techniques for two decades, at which time a transcendent accompanied by seven jade lads and seven jade maidens descends into Pei's courtyard. The transcendent identifies himself as Master Red Pine and informs Pei that he should cease practicing all of the techniques he had previously learned, in order to focus his efforts on one technique, visualization of the Five Numina (wuling 五靈). This ritual involved invoking the names of the five directional gods and then causing them to appear through meditation. Through contact with these gods, a practitioner could obtain a perfected Dao and undergo transfiguration as a perfected being. Once Red Pine conveys this directive, he disappears and has no further relationship or communication with Pei.

In the wake of his visit from Red Pine, Pei retires from official life and dedicates himself to the Five Numina method, embracing the well-worn trope of retirement and seclusion that permeates the life narratives of Daoist adepts. Eventually, Pei feigns a fatal illness, then leaves to settle in a mountain cave. He practices meditation on the Five Numina for twenty-two years, during which time five gods dressed in turbans of different colors pay him a visit. Each of these gods give him scriptures and esoteric foodstuffs. He reads all of these scriptures and consumes the foods. Three months later, these gifts enable Pei to travel vast distances across the universe and give him godlike powers to command demons to do his bidding. He then roams throughout the world, and when he returns to his cave, a god appears and gives him an esoteric scripture.

Pei then travels westward across drifting sands to the shores of a river flowing from the Kunlun Mountains 崑崙山, far to the west of China. Upon arriving at the riverbank, Pei encounters a divine being who informs him of the final techniques for achieving perfection. Pei practices these techniques for eleven years and then embarks on a long cosmic journey, during which he encounters other divine beings. In the end, Pei is invested as a perfected being.

---

49 Lord Pei recited parts of *Scripture of the Most High Treasure God* (*Taishang baoshenjing* 太上寶神經), and on July 27, 365, revealed bodily practices through Yang. See *DZ* 1016, 9.6a–9a. See Kroll 2003, 159.

Pei's life narrative is followed by three sections containing additional information concerning Lord Pei. First is a brief description of Mt. Xixuan 西玄山, the place where Pei is thought to now rule as a perfected being. There is a description of the peaks' measurements and their palaces and grottos, as well as the distances between them. Second is a description of techniques for refined contemplation revealed by Master Jiang 蔣先生 to Zhi Ziyuan, Pei's first master at the monastery. Third is a brief outline of the benefits of conducting Daoist practices in a private chamber.

After this, the author provides more information about the teachings Lord Pei received from Zhi Ziyuan. All of these teachings focus on methods to be performed on the Eight Nodal Days (bajie ri 八節日), that is, the equinoxes, solstices, and the first day of each of the four seasons. The writer includes a pastiche of quotes from many scriptures to bolster and expand on Zhi's claims about the efficacy of the autumnal equinox. An adept must find a remote place to seek absolution for his transgressions, a circumstance underscoring the solitary nature of many of these methods. The writer concludes by reiterating the importance of the equinox as the day of "autumnal judgment" (qiupan zhi ri 秋判之日), the "day of distinguishing life and death" (shengsi zhi ri 生死之日).

This is followed by a lengthy elaboration of Pei's training, the eleven years of practice that completed his transformation. This section represents a significant addendum to the earlier text. The two methods discussed in this section complement one another. The first involves meditating with the power of solar rays and the Five Imperial Sun Lords 五帝日君. The second employs the power of lunar rays to draw near the Five Imperial Lunar Ladies 月中五帝夫人. The centerpiece of these rituals are the two texts *Most High Writs of the Streaming Regalia* (*Taishang yuyi wen* 太上鬱儀文) and the *Most High Stanza on Knotted Spangles* (*Taishang jielin zhang* 太上結璘章).[50]

The hagiography concludes with a list of the books that Pei acquired over his lifetime and two recipes that he received early in his training. The first recipe is for *Wolfiporia extensa*, or poria (fuling 茯苓), a fungal body growing on the roots of pine trees. The second is for preparing *huma* 胡麻, a term that was used in medieval China to refer to a number of different plants, most commonly sesame (*Sesamum orientale*) or flax (*Linum usitatissimum*).[51]

---

50 For a detailed discussion of these rituals from this hagiography, see Esposito 2004, 355–356.
51 For more information on and relevant studies of *fuling* and *huma*, see Pettit and Wells 2020, 20–21.

Traditions of Lord Su, Upper Chamberlain of the Mysterious Continent

Su Lin was the alleged teacher of Zhou Yishan, known in this text as Zhou Jitong 周季通. The biography is dictated in Zhou's voice. Thus, some of the information contained in the following biography is also found in the *Inner Tradition of the Perfected Purple Yang*. Some of this information may therefore originate with the earliest revelations of the Supreme Purity tradition. However, the version found in the 104th fascicle of the *Seven Slips from a Cloudy Bookbag*, translated below, lacks the formulas and meditation techniques found in the biography of Su Lin as preserved in Zhou's hagiography and other sources.[52] This biography is the shortest text presented in this collection.

The hagiography begins with a brief description of Su's ambitions and subsequent travels. In the state of Zhao 趙, he takes Master Qin Gao 琴高先生 as his teacher. Although he learns macrobiotic techniques and meditative practices from Qin Gao, his ambitions lead him to a new teacher, Master Qiu 仇先生 of Mt. Hua 華山, described as a transcendent being. From Master Qiu, Su learns a ritual for nourishing his spiritual embryo and a method for returning his spirit and guarding his cloud-soul (hun 魂), a kind of soul that was thought to exist in the human body while alive, but that would rise into the heavens after death. However, Qiu claims that Su is already destined to become a transcendent and so sends him to yet another teacher, Juanzi 涓子, who is also a perfected being.

From Juanzi, Lord Su learns how to eliminate the Three Corpses (sanshi 三尸) and grain worms (guchong 穀蟲), parasitic beings and demonic creatures that feed off the human body. They are present in the human body at birth and reside in the three bodily regions (head, heart, abdomen). They are imagined to invite disease-causing agents into the body and report a host's transgressions. Eliminating them from the body results in long life. The text includes a lengthy description of the Three Corpses, their names, and what they attack in the body. It then describes the pills to expel the worms and the order in which they should be taken. Juanzi is then summoned to fill a celestial office, and Lord Su finds in his chamber a text outlining other techniques and details about Juanzi's journey to become a perfected being. The author of the text then defines a few of the terms found in the text Juanzi left for Lord Su, and then recounts Su's travels and efforts to attain perfection. Shortly before he ascends, Lord Su is said to be selling straw shoes in the marketplace, which is the point in the *Inner Tradition of the Perfected Purple Yang* when Zhou Jitong encounters Su.

---

52 Robinet 1984, 2.367.

Lord Su ascends in broad daylight and the hagiography provides a description of his heavenly entourage and his official titles. Jitong ends the biography with his personal testimony that he saw his master ascend into the heavens and that he is leaving behind this written record for people to know what happened.

Inner Tradition of Lord Wang, Perfected Being of Pure Vacuity

Wang Zideng was a god who bestowed revelations on Yang Xi, and was said to be the master of Wei Huacun, whose hagiography is also featured in this collection. The eleventh-century edition attributes the authorship of Wang Zideng's biography to Wei Huacun. According to Tao Hongjing, a copy of Lord Wang's hagiography written in Yang Xi's hand existed at the end of the fifth century, and he added this manuscript to his collection at Mt. Mao.[53]

The present redaction of Lord Wang's hagiography begins with a lengthy account of his ancestry and parents. According to the text, Wang was born in 36 BCE into a Sogdian family. His father was a highly ranked Han official, and his mother was a descendant of Sima Qian. A short time after marrying the daughter of a prominent official, Wang's dream of becoming a perfected being leads him to abandon his family to move into a mountain retreat. After Wang has lived as a recluse for nine years, a heavenly retinue of officials visit him in his retreat. Ziwen of Xiliang 西梁子文, a perfected being, reveals that it is his responsibility to test and evaluate adepts, as well as to appoint and promote those who are bona fide perfected. This heavenly official recognizes Wang's hard work at his mountain retreat and informs him that his name has been recorded in heavenly registers, and that he has been given a celestial title.

After this initial visit from heavenly officials, Wang moves to a new mountain retreat and continues his practice. His zeal and dedication lead to the arrival of the Perfected Being of the Western Citadel, who has been appointed as Wang's heavenly master. In their first interaction, Wang's new teacher explains why he has yet to succeed in his endeavors despite receiving a heavenly title and making earnest efforts to achieve longevity. He then provides Wang with a collection of thirty-one fascicles of perfected scriptures after Wang swears an oath and pledges to follow the proper protocols for their subsequent transmission.

After receiving these scriptures, the Perfected Being of the Western Citadel instructs Wang to visualize the Mysterious Continent, the administrative district of the Most High Elder 太上丈人, and in mere seconds, master and disciple arrive there together. The Perfected Being of the Western Citadel

---

53 See *DZ* 1016, 12.13b, 14.17b, 20.2b; Robinet 1984, 2.370.

leads Wang to call upon the Most High Elder. This high god and Wang's master appear to be close intimates as they sit down together arm-in-arm and have a private conversation. Eventually, they ask Wang to join them and lay out a succulent feast, after which the Most High Elder states that Wang is fated to become a divine transcendent. The Lord Who Governs over the Transcendent Dao 主仙道君 next instructs his servants to give Wang two fascicles of texts and divine elixirs, which he drinks. After this, Wang returns to the Western Citadel where, after nine years, he achieves the Dao.

Wang's transcendence is followed by a description of his celestial travels on his flying chariot. Wang's journey takes him in each of the four cardinal directions to meet divine beings, who give him scriptures and other items, as well as to various heavenly locations to visit other deities, from whom he receives more scriptures and divine elixirs. After engaging in a final fast, Lord Wang travels to meet the Grand Simplicity Lord of the Three Primes' High Dao 太素三元上道君, at which time his appointment as a god is confirmed. The hagiography concludes with a list of the texts governed by Wang, as well as a description of the symbols of his heavenly position.

Inner Tradition of the Lady of the Southern Sacred Peak, Primal Lord of Purple Vacuity

Wei Huacun was the principal divinity who transmitted scriptures to Yang Xi. Through her intimate relationship with Yang, Wei became the first Grand Master (zongshi 宗師) of the Supreme Purity tradition. No extant copy of Lady Wei's hagiography is considered by scholars to be complete or authoritative. Tao Hongjing's fifth-century *Secret Instructions for the Ascent to Perfection* (*Dengzhen yinjue* 登真隱訣, DZ 421) contains only a few relevant details about Wei's life. However, her hagiography surely circulated in some form and was known to early Tang bibliographers, who, as mentioned above, listed it in the "Bibliographic Treatise" of the *History of the Sui*. The most extensive extant versions of her hagiography date from the Song dynasty and are found in collections of the period such as *Extensive Records of the Taiping Era*, *Imperial Reader of the Taiping Era*, and *Seven Slips from a Cloudy Bookbag*. The version of Wei's hagiography from the latter was embedded within a treatise (fascicle 4) detailing key figures in the transmission of Daoist scriptures. The excerpt is clearly abridged and is missing details about her later life that surely would have been included in other now-lost versions of her story, yet it is the most complete version of Wei's hagiography and is the one we have chosen to translate for this volume.

The text begins with a brief personal history that locates Wei and her family in the decades just prior to Yang Xi's employment with the Xu family. Wei's family was from Rencheng 任城 in present-day Shandong

Province. Her father, Wei Shu 魏舒 (209–290), was an official during the reign of Emperor Wu (Sima Yan 司馬炎, r. 266–290) of the Western Jin dynasty and served in a variety of important posts. Shu arranges for Wei to be married to Liu Yi 劉乂 from Nanyang 南陽 (present-day Henan Province). But Wei Shu's plans contrast with Wei Huacun's wishes, as she had been inclined toward Daoist practice from a young age. Wei agrees to be married, but the duties of being a wife and mother interfere with her yearning for the Dao. After her children become adults, Wei announces her intentions to withdraw from her family to pursue her interactions with the Perfected.

Wei next spends one hundred days meditating in her chamber, whereupon she is visited by a group of four perfected beings. The author of this work notes that bystanders could not see this extraordinary scene; only Wei is able to perceive them. The four perfected introduce themselves. The most crucial of these gods is Wang Zideng, who praises Wei's efforts to cultivate herself. Wang is identified as Lady Wei's master and teacher, who will lead her toward securing a divine appointment as a Daoist goddess.

Wei replies with an extended self-description focused on her character and physical qualities. The confession is unreservedly negative, denigrating her body, belittling her practice, and questioning her dedication, all while positioning herself as the hapless denizen of a corrupt and defiled world. This deeply humble self-description parallels the one found in Wang Zideng's hagiography, but is both longer and more extreme. The perfected assure Wei that she can overcome all of these shortcomings, owing to her fondness for the Dao, her sincerity, and the karmic circumstances of her birth. Wang Zideng's attendants then bestow eight scriptures upon Wei. In the abridged ending, the author acknowledges that several more were given to Wei at a later time.

Traditions of the Perfected Director of Destinies, Grand Prime Perfected Being and Upper Chamberlain of the Eastern Sacred Peak

Mao Ying, or Lord Mao, is one of the founding divinities of Supreme Purity Daoism. Ying's family was from the Xianyang 咸陽 area and had long served the Qin state. Together with his two younger siblings, Mao Gu 茅固 and Mao Zhong 茅衷, he moved from Shaanxi to Jiangsu and settled on the three peaks of Mt. Gouqu 句曲山. There are three principal versions of Lord Mao's biography: that of the *Seven Slips from a Cloudy Bookbag* translated here, an earlier version found in Ge Hong's *Traditions of Divine Transcendents*, and a third found in fascicle 5 of the *Monograph on Mt. Mao* compiled in the early 1300s by Liu Dabin. Ge Hong's version is shorter and has little connection to Lord Mao's Supreme Purity pedigree, while Liu Dabin's version is longer and contains additional material.[54]

The hagiography begins with a family history that details the activities of Ying's ancestors. Some of Ying's forebears served the Qin state as military officials during its rise, while others avoided official life as hermits or farmers, as did Ying's father. At the age of eighteen, Ying is said to have left home to live in the mountains for six years, reading *Laozi* and the commentaries to *Zhou Changes* (*Zhouyi* 周易). After receiving visions of jade maidens, he sets off to find Lord Wang and the Western Citadel. Twenty years later Lord Wang takes Ying to see the Queen Mother of the West, from whom he receives numerous texts and talismans.

Returning to the human world, Ying lives as a hermit until the age of forty-nine, when he finally returns home to his family. He is reprimanded by his father for unfilial behavior, but eventually convinces him that he has attained the Dao. Shortly after, Ying's younger brothers are called to official appointments in the Han administration and seen off with a great feast. Ying is later called to his celestial appointment and seen off in a similar fashion. He then travels to Mt. Gouqu, which locals have renamed Mt. Mao in his honor.

Ying is then joined by his brothers, who have in the meantime heard of Ying's remarkable accomplishments. Ying instructs his brothers and gives them texts. Despite their advanced age, they are able to achieve transcendence and are invested by a celestial officer with duties and positions related to governing Mt. Mao. After this, the Five Emperors arrive with officials, and they provide Ying with his titles and symbols of office. These are conveyed in a lengthy sequence of verse stanzas that make up the end of the hagiography. After this, Ying bade farewell to his brothers, who remained behind to govern Mt. Mao. The biography concludes with a folk song that originated with these miraculous events.

Inner Tradition of Han Emperor Wu

This narrative tells the story of the encounter of Han Emperor Wu (Liu Che 劉徹, 156–87 BCE) with the Queen Mother of the West in 110 BCE and its aftermath. Unlike the other saints in Yang's hagiographies, Han Emperor Wu is a well-known historical figure who reigned for over fifty years from 141 to 87 BCE. He presided over the development of a strong, centralized state and the unprecedented territorial expansion of the Han empire. The contemporary account of the emperor's calendarist and astrologer Sima Qian attests to the emperor's interest in attaining immortality, employing

---

54 Robinet 1984, 2.390.

masters of esoterica, and innovating in ritual sacrifices.⁵⁵ Thus, while there is no extant record of a visit from the Queen Mother of the West, many of the people and events mentioned in this hagiography, such as Dongfang Shuo 東方朔 (ca. 160–93 BCE) and imperial sacrifices, are attested in other sources.⁵⁶

The version of this story included in the *Daoist Canon*, which we translate below, begins with a brief description of Emperor Wu's fondness for the arts of longevity and a sacrifice he made on Mt. Song in 110 BCE. After this sacrifice, the emperor is relaxing with two advisors, Dongfang Shuo and Dong Zhongshu 董仲舒 (179–104 BCE), when he is visited by a jade maiden named Wang Zideng, who announces that he will be visited by the Queen Mother of the West on the seventh day of the seventh lunar month. The emperor then fasts and prepares a sumptuous banquet in preparation for the Queen Mother of the West's arrival, who arrives at the appointed time with a heavenly entourage of thousands of attendants.

After they sit, the Queen Mother of the West unveils her own feast of exotic foods accompanied by an orchestra of celestial musicians. Once the feast ends, Emperor Wu confesses his shortcomings to the Queen Mother of the West but begs that she still give him the methods for transcendence, particularly oral instructions supplementing the techniques that he previously tried. The Queen Mother of the West explains that Wu's many licentious habits, military campaigns, and executions are all impurities that will cut his life short. She then instructs the emperor with the words taught to her by the Celestial King of Primordial Commencement 元始天王, which include information about classes of drugs and teachings about nourishing qi. After this, the Queen Mother of the West prepares to leave, but the emperor begs her to stay. At this point, the Queen Mother of the West summons the Lady of the Upper Prime to join them.

In a short while, the Lady of the Upper Prime appears. After greeting the emperor and the Queen Mother of the West, the Lady describes in detail the shortcomings of the emperor's character and behavior and urges him to change his ways. The emperor promises to heed her words, but then suddenly spies a text called *Charts of the True Forms of the Five Sacred Peaks* (*Wuyue zhenxing tu* 五嶽真形圖) in the Queen Mother of the West's bookbag and asks about it. Despite her misgivings, the Queen Mother agrees to give this text to the emperor. However, the Lady of the Upper Prime informs him that this text will do him little good without the

---

55 Sima Qian's biography of Emperor Wu is found in fascicle 12 of his *Records of the Historian*. Ban Gu's biography in fascicle 6 of his *History of the Former Han* attests to similar interests.

56 Dongfang Shuo's biography in fascicle 65 of the *History of the Former Han* is perhaps the most complete account of his life and activities at court.

so-called *Twelve Texts* (*Shi'er shi* 十二事), which she lists.⁵⁷ Emperor Wu asks for the texts, but the Lady of the Upper Prime states that she does not possess them, but that she hopes the emperor will find them after some searching. The emperor begs for the texts, kowtowing on the ground until blood runs down his face.

A brief argument ensues between the Queen Mother of the West and the Lady of the Upper Prime over when and how it is appropriate to transmit texts. The Queen Mother of the West states that the emperor's sincerity and desire for transcendence makes him worthy of the texts, despite his shortcomings. The Lady of the Upper Prime finally relents, but because only a man may transmit the *Twelve Texts* to another man, she calls upon a male god, the Lesser Lad of Azure Perfection 青真小童, who lives in the eastern heavens opposite the Queen Mother of the West, to transmit the texts instead. After the *Twelve Texts* are delivered, she incants over them and explains to the emperor their names, how to use them, when he may transmit them to others, and the penalties for recklessly divulging their contents. The Queen Mother of the West then invests the emperor with the *Charts of the True Forms of the Five Sacred Peaks* and suggests that he transmit these two collections of texts to two of his advisors, Dong Zhongshu, a classical scholar, and Li Shaojun 李少君, a master of methods at court. Dongfang Shuo is then revealed to be a divine being.

The banquet concludes with the emperor promising to heed the instructions of the two goddesses, reform his errant ways, and devote himself to transcendence. He continues to make sacrifices at Sacred Peaks but is unable to quell his carnal desires or curb his violent appetites. After six years, the Queen Mother of the West orders fire to rain down from heaven and consume the texts that she and the Lady of the Upper Prime had given the emperor. Filled with regret, the emperor continues to make sacrifices and plead with the heavens for another chance, but never receives an answer. Despite conducting multiple imperial tours and sacrifices at the Sacred Peaks, the emperor dies in 87 BCE and is entombed. The text concludes with several unusual circumstances surrounding his death, including strange sounds and mists around his tumulus and the appearance of funerary objects from the tomb in marketplaces and caves. The author hints that the presence of these objects may mean that the emperor escaped death via esoteric techniques.

---

57 For a discussion of the term *shi* 事 as conveying the abstract notion of texts in early historiography, see Fahr 2021, 195–196.

清靈真人裴君傳
弟子鄧雲子撰

清靈真人裴君，字玄仁。右扶風夏陽人也。以漢孝文帝二年，君始生焉。為人清明，顏儀整素，善於言笑。目有精光，垂臂下膝，聲氣高徹，呼如鍾鳴。家奉佛道。年十餘歲，晝夜不寐，精思讀經。

嘗於四月八日，與馮翊趙康子、上黨皓季成，共載詣佛圖。時天陰雨，忽有賤人著故布單衣，巾黃巾，詣君車後索載。君禮而問之，不答，君下車以載之。康子、季成並大怒，呵問：「何等人而上吾車乎？」

君乃陳諭，遂聽俱載。君自徒行在後，顏無變色，寄載人自若，亦不以為慙也。將至佛圖，乃曰：「吾家近在此。」乃下車，奄然失之。

---

1 An administrative district of the Han capital, Chang'an 長安, named for a bureaucratic post. Ban Gu 1997, 1546.
2 The posthumous title of Liu Heng 劉恆 (200–157 BCE), who reigned as Emperor Wen of the Han (180–157 BCE), which places Pei's birth at approximately 178 BCE.
3 Having long arms is one of the thirty-two marks of a Buddha. A white tuft shining between the eyebrows is also one of the marks, but it is unclear if that is what is implied by his eyes having a "radiant glow." Xingyundashi 2003, 507–510.
4 Scholars date the entry of Buddhism in China to the first or second century CE, so the claim that Pei's family was Buddhist appears dubious. However, other Yang Xi hagiographies

Traditions of Lord Pei, the Perfected Being of Pure Numinosity
Compiled by his disciple Deng Yunzi

The Perfected of Pure Numinosity, Lord Pei, styled Xuanren, was from Xiayang[1] in You Fufeng Commandery. His life began in the second year of Han Emperor Wen the Filial.[2] His conduct was pure and bright, and he maintained a fastidious yet simple appearance. He was clever in speech and good at telling jokes. His eyes had a radiant glow, and his forearms hung past his knees.[3] His voice resounded like the peal of a bell whenever he spoke. His household venerated the Dao of the Buddha, and even when he reached adolescence, he devoted himself day and night to contemplation and reading scriptures.[4]

One time, on the eighth day of the fourth lunar month, he took a carriage with Zhao Kangzi of Fengyi and Gao Jicheng of Shangdang and went to a Buddhist temple.[5] At the time the sky was dark and rainy when suddenly an indigent man—dressed only in old, unlined plain clothes with his head wrapped in a yellow turban—approached the back of their carriage.[6] Lord Pei was respectful and extended a greeting to him, but the man did not reply. Lord Pei then got down from the carriage and allowed the stranger to board. Kangzi and Jicheng were both irate and scolded him, "How can such a low-class person board our carriage?"

Lord Pei explained his reasons to his friends; they acquiesced and allowed the stranger to ride with them. Lord Pei walked along behind, his countenance never changing. Meanwhile, the stranger they picked up was composed and unashamed to sit in the carriage. As they approached the Buddhist temple, the stranger said, "My home is near here." He then stepped down from the carriage and quickly vanished.

---

mention connections with Central Asia (see Lord Wang's Sogdian origins), so there is a possibility that Yang imagined that these figures had an early connection to Buddhism.

5   Literally, a Buddhist pagoda, but here a metonym for the monastic complex. The eighth day of the fourth lunar month is widely recognized as the birthday of the historical Buddha, so presumably there were many carriages and pedestrians making the trek to the temple on this day. See Xingyundashi 2003, 2746. Fengyi was an administrative district of the Han capital, Chang'an (Ban Gu 1997, 1545). Shangdang was a large administrative unit in present-day Shanxi Province (Ban Gu 1997, 1553).

6   Later in this hagiography (see p. 23 below), one of the spirits who appear to Pei is also identified as wearing a yellow turban, so this is likely foreshadowing.

佛圖中道人支子元者，亦頗知道。宿舊人傳之云，已年一百七十歲。見君而歡曰：「吾從少至老，見人多矣！而未嘗見如子者。」乃延君入曲室之中，幽靜之房。大設豐饌，飲食既畢，將君更移隱處。呼之共坐，乃謂曰：「吾善相人，莫如爾者。子目中珠子正似北斗瑤光星，自背已下象如河魁，既有貴爵，又當神仙，天下志願，子寶享焉。然津梁未啟，七氣未淳，不見妙事，亦無緣而成也。」

因以所修祕術，密以告君，道人曰：

「此長生內術，世莫得知。吾昔遊焦山及鼈祖之阿，遇仙人蔣先生者，乃赤將子輿也，以神訣五首授吾，奉而行之，於今一百七年矣。氣力輕壯，不覺衰老。但行之不勤，多失真志，不能去世。故雖延年，不得神仙也。猶是行之多違，精思不至之罪也。今以教子，子祕而慎傳之。

第一、思存五星，以體象五靈。存之法：常

---

7   The term "quiet" here describes the subtle and silent ways of goddesses (Knechtges 1982, 273; Knechtges 1996, 345).
8   Physiognomy has a long pedigree in Chinese literature. See Durrant et al. 2016, 461.
9   The Gemmy Light is Eta Ursae Majoris (Alkaid), a star in the constellation of Ursa Major. The River Kui is a six-star constellation near the bowl of Ursa Major. See Schafer 1977a, 121–125; Schlegel 1967, 530. For more on the bodily marks of transcendence in Supreme Purity texts, see Bokenkamp 1997, 298.
10 In Buddhist texts of this period, "ferrying and bridging" is a term referring to the great acts of salvation that a Buddha or bodhisattva performs at the end of life. See Mather 2002, 53; Xu Zhen'e 1989, 2.56–57. "Seven qi" likely refers to the seven white-souls (*po*)

At this temple there was a Buddhist monk named Zhi Ziyuan who knew the Dao well. An old friend of his passed on the tale that Zhi had already lived for 170 years. On seeing Lord Pei, he said with joy, "Over the course of my life, I have seen so many people, yet I have never seen one like you." He then led Lord Pei into a dark and quiet room within a secret chamber.[7] There they laid out a great feast, and once their meal had ended, he took Lord Pei to an even more secluded location. He asked Pei to sit, then said, "I am skilled at physiognomy,[8] and there is no one like you. Your pupils are like the Gemmy Light of the Dipper, and the lower part of your back resembles the River Kui.[9] You will not only enjoy a title of nobility, but are also destined for transcendence. You will possess and enjoy all that the whole world desires. But your ferrying and bridging have not yet begun, and your seven qi are not yet purified.[10] If you do not encounter something wondrous, you lack the karmic affinity to achieve completion."

The monk then privately told Lord Pei about esoteric techniques he had cultivated:

"No one in the world has ever gained knowledge of these esoteric techniques of longevity. Many years ago, I traveled to Mt. Jiao, and to the slopes of Mt. Biezu, and happened upon the transcendent Master Jiang, who is actually Chijiang Ziyu.[11] He transmitted five Divine Instructions to me. It has been 170 years since I received and began practicing them. I am still hale and hearty and do not feel the effects of old age. Yet I have been lax in my practice and have lost my resolve for perfection, so I am unable to leave this world. Thus, I have only prolonged my years and have not attained divine transcendence. For I have practiced like this with many transgressions and am guilty of lacking single-minded determination. You must keep what I teach you now secret and transmit it only with great care.

"In the first technique, call to mind and visualize the five planets,[12] with their bodies resembling the Five Numina. The ritual for visualization: always

---

that have yet to be refined through esoteric meditative techniques. See Bokenkamp 1997, 283, 324–326.

11 According to the *Arrayed Traditions of Transcendents*, Chijiang Ziyu lived in the time of the Yellow Emperor. He later served as an official in the reign of Yao, abstained from grains, rode whirlwinds into the air to chase the wind, and sold raw silk in the market. See Wang Shuming 2007, 7.

12 Mercury, Venus, Earth, Mars, and Jupiter. In his "Rhapsody on the Western Capital" ("Xidu fu" 西都賦), Ban Gu writes that the palace at Chang'an "embodied" (*tixiang*) Heaven and Earth, the same word used to describe how the Daoist adept embodies the planets in his body. See Knechtges 1982, 24, 115; Xiao Tong 1983, 24.

於密室以夜半後生氣之時服挹五方之氣。於寢牀上平坐,向月建所在,先叩齒九通,咽液三十過。畢,存想五星,使北方辰星在頭上,東方歲星在左,西方太白星在右,南方熒惑星在膝中間,中央鎮星在心中。久久行之,出入遠行。常思不忘,無所不却,萬禍所不能干也。後當奄見五老人,則是五星精神也。若見者當問以飛仙之道,五神共扶人身形白日昇天。

第二、初以甲子上旬直開除之日為始。以生氣之時夜半之後。勿以大醉大飽,身體不精,皆生疾病也。當精思遠念,於是男女可行長生之道。其法要祕,非賢勿傳。使男女並取生氣,含養精血。此非外法,專採陰益陽也。若行之如法,則氣液雲行,精醴凝和,不期老少之皆返童矣。凡入靖,先須忘

13 According to the *Classic of Rites* (*Liji* 禮記), this qi refers to the air that arises in the last month of spring. See Wang Wenjin 2001, 205. Daoist writers, on the other hand, see vital qi as existing all year, and calculate its amount by determining the yin and yang qi present at a particular time of day.

14 This is determined by the position of the handle of the Big Dipper at the beginning of each lunar month. The implication here is that the adept should orient himself toward the dipper handle rather than in an arbitrary cardinal direction. See Zhang Shuangdi 1997, 281 n. 53; Major et. al. 2010, 127. See also Tseng-kuei Liu 2008, 899.

in a sealed chamber after the midnight hour, when there is vital qi,[13] imbibe the qi of the five directions. Sit upright on your bed and position yourself facing the proper direction for the month.[14] First click your teeth nine times, and then swallow thirty times. When finished, visualize and contemplate the deities of the five planets, causing the Chronographic Star of the North to be above your head, the Year Star of the East to be on your left, the Grand White Star of the West to be on your right, the Dazzling Deluder Star of the South to be between your knees, and the Quelling Star of the Center to be in your heart.[15] Do this for a long time, both at home and abroad and even on a distant journey. If you always are mindful of it and do not forget this practice, you can overcome anything, for the myriad calamities will not befall you. After a while, if you suddenly see five old men, these are the essential spirits of the five planets. If you see them, be sure to ask about the way of flying transcendent beings, by which means these five spirits support the human body so that it can ascend to the heavens in broad daylight.

"As for the second technique, begin on the first ten days of the month on *kai* and *chu* days.[16] Select a time after midnight when there is vital qi. You should never do this when too drunk or too full, or when you lack energy, for you will inevitably become sick. When you practice refined contemplation, keep longings far away, so that men and women can put into practice the Dao of longevity. The procedure is absolutely secret and should not be transmitted to an unworthy person. Both men and women can gain vital qi, and this will help supplement their seminal essence and blood.[17] This technique is not like those profane methods that focus on procuring yin to benefit yang.[18] If one follows the technique, one's qi and bodily fluids will flow through the body, thus allowing one's vital fluids to mix together. No matter how old or young a person is, their youthful appearance will return. Upon entering your oratory, you must forget both

---

15 The stars in order here are Mercury, Jupiter, Venus, Mars, and Saturn. For more on the nomenclature of the planets, see footnotes 45–51 below.

16 We have benefited from Henri Maspero's interpretation and translation, especially of the incantation below (1981, 522–523). Ge Hong identifies the same days for entering famous mountains in fascicle 17 of his *Inner Chapters of the Master Embracing Simplicity*. See Ge Hong 1996, 303. The idea that rituals should be undertaken on certain days and times was entrenched in Chinese thought many centuries prior to this text. For more on time taboos, see Tseng-kuei Liu 2008, 895–901.

17 For the nature of seminal essences in men and women, see Schipper 1993, 106–107, 156–157.

18 For Raz (2008, 116–117), such passages signal that different Daoist groups in the fourth or fifth century began criticizing early explicitly physical sexual practices such as merging qi (heqi 合氣).

形忘物，然後叩齒七通而咒曰：

白元金精
五華敷生
中央黃老君
和魂攝精
皇上太精
凝液骨靈
無上太真
六氣內纏
上精玄老
還神補腦
使我合會
鍊胎守寶

祝畢，男子守腎固精，煉炁從夾脊遡上泥丸，號曰「還元」。女子守心養神，煉火不動，以兩乳炁下腎，夾腎上行，亦到泥丸，號曰「化真」。養之丹扃，百日通靈。若久久行之，自然成真，長生住世，不死之道也。

19 The name of one of five spirits collectively called the Five Spirits of Taiyi (Taiyi wushen 太一五神), who in the *Cavernous Perfection Supreme One Imperial Lord's Grand Elixir Hidden Book from the Mysterious Scripture of Cavernous Perfection* (*Dongzhen taiyi dijun taidan yinshu dongzhen xuanjing* 洞真太一帝君太丹隱書洞真玄經, *DZ* 1330, 22b), was said to wield control over cloud-souls and white-souls. For more, see Chang Chao-jan 1998, chapter 3.

20 In the second stanza of the *Most High Jade Classic of the Yellow Court's Inner Phosphors* (*Taishang huangting neijing yujing* 太上黃庭內景玉經, *DZ* 331, 1b), the five blossoms are the five breaths of the five directions that nourish an adept's "numinous root" (linggen 靈根), that is, the tongue, during visualization exercises. See Schipper 1975, 63.

your body and the external world, and then click your teeth seven times before making the following incantation:

> May the metal essence of the White Prime[19]
> Spread life throughout my five blossoms.[20]
> May the Yellow Venerable Lord of the center
> Harmonize my cloud-souls and order my essences.
> May the grand essence of the August One on high
> Solidify and meld the numina in my bones.[21]
> May the Most High Grand Perfected's
> Six Qi[22] coil within,
> And thus send essence up to the Mysterious Elder,
> While reverting my spirits and replenishing my brain.[23]
> And may this cause me to merge and combine my essences,[24]
> To refine my embryo while guarding my treasure.

"When the incantation is finished, a male adept guards his kidneys to stabilize his spermatic essence. Then he refines qi by guiding it along his spine all the way up to his Muddy Pellet.[25] This is called 'Reverting to the Prime.' A female adept guards her heart-mind to nourish her spirit. She refines this fire without letting it move. She sends this qi down from her breasts to her kidneys. Then she sends it upward between the kidneys until it reaches her Muddy Pellet as well. This is called 'Transformed into Perfection.' Adepts will be able to communicate with spirits if they cultivate with a cinnabar crossbar[26] for one hundred days. If one practices this technique for a long time, one will spontaneously become a perfected being who can live long in this world. This is the Dao of preventing death.

---

21 Signaling that the five qi and essences meld together with the divine bones and marrow of an adept.
22 Kroll identifies these as yin, yang, wind, rain, darkness, and light (1996, 665).
23 On the concept of circulating spermatic essence in one's brain, see Strickmann 1979, 173. This method seems designed to replace the circulation of essence to the brain.
24 Combining one's vapors or essences builds on a rich history of sexual cultivation terminology, such as "conjoining yin and yang" (he yinyang 合陰陽) and "conjoining forms" (jiexing 接形). See Harper 1998, 135. Here, however, the author wishes the adept to engage in such acts as meditation rather than coitus.
25 The "Muddy Pellet" refers to the brain within a Daoist adept in which high celestial gods reside. See Pettit and Chang 2020, 160.
26 This is when the doorway into an adept's cinnabar field is blocked off to the outside by a crossbar. Here "cinnabar crossbar" refers to the sustained focus an adept must have to engage in these meditative practices.

第三、用《五行紫文》以除三尸。常用朔望之日日中時，臨目南向。臨目者，當閉而不閉也。心存兩目中出青氣，心中出赤氣，臍中出黃氣，於是三氣相繞，合為一氣，以貫一身。須臾內外洞徹，如火光之狀。良久，乃叩齒十四通，咽液十四過，畢。此鍊形之道，除尸蟲之法也。久而行之，體有五香之氣，目明耳聰，長生不死。

　　第四、名曰陰德致神仙之道。其文曰：『常以甲子日沐浴，竟甲子上旬日。當燒香於所止床之左右。久久行之，天仙玉女下降也。』

　　又一法：當養白犬白雞。犬名曰白靈，雞名曰白精。諸八節日及行入五嶽，乃登名山諸有神仙之所在處。密放雞犬於其間，去勿廻顧。天真仙官當與子芝英靈草矣。

　　又一法：作素奏，使長一尺二寸，丹書其文曰：『某郡縣鄉里某，欲得長生，登仙度世，飛行上清。真人至神、五嶽羣靈、

27　The title *Purple Writs of the Five Phases* (*Wuxing ziwen* 五行紫文) does not match any names of scriptures in the *Zhengtong* canon. The "Three Corpses," or corpse worms, are a form of demonic haunting that may be either ritual contamination of dead bodies or parasites within the human body. See Kubo Noritada 1956; Li Jianmin 2008; Huang 2012, 52–53.

28　By the early Song dynasty, the "five aromas" referred to five exotic aromatic ingredients, a definition likely rooted in esoteric Buddhist traditions of the Tang dynasty, where these ingredients were used in the construction of altars (Xingyundashi 2003, 1126a–b). A passage from the *Pearlbag of the Three Caverns* (*Sandong zhunang* 三洞珠囊, *DZ* 1139)

"For the third technique, use the Purple Writs of the Five Phases to purge yourself of the Three Corpses.[27] At noon on the days of a new or full moon, face south and nearly close your eyes. 'Nearly closing your eyes' means that they will appear shut but are not really shut.[i] Visualize an azure qi emerging from between your eyes, a red qi emerging from your heart, and a yellow qi emerging from your navel. These three qi will coil around your body, merging into a single qi, and permeate through your entire body. Inner and outer will be immediately transparent, as if illuminated by the light of a fire. After a long time, click your teeth fourteen times, swallow fourteen times, then stop. This Dao is to refine your form through a method to expel your corpse worms. If you practice this for a long time, your body will smell of the five aromas,[28] your vision will be clear, and your hearing sensitive, and you will attain longevity and never die.

"The fourth technique is called the Dao of Bringing on Divine Transcendence through Secret Virtues.[29] Its scripture reads, 'Always take baths on *jiazi* days, and do this until the first ten days of the month are over.[30] You should burn incense to the left and right of your bed. The celestial transcendents and jade maidens will descend if you practice this for a long time.'

"There is another method: You must raise a white dog and a white chicken.[31] The dog is called 'White Numen'; the chicken 'White Essence.' Travel to the Five Sacred Peaks on the Eight Nodal Days to ascend to the dwelling places of divine transcendents on each of these famous mountains. Secretly leave the chicken and dog there, and do not look back as you leave. The celestial perfected and transcendent officials will then give you mushroom blossoms and numinous herbs.

"There is another method: Write the following in cinnabar ink on a white memorial that is one foot, two inches long, saying, 'I, (name), from (prefecture/county/village), desire to achieve long life, escape this world through transcendence, and fly up into the Supreme Purity heavens. I implore the highest spirits of the perfected, the assembled spirits of the Five

---

    defines it as *Aristolochia recurvilabra* (qingmu xiang 青木香), a plant similar to birthwort. See Read 1977, 49–50.

29 This term frequently appears in pre-Qin, Han, and post-Han literature, variously connoting feminine domains of power, virtuous actions conducted in secret and repaid with heavenly rewards, and earthly forces.

30 In other words, *jiazi* days that fall on the first ten days of every month are suitable for bathing.

31 According to the *Inner Chapters of the Master Embracing Simplicity*, fascicle 11, leading a white dog and carrying a white chicken are also required to pacify spirits when entering mountains and searching for numinous mushrooms (Ge Hong 1996, 202).

三官九府,乞除罪名。』

　　書奏畢,以青絲係金鐶一雙,合以纏奏。再拜北向。置奏石上,因以火燒成灰。乃藏鐶於密石間而去,勿反顧。無鐶,可用條脫一雙以代鐶。古人名為縱容珠子也。慎與多口嫉妬之人道之。非但無益,乃更致禍。如此十過,天上五帝,三官九府,更相屬勑,除人罪過,著名生錄,刊定仙籍。

　　入山求芝草靈藥,所欲皆得。山神玉女,自來營衛。狼虎百害,不敢犯近。神靈祐助,常欲使人得道,開人心意。惡鬼老魅,不敢試人。

　　行此道,易成而無患。若道士不知此術,入山必多不利,數為鬼物所試。在人間則多轗軻疾病,財物不昌,所願不從。若能行此道,長生神仙。

　　第五、太極真人常以立春之日日中時,會諸仙人於太極宮。刻玉簡,記仙名。常以其夕夜半時,正北向,仰視北極,再拜頓首。陳乞己罪多少之數,求解釋之意。畢,復再拜乃止。

32　The Three Officials of Heaven, Earth, and Water inspect the actions of human beings on specific days of the year (Stein 1979, 70). In Yang Xi's revelations, the "Nine Bureaus" or "Nine Palaces" (jiugong 九宮) refers to official residences in the Kunlun Mountains where a bevy of transcendent and perfected beings serve as officials, hearing cases brought before them from Daoist adepts who request that heavenly records of their allotted fate be changed on account of their observances of Daoist precepts. *DZ* 1016, 5.15a–b.

Sacred Peaks, the Three Offices, and the Nine Bureaus to strike my sinful name from the heavenly records.'[32]

"After you finish writing the memorial, wrap up the document with a pair of golden rings twined with an azure string. Face north and bow twice. Then place the memorial on a stone and burn it until it turns to ash. Afterward, hide the rings in a secret space amid the rocks and do not look back as you leave. If you do not have golden rings, you can also use a pair of coiled armbands as a substitute. This is what the ancients called 'Tolerant Pearl.' Be careful not to speak of this to people prone to gossip and jealousy. That would be of no benefit to you, and it would only bring more misfortune. Once you do this ten times, the heavenly Five Emperors and Three Offices and Nine Bureaus will each issue an edict that will remove your transgressions, inscribe your name on the Register of the Living, and confirm your place in the rosters of transcendent beings.

"When you enter the mountains seeking mushrooms and numinous medicines, you will find all you desire. Mountain spirits and jade maidens will come to your defense of their own accord. Wolves, tigers, and ferocious beasts will not dare approach you. All these divine numina will bless and protect you, for they constantly desire to serve people in the attainment of the Dao and open their minds. Evil ghosts and primeval bogies will not dare test them.

"If you practice this Dao, you will be carefree from any worries, and find it easy to achieve. If a Daoist adept does not know about this technique, he will encounter many hardships when entering the mountains, for he will repeatedly be tested by demonic beings. Even in the city he will encounter many setbacks and illnesses, his wealth will not grow, and all will run counter to his wishes. If, however, you can practice this Dao, it will lead to long life as a divine transcendent.

"As for the fifth technique: the Perfected of the Grand Bourne regularly convene meetings with transcendents at the Grand Bourne Palace at midday on the day of the inception of spring.[33] They inscribe jade slips to record the names of transcendents. Always face north on this night, and at midnight look up to the Northern Bourne[34] and bow twice while knocking your head on the floor. Report all of your transgressions, however many or few, and plead with them, expressing your hope to seek absolution. When this is over, bow twice again to end the ritual.

---

33 The first day of the spring solar season, usually February 4.
34 The pole star at one end of the axis around which all stars rotated. See Needham and Wang 1959, 261; Knechtges 1982, 188; Schafer 1977a, 44.

至春分之日日中時，崑崙瑤臺太素真人會諸仙官，校定真經。

　　至立夏之日日中時，上清五帝會諸仙人於紫微宮。見四真人論求道者之功過。

　　至夏至之日日中時，天上三官會於司命、河侯。校定萬民罪福，增年減筭。

　　至立秋之日日中時，五嶽諸真人詣中央黃老君於黃房雲庭山。會仙官於日中，定天下神圖靈藥。

　　至秋分之日日中時，上皇大帝乃登玉清靈闕太微之觀。會太上三老君、北極諸真公、八海大神、五嶽尊靈，仙官萬萬。共集議定天下萬兆之罪福，學道之勤懈。一一條列，副之司命。

　　至立冬之日日中時，陽臺真人會詣仙官玉女。定新得道始入仙錄之人。

35　The god who will give Lord Pei the scriptures needed for his apotheosis as a perfected god. It is likely that this is the same as the Perfected Lord of Grand Simplicity, who was appointed as a precentor to Lord Li. Bokenkamp 1997, 355.

36　One of three constellations, along with the Grand Tenuity (Taiwei yuan 太微垣) and Heaven's Marketplace (Tianshi yuan 天市垣). See Kroll 2015, 576.

"On the vernal equinox, at midday, the Perfected Being of Grand Simplicity[35] from the Jasper Terrace of Mt. Kunlun convenes a meeting of transcendent officials to collate and confirm the accuracy of the perfected scriptures.

"On the first day of summer, at midday, the Five Emperors of the Supreme Purity convene a meeting with transcendents at the Palace of Purple Tenuity.[36] The Emperors will meet with the Four Perfected to evaluate the achievements and missteps of all those who seek the Dao.

"On the summer solstice, at midday, the Three Officials of Heaven on High convene a meeting with the Director of Destinies and the River Marquis. They record the faults and strengths of the people, and will add or subtract years from their lifespans.

"On the first day of autumn, at midday, the perfected beings of the Five Sacred Peaks go to the Yellow Chamber at Mt. Yunting to call upon the Central Yellow Lord Lao. They convene all the transcendent officials at midday to configure the divine diagrams and concoct numinous medicines of the realm.

"On the autumnal equinox, at midday, the Great Emperor of Higher Sovereignty will ascend to the observatory at the Grand Tenuity Palace between the numinous pylons of the Jade Purity heaven. He will convene a meeting with the Three Elder Lords on High, transcendent dukes of the Northern Culmen, the great gods of the Eight Seas, the worthy numina of the Five Sacred Peaks, and the hundred million transcendent officials. Together they will determine the transgressions and good deeds of every person, as well as the diligence and laxness of those who study the Dao. They will list them out one by one and send a copy to the Director of Destinies.

"On the first day of winter, at midday, the perfected beings of the Solar Terrace[37] convene a meeting with the various transcendent officials and jade maidens. They will confirm those people who have recently achieved the Dao and are to be entered into the registers of transcendents.

---

37 This term predates Daoist scriptures and has the ordinary meaning of a high platform that receives sun and stays dry (see Knechtges 1982, 444). In Supreme Purity scriptures, however, it is an alternate name for the chthonic regions of Mt. Wangwu 王屋山 (see DZ 1016, 5.14b; Yoshikawa Tadao and Mugitani Kunio, 2000, 208 n. 35; Smith 2020, 67 n. 173). It is unclear if this passage refers to Mt. Wangwu or is a more general term for grotto-heavens.

至冬至之日，日中時，天真眾仙諸方諸東華大宮。見東海青童君，刻定眾仙籍金書內字。

常以八節日夜半日中，謝七世祖父母及身中罪過，罪過自除也。久行之，神仙不死。

夫秋分日者，太上神真觀試萬仙，自非真正者，不可輕用其日謝罪也。真人仙官，以八節日日中時共會集，三日乃解。欲修道者，當先齋戒，勿失之也。

又一法：每至八節日，常當行入五嶽，或神仙真人所棲名山之處也。每於深僻隱巖之中，密燒香乞願，祝曰：

玄上九靈
太真高神
使某長生
所欲從心
百福如願
壽如靈山
謹以節日
登巖請生

畢，因散香於左右，勿顧而返。常能行此，必長生神仙，所欲如心。玉女詣房，眾靈衛身也。

"On the winter solstice, at midday, the heavenly perfected and the assemblies of transcendents go to the Eastern Florescence Great Palace of the Fangzhu Isles.[ii] They will have an audience with the Azure Lad Lord[38] of the Eastern Seas to carve and set the registers of transcendents by writing their secret names in gold.

"Always at noon or at midnight on these Eight Nodal Days, repent for the transgressions of your fathers and mothers for seven generations, as well as your own, for these transgressions will be absolved without fail. If you do this for a long time, you will live long as a divine transcendent.

"The autumnal equinox is the day on which the highest divine perfected inspect and test the myriad transcendents, and therefore those who are not legitimate perfected beings should not frivolously use this day to confess their transgressions. Perfected beings and transcendent officers convene at midday during the Eight Nodal Days, disbanding only after three days. If you want to cultivate the Dao, you must fast and observe the precepts in the days prior without fail.

"There is another method: On each of the Eight Nodal Days, travel to one of the Five Sacred Peaks, or a famous mountain where divine transcendents and perfected beings reside.[iii] Each time you come to a cliff hidden in a deep, remote place, secretly light incense in supplication and incant,

> O Nine Numina of the highest mysteries,
> Grand perfected and high spirits,
> Grant (your name) long life.
> What my mind desires will be as I wish.
> A hundred blessings will come as I wish.
> I will live as long as a numinous mountain.
> On this nodal day, I have respectfully
> Ascended this cliff to beg for more life.

"Once you have completed this, waft incense to your left and right and don't look back as you leave. If you are able to practice this regularly, you will live as long as a divine transcendent and have all that you desire. Jade maidens will visit your bedchamber, and you will be protected by throngs of spirits.

---

38 For more on this figure, see Smith 2011, 803.

若或有棲遁冥契,而不獲登山者,寄心啓願。精意向真,亦與身詣名山者無異。每事決在心誠密暢,求真堅正,乃獲之也。

此赤將子輿五首隱訣內道要事畢矣。」

君乃再拜,而奉要言還歸。精思行之,常處隱室。不棲名好。乃服食茯苓,餌卉醴華腴。積十一年,夜視有光,常能不息,從旦至中。

年二十三,本郡所命為功曹,君不應命。尋又州辟主簿,轉別駕,舉秀才。詣長安,拜博士高第,轉尚書選曹郎、御史中丞、散騎常侍、侍中。出為北軍中候,以伐匈奴有功,封灘陽侯。

後遷冀州刺史。別駕劉安之時年四十五。初迎君為主簿,後轉別駕。亦知仙道,

---

39 A hidden contract, or otherworldly covenant, is a pact that an adept makes when joining or according with higher powers. According to Yang Xi, it happens when an adept's mind is purified from all filthy, mundane thoughts. See *DZ* 1016, 2.17b; Smith 2013, 135. "Dwelling in seclusion" is a term commonly used to refer to worthy officials living in seclusion during the early medieval period. See Fang Xuanling 1997, 1805.
40 Below (p. 63), the author defines this as honey.

"Adepts who dwell in seclusion to make hidden contracts, yet have no way to ascend a mountain, should make their minds known to convey their wishes.[39] If they strive toward perfection with the utmost zeal, there will be no difference between them and adepts who go to a famous mountain. All such matters are determined by secretly conveying your heart's sincerity. So if you are resolute and forthright in seeking perfection, you will surely achieve it.

"This completes the essential matters of the inner teachings from Chijiang Ziyu's five stanzas of esoteric instructions."

Lord Pei bowed twice and accepted these indispensable words, and then returned home. He practiced refined contemplation and would stay for long periods in his oratory. He never became well known. He ingested poria and the grassy liquor of flower oil.[40] After doing this for eleven years, he could see at night as if there were light and could often go the whole morning without breathing.

When he was twenty-three,[41] Pei was appointed by the prefect of his local commandery to serve in the Bureau of Merit, but he did not accept the appointment. Shortly thereafter he was again appointed, as registrar, by the regional government, and then promoted to lieutenant governor and recommended as a Cultivated Talent. He went to the capital of Chang'an, where he was honored as an erudite of the highest rank, and transferred from the position of gentleman of senior appointments to palace deputy of the Censorate, cavalier attendant-in-ordinary, and palace attendant. He was sent out to the frontier as the watch officer of the Northern Army and was enfeoffed as marquis of Suiyang[42] for his many victories against the Xiongnu.

Later, Pei was promoted to regional inspector for Jizhou.[43] Lieutenant governor Liu Anzhi was forty-five years old at that time.[44] Back when he first met Lord Pei, Liu was only a registrar, but had since been made lieutenant governor. Liu also knew a great deal about the Dao of transcendence, and

---

41 The Chinese count the time in vivo as the first year of life, so by the Western calculation, Lord Pei would have been 22. This holds true for all ages found here.
42 A variant for Suiyang 睢陽 (Morohashi Tetsuji 1955–1960, 7.309c), a city that is in the southern part of present-day Shangqiu County 商丘縣 in Henan Province. See Zang Lihe 1972, 1040d.
43 An area now called Baixiang County 柏鄉縣 in Hebei Province (Zang Lihe 1972, 1212b).
44 In *Essence of Supreme Secrets* (*Wushang biyao* 無上祕要, *DZ* 1138, 54.9b) (Lagerwey 1981, 164), Liu is identified as Huang Chuping 黃初平, also known as the Red Lord of the Southern Sacred Peak (Nanyue chijun 南嶽赤君). He took up life as a hermit at Mt. Jinhua 金華山 and changed his name to Liu Anzhi.

飲食黃精,積二十餘年,身輕,面有華光。數與君俱齋靜室中。

以正月上旬,君沐浴齋于靜室。至三月,奄有仙人乘白鹿。從玉童玉女各七人,從天中來下在庭中。他人莫之見。君拜頓首,乞請一言。仙人曰:「我南嶽真人赤松子也。聞子好道,故來相過。君何所修行乎?」

君長跪自陳所奉行,凡百二十事。松子曰:「勤存五靈,別當授子真道。」奄然而去。

君於是乃求解去官,自稱篤疾。欲詣太上請命。遂棄官委家,逃遊名山,尋此微妙。別駕劉安之從焉。

君時年四十五,帝累徵召,一不應命。逼之不已,君乃北遊到陽浴山,以避人間之網羅也。遂入石室北洞中,學道精思,無所不至。安之不能久處山中,時復出於人間。君於後將雲子去,乃登太華山,入西洞玄石室裏。

積二十二年,奄見五老人皆巾來詣。君再拜頓首,乞請神訣,乃出神芝見賜。

---

45 *Polygonatum*, a common plant consumed by Daoist adepts to enable them to ascend to the heavens. See Campany 2002, 338.

46 While we could find no mention of Mt. Yangyu elsewhere, it is likely a phonetic and/or graphic loan for Yanggu 陽谷 or Yangyu 暘谷, the mountains of the east where the sun rises. See Kroll 1984, 15 n. 70; Schafer 1977b, 133 n. 52. But the mountain here seems to refer to a location within China, and the mention of a northern cave leads Schafer to see this name as a possible variant of Mt. Yangluo 陽洛山, a cluster of mountain peaks fifty *li* north of the city of Qinyang 沁陽 in Shanxi Province.

for twenty years had consumed Solomon's seal,[45] thus making his body light and his face glow. Pei and Liu often conducted fasts together in an oratory.

During the first ten days of the first lunar month, Lord Pei bathed himself and fasted in his oratory. In the third month, a transcendent riding a white deer suddenly appeared. He was accompanied by seven jade lads and seven jade maidens, who all descended into Lord Pei's courtyard from heaven. No one else saw them. Lord Pei respectfully kowtowed and begged for advice. The transcendent said, "I am Master Red Pine, Perfected of the Southern Sacred Peak. I have heard that you are fond of the Dao, so I have come to see you. What techniques of cultivation have you practiced?"

Lord Pei knelt down on his knees and explained the 120 methods he had already tried. Master Red Pine replied, "Focus on visualizing the Five Numina, after which I will bestow a Dao of perfection upon you." With these words, he suddenly departed.

After this, Lord Pei, claiming he had a fatal illness, requested to leave his official post. He hoped, he said, to beseech Lord Lao the Most High to save his life. He then quit his post, left his family, and fled to the famous mountains in pursuit of subtle mysteries. Lieutenant Governor Liu Anzhi accompanied him.

When Lord Pei was forty-five, the emperor repeatedly summoned Pei back to office, but he never once complied with these orders. Because he was endlessly pressed to return to office, Lord Pei traveled north to Mt. Yangyu[46] to escape the snares of the human world. He entered a stone chamber in the northern grotto of Mt. Yangyu, where he studied the Dao through refined contemplation, mastering everything. Liu Anzhi, however, could not dwell in the mountains for long periods, so he repeatedly returned to the human realm. Afterward, Lord Pei left for Mt. Taihua with his disciple Deng Yunzi[47] and entered a dark stone chamber in the western grotto.

After twenty-two years, he suddenly saw five elderly men in turbans who had come to pay a visit.[48] Lord Pei respectfully kowtowed twice and entreated them for divine instruction. They showed him divine mushrooms, which they presented as gifts.

---

47 Identified as the collator of this text in the subtitle of the hagiography.
48 The titles and names of the five lords and information about their attendant deities is included in the text "A Superior Method for Beckoning the Five Star Lords by Returning the Spirits to Soar into the Empyrean and Ascend into Space" ("Huishen feixiao dengkong zhao wuxing shangfa" 迴神飛霄登空招五星上法), collected in *DZ* 1138, 97.1a–3b (Lagerwey 1981, 206–207).

一老人巾青巾，著青衣。柱青杖，帶《通光陽霞》之符。乃東方歲星之大神也。以青華之芝見賜，出青書一卷，是《紫微始青道經》也。

又一老人巾蒼巾，著蒼衣。柱蒼杖，帶《鬱真簫鳳》之符。乃北方辰星之大神也，以蒼華之芝見賜，出《蒼元上籙》《北斗真經》《中命四旋經》四卷見授。

又一老人，巾白巾，著白衣，柱白杖，帶《皓靈扶希》之符，乃西方太白星之大神也，以白華之芝見賜，出《太素玉籙》《寶玄真經》三卷見授。

又一老人巾赤巾，著赤衣，柱赤杖，帶《四明朱碧》之符，乃南方熒惑星之大神也，以丹華之芝見賜，出《龍胎太和丹經》二卷見授。

又一老人，巾黃巾，著黃衣，柱黃杖，帶《中元八維玉門》之符，乃中央鎮星之大神也，以黃華之芝見賜，出《四氣上樞太元黃書》八卷見授。乃五星之精，天之大神也。

君再拜，服此神芝，讀神經，十旬之間，視見萬里之外，能日步千里，能隱能彰，役使鬼神。

乃遊行天下，東到青丘。遇谷希子青帝君，

---

49 Jupiter. See Schafer 1977a, 63–64.
50 Mercury. See Schafer 1977a, 213–214.
51 On the correlation of Venus with the western direction and the color white, as well as similar terms for Mars (south) and Saturn (center) below, see Schafer 1977a, 212.
52 Yang Xi uses the term "dragon embryo" in his revelations to refer to a transcendent drug that one swallows to avoid death. See *DZ* 1016, 14.16b; Yoshikawa Tadao and Mugitani Kunio 2000, 534.

The first elder wore an azure turban and was dressed in an azure robe. He leaned on an azure staff and hung a *Penetrating Solar Auroras* talisman from his belt. He was the great god of the Eastern Year Star.[49] He gave Pei an azure-blossom mushroom and an azure book in one fascicle titled *Scripture of Purple Tenuity's Inaugural Azure Dao*.

The next elder wore a deep-gray-blue turban and was dressed in a deep-gray-blue robe. He leaned on a deep-gray-blue staff and hung a *Piping Phoenix of Embellished Perfection* talisman from his belt. He was the great spirit of the Chronographic Star of the North.[50] He gave Pei a gray-blue-blossom mushroom and *Upper Register of the Gray-Blue Prime, Perfected Scripture of the Northern Dipper*, and *Four Revolutions of the Central Mandate*, three works in four fascicles.

The next elder wore a white turban and was dressed in a white robe. He leaned on a white staff and hung a *Hoary Numen That Grasps the Imperceptible* talisman from his belt. He was the great god of the Grand White Star of the West.[51] He gave Pei a white-blossom mushroom and *Jade Register of Grand Simplicity* and *Perfected Scripture of Precious Mystery*, two works in three fascicles.

The next elder wore a red turban and was dressed in a red robe. He leaned on a red staff and hung a *Four Lights of the Vermillion Discs* talisman from his belt. He was the great god of the Dazzling Star of the South. He gave Pei a cinnabar-blossom mushroom and *Cinnabar Scripture of Grand Harmony of the Dragon Embryo*, a work in two fascicles.[52]

The next elder wore a yellow turban and was dressed in a yellow robe. He leaned on a yellow staff and hung a *Central Prime of the Jade Gate's Eight Directions* talisman from his belt. He was the great god of the Quelling Star of the Center. He gave Pei a yellow-blossom mushroom and *The Grand Primal Yellow Book of the Upper Pivot of the Four Qi*, a work in eight fascicles. These essences of the Five Stars are great gods of heaven.

Lord Pei bowed twice, consumed these divine mushrooms, and read the divine scriptures. Within one hundred days, he could look out and see for ten thousand miles, walk one thousand miles in a single day, disappear and reappear, and command demons and gods.

He roamed freely throughout the world and arrived in the east at the Azure Hillocks.[53] He encountered the Azure Imperial Lord, Master Guxi,[54] and

---

53 The *Inner Chapters of the Master Embracing Simplicity*, fascicle 18 (Ge Hong 1996, 323), talks about the Yellow Emperor heading there and obtaining scriptures.
54 Appearing in Yang Xi's revelations as a high god with a rank similar to Xu Mi or Xu Hui (*DZ* 1016, 4.13a; Smith 2013, 287 n. 175), and also as the right transcendent sire flanked by Master Red Pine, the left transcendent sire (*DZ* 1016, 5.5a; Smith 2020, 47).

授以青精日水,飲食青芝。還到太山,遇司命君,授以《上皇金籙》。

乃西到流沙濱,白水岸。遇太素真人乘龍雲軿,建紫晨巾,以紫羽為蓋,仗七色之節。侍從神童玉女各二百許人。在白水沙洲,空山之上方遊觀金城。鳴玉鐘,舞華幢。望在空山之上,往而不至。

君乃身投長淵,浮白水。冒洪波,越沙岸。嶮巇沈溺,遂登空山。見而拜焉,頓頭稽顙,乞請真訣。太素真人笑曰:「危乎濟哉!子今日始當得之矣。」因口教服二景飛華上奔日月之法。又授《太上隱書》,告君曰:「此足以為真矣。」

遂留空山上,修二景引日法,誦《隱書》。積十一年,太素真人曰:「子道已成矣」。因以景雲龍輿見載,羽蓋華寶之儀。

詣太素宮,見上清三元君。君當爾之時,亦不知在何處也。三元君治太素宮,諸仙童玉女侍者有千餘人。

55 "Higher Luminaries" refers to a distant age in the past when many of the heavenly scriptures were compiled (Robinet 1984, 1.112–113).
56 A mythical river flowing from the Kunlun Mountains (*DZ* 1016, 1.3b; Smith 2013, 33). According to commentary by Wang Yi 王逸 (ca. 89–158 CE) to "Encountering Sorrow" ("Lisao" 離騷), the *Master of Huainan* states that drinking from the Baishui River will impart immortality (Jin Kaicheng 1999, 201).
57 The term "metal fortress" may refer to lands around the capital, but here is used in the sense of a strategic and impregnable location.

received solar water with azure essence and consumed its azure mushroom. Returning to Mt. Taihua, he met his lordship, the director of destinies, and was invested with the *Gold Register of the Higher Luminaries*.[55]

Pei then traveled west and came to the drifting sands leading to the shores of the White River.[56] There he had a close encounter with the Perfected Being of Grand Simplicity, who rode a cloudy phaeton yoked to dragons, wore a Purple Dawn turban capped with purple feathers, and held a seven-colored tipstaff. Divine lads and jade maidens, nearly two hundred each, followed behind. While traversing the sandbars of the White River, he could see a metal fortress in the distance atop Mt. Kong.[57] Jade bells were ringing and floriate streamers swirled about. While Pei could see all of this, he, it seemed, could never draw any closer to the shore leading to Mt. Kong.

Lord Pei next jumped headlong into a deep abyss, plunging into the White River. He was tossed about on its roaring currents until he finally crossed to the other shore. After nearly drowning in the dangerous waters, he began his ascent to the top of Mt. Kong. When Pei was granted an audience with the Perfected Being, he clasped his hands in obeisance and then touched his head to the floor as he kowtowed to request the secret formula for perfection. The Perfected Being of Grand Simplicity smiled and said, "It is dangerous to cross that river! From this day forward you shall have what you seek." Thereupon he taught Pei the method for ascending to the sun and moon by consuming the soaring blossom of Two Phosphors. He gave Pei *The Hidden Writings of the Most High*,[58] and told Lord Pei, "This will enable you to reach perfection."

Pei remained atop Mt. Kong to cultivate the method of drawing in solar essences through ingesting the two phosphors, and to recite *The Hidden Writings*. After eleven years, the Perfected Being of Grand Simplicity said, "You have completed this Dao." Then Pei was carried on a dragon carriage of shining clouds covered with a feathered canopy and ornate jewels.

Next, Pei visited the Palace of Grand Simplicity, where he had an audience with the Three Primal Lords.[59] But when Pei came before the lords, he was not quite sure where he was. These three Primal Lords governed the Palace of Grand Simplicity with their retinue of more than a thousand

---

58 This scripture appears throughout early medieval scriptures and is often paired together with the *Perfected Scripture of the Eight Immaculates* (*Basu zhenjing* 八素真經). See *DZ* 1016, 5.3a; *DZ* 1138, 23.10a; Bokenkamp 1997, 371 n. 36; Smith 2020, 35 n. 13.
59 Meaning the three goddesses linked to the Three Immaculates (sansu 三素) or the three-colored qi of the heavens. They are seen as the mothers of the three gods in a person's Grotto-Room. See Kroll 2003, 203 n. 127.

以黃金為屋,青玉為牀。君既詣金闕,再拜稽首。三元君以《玉璽金真》見賜,玉女二十四人玉童三十二人見侍。

乃乘飛雲中輦復北遊,詣太極宮。見太極四真人,四真人見授《神虎》符、流金火鈴。乃詣太微宮受書為清靈真人,治清靈宮。佩三華寶衣,乘飛龍景輿,仗青旍、玉鉞、七色之節,遊行上清九宮。

西玄者,葛衍山之別名。葛衍有三山相連:西為西玄,東為鬱絕根山,中央名葛衍山。三山有三府,名曰三宮。西玄山為清靈宮,葛衍山為紫陽宮,鬱絕根山為極真宮。

三山纏固萬三千里,高二千七百里。下有洞庭,潛行地中,通玄洲崑崙府也。西玄山下有洞臺,方圓千里。金城九重,有玉堂蘭室。東西宮殿,中有四百二十真人處焉。其樹則絳碧,草則芝英。其鳥獸則麒麟鳳凰。距崑崙七萬里,其間有高暉山,上有洞光如日。葛衍、西玄、鬱絕根三山也。

道人支子元受蔣先生入室精思,存

---

60 According to Yang Xi, Lord Lao wears a *Divine Tiger* talisman, which is the same text Xu Mi copied from Yang Xi (*DZ* 1016, 8.13b). See Smith 2020, 2.34 n. 10, 281 n. 213. Fire bells are a common accoutrement of Daoist deities, who use them to ward off demons and other evil forces. See Mugitani Kunio 2011a, 532–533; Pettit and Chang 2020, 167; *DZ* 1016, 5.4a; *DZ* 421, 1.7.

transcendent lads and jade maidens. Their chambers were made of pure gold and their couches were made of azure jade. When Pei came before the Golden Porte, he bowed twice and kowtowed. The Three Primal Lords bestowed the *Jade Seal of Golden Perfection* on Pei and gave him twenty-four jade maidens and thirty-two jade lads to serve as his attendants.

Pei then got back in his carriage and soared northward among the clouds until he reached the Grand Bourne Palace. He called upon the Four Perfected Beings of the Grand Bourne, who gave Pei a *Divine Tiger* talisman and fiery bells of liquid gold.[60] Pei then visited the Palace of Grand Tenuity, where he received a document confirming him as the Perfected Being of Pure Numinosity, who would rule over the Palace of Pure Numinosity.[iv] He wore fine garments of three blossoms; rode a luminescent chariot of flying dragons; carried an azure pennant, jade axe, and seven-colored tipstaff; and traveled throughout the Nine Palaces of the Supreme Purity.

Mt. Xixuan is an alternative name for Mt. Geyan.[61] There, three peaks are linked together: the westernmost is Mt. Xixuan, the easternmost is Mt. Yujuegen, and the middle is named Mt. Geyan. Each peak has a subterranean bureau, and the three are collectively called the Three Palaces. The Palace of Pure Numinosity is built on Mt. Xixuan, the Palace of Purple Solarity on Mt. Geyan, and the Palace of Utmost Perfection on Mt. Yujuegen.

The circumference around the three peaks is exactly 13,000 miles, and each is 2,700 miles tall. There is a grotto hall under each peak, through which one can travel underground all the way to the bureaus of Mt. Kunlun of the Mystic Continent.[62] The grotto terrace beneath Mt. Xixuan is square and has a perimeter of one thousand miles in each direction.[63] Its golden walls are arrayed in nine concentric circles, within which there are jade halls and orchid chambers. There are palaces along its east-west axis that house 420 perfected beings. Its trees are scarlet and cyan, and its lawn consists of flowering numinous mushrooms. The birds and beasts all resemble kirins and phoenixes. Mt. Xixuan is seventy thousand miles from Kunlun, and between these two is Mt. Gaohui, which has a penetrating beam of light as bright as the sun. It shines on the three peaks Geyan, Xixuan, and Yujuegen.

Master Jiang transmitted to the Daoist adept Zhi Ziyuan a ritual method for practicing refined contemplation in an oratory to visualize the spiritual

---

61 Zhou Yishan's hagiography states that he ruled from the Golden Court on Mt. Geyan. See Miller 2008, 150.
62 In *Record of the Ten Continents* (*Shizhou ji* 十洲記, DZ 598), this consists of lands far to the northwest of the human world that face the northwest gate of Heaven. The Mysterious Metropolis (Xuandu 玄都) is located there. See Smith 1990, 91.
63 Meaning that each side of the square cavern and the diameter of its round top were one thousand *li* long.

五靈之神光，服氣之法。常以夜半之時，靜室獨處。平坐向東，瞑目陰呪曰：

蒼無皓靈
少陽先生
九氣還肝
使我魂寧
上帝玉籙
名上太清

畢，因閉氣九息，咽液九過，叩齒九通。次南向，瞑目陰呪曰：

赤庭絳雲
上有高真
三氣歸心
是我丹元
太微綠字
書名神仙

畢，因閉氣三息，咽液三過，叩齒三通。次西向，瞑目陰呪曰：

素元洞虛
天真神廬
七氣守肺
與神同居
白玉金字
九帝之書
使我飛仙
死名已除

luminescence of the Five Numina and imbibe qi. This is to be done in the middle of the night when you are alone in your oratory. Sit upright while facing east, and whisper this incantation with your eyes closed:

> Great Numen of Verdant Nothingness,[v]
> Master of the Lesser Yang:[64]
> With the nine qi restore my liver
> So that my cloud-souls will be at peace.
> Rise to the jade registers of the emperors
> To mark my name high in Grand Purity.

When finished, stop breathing for a count to nine, swallow nine times, and click your teeth nine times. Next, face south, close your eyes, and whisper this incantation with your eyes closed:

> Scarlet Cloud of the Red Courtyard,
> The high perfected being above:
> With the three qi, give my heart refuge,
> So that they may become my Cinnabar Prime.
> Make green letters[65] of Grand Tenuity
> Inscribe the names of divine transcendents.

When finished, stop breathing for a count to three, swallow three times, and click your teeth three times. Then face west and whisper this incantation with your eyes closed:

> The Immaculate Prime of the Grotto Barrens
> The divine shanty of the celestial perfected:
> With the seven qi guard my lungs,
> So that I may live among the gods.
> In golden letters atop white jade
> Is the book of the Nine Emperors.
> May it cause me to become a flying transcendent,
> Whose time of death will henceforth be erased.

---

64 "Lesser Yang" is a term referring to the palaces in the eastern direction, both those buildings on earth (Knechtges 1987, 254 n. 17) and those in places far beyond earth (Morohashi Tetsuji 1955–1960, 2.96c).

65 In ancient times, "green letters" referred to auspicious signs that King Yu of the Xia received in a river (Fang Xuanling 1997, 408). By medieval times, it meant imperial commendations, and Daoists used the same phrase to describe their names in heavenly registers (Pettit and Chang 2020, 316 n. 8).

畢，因閉氣七息，咽液七過，叩齒七通。次向生年之本命處，瞑目陰呪曰：

黃元中帝
本命之神
一氣侍脾
使我得真
老君玄籙
書名神仙
長生久視
與命永存

畢，因閉氣一息，咽液一過，叩齒一通。次北向，瞑目陰呪曰：

玄元北極
太上之機
五氣衛腎
龜玉參差
神名玉札
年同二儀
役使六甲
以致八威

---

66 In *Analects of Confucius* 16.1, the characters *gui* and *yu* refer to precious objects; here they are used as a metaphor for the adept's body.
67 "Two Mechanisms" here refers to Heaven and Earth. The adept is asserting that he will live forever.

When finished, stop breathing for a count to seven, swallow seven times, and click your teeth seven times. Then face the direction associated with your natal year, and whisper this incantation with your eyes closed:

> The Central Emperor of the Yellow Prime
> Is the god of the year in which I was born.
> With a single qi, attend to my spleen
> And enable me to attain perfection.
> On the mysterious registers of Lord Lao,
> Record my name as a divine transcendent.
> So as to lengthen my life and extend my being,
> So that my life will be preserved forever.

After this, stop breathing for a count of one, swallow once, and click your teeth once. Then face north and whisper this incantation with your eyes closed:

> Mystic Prime of the Northern Bourne,
> The uppermost motive force:
> With the five qi, guard my kidneys,
> And places where tortoiseshell and jade are askew.[66]
> May my divine name will appear on jade slips
> So that my age will match the Two Mechanisms.[67]
> Send forth the six Jia officers,
> And call upon the eight mighty ones.[68]

---

68 The *Four Commentaries on the Miraculous Scripture of the Highest Form of the Primordial Commencement's Immeasurable Powers of Salvation* (*Yuanshi wuliang duren shangpin miaojing sizhu* 元始無量度人上品妙經四註, *DZ* 87, 2.6b), defines them as dragons, kirins, tigers, leopards, lions, snakes, pegasuses, and vicious beasts.

畢，因閉氣五息，咽液五過，叩齒五通。爾乃存五方之氣都畢，又咽液九過，北向再拜，陰呪曰：

謹白太上太極四真君
請存五方五靈神
使某相見得語言

畢乃精思。

此一法，存五靈先服氣陰祝之道。與出中庭存法等耳。此法乃逕要不煩，又於靜思易也。裴君後重更授傳如此。於靜室祝時，亦先存五靈在體中使備，然後服氣爾。庭中之法，所修煩多難行，又於致神之驗，不勝於靜室之速也。後出要言，祕之勿傳。庭中之法，以勸於始學，使不懈怠爾。篤而言之，室中為要法。

支子元受蔣先生第五首之訣，以八節之日存思。陳已立身已來罪過多少之數，輸誠自狀已。上希天皇、諸真開寫之祐，剋身歸善，以求長生神仙者也。

蓋秋分之節者，氣處清靈太和之正日也。眾真諸仙，是其日皆聽訟焉。又地上剌姦吏部，境域諸仙官，並斜奏所在道士之功過，及萬民有罪應死生者也。

69 Yang Xi describes Pure Numinosity as primordial qi, which an adept must constantly consume in his quest to attain a perfected body. Here the idea is that the autumnal equinox marks the day when this rarefied energy is most perfectly formed. See Kroll 2003, 181–182; Smith 2013, 187 n. 109.

When finished, stop breathing for a count to five, swallow five times, and click your teeth five times. When your visualizations of the qi of the five directions are thus complete, swallow again nine times and bow twice facing north and whisper this incantation:

I reverently inform the Four Perfected Lords of the Grand Bourne:
May I now visualize the five numinous gods of the five directions
So that they will appear before (your name), in order that I can speak
    with them.

After this, practice refined contemplation.

This method is the Dao of visualizing the Five Numina, in which one first ingests qi and afterward makes whispered incantations. This is of the same caliber as the method of visualizing the Three Primes in the Central Courtyard. This method is not only straightforward and not cumbersome, but also makes quiet meditation easier. Lord Pei later revised the method and transmitted it as follows. When making incantations in your oratory, fully visualize all Five Numina in your body before beginning to imbibe qi. The method of the Central Courtyard is full of details tedious to cultivate and difficult to practice, yet it is no faster in causing the spirits to come to you than doing it in the oratory. These essential words bestowed by Pei later in life should be kept secret and not transmitted. The Central Courtyard method is for encouraging those just beginning their studies, since it enables them to guard against idleness. But to be honest, practicing in an oratory is the most important method.

After receiving Mr. Jiang's five formulas, Zhi Ziyuan visualized and meditated upon these spirits on the Eight Nodal Days. He reported the full number of transgressions he had committed since birth, and the number of times he had committed them, earnestly setting forth an account of his failings. His most fervent hope was that the Celestial Sovereign and all of the perfected beings would bless him by copying each one down, so that he would restrain his mortal body and return to the good in order to pursue long life as a divine transcendent.

Now, the autumnal equinox is the nodal day when qi is lodged in Pure Numinosity, the day of Grand Harmony.[69] The multitude of the perfected and various transcendents listen to litigations on this day. Moreover, the terrestrial investigators of corruption of the Board of Personnel,[70] in conjunction with transcendent officers in various locales, will make a report on the meritorious acts and failings of Daoist adepts, as well the transgressions of commoners whose lifespan and death should be adjusted.

---

70 In charge of recruitment and supervision of officials. See Rogers 1968, 274 n. 640.

《仙忌真記》曰:「子欲昇天慎秋分,罪無大小皆上聞。以罪求仙仙甚難。是故學道為心寒。」此是朱火丹陵仲陽先生之要言矣。

秋分氣調日和,中順天地者也。夫火炎之氣摧於凋落之勢,玄水包津胎於金生之府,乃太陽光轉少陽,藏養天地。於是所以定剛柔之際,合二象之序。煥成流明,乃別陰陽、三元。寔八節之標日,求道之要梯矣。

每至其日日中之時,上皇太帝君玉尊陛下,乃登廣寒上清靈宅。太空之闕丹城紫臺長錦玉樓。君真集于太微之觀。上關九天之真皇。中要太上三老君、北極諸真及八海大神。下命五嶽名山諸得道者,尊靈萬萬,並會于陽寥之殿。

共集議定天下萬民之罪福,記學道求仙者之勤疏。議犯過日月、修行善惡、刑罰之科、生死之狀。各隨其所屬部境,根源條例,副之司命,書之皇錄。罪福

---

71 Our translation is based on Bokenkamp's translation of this passage (1997, 366).
72 Identified in *Upper Scripture of the Grand Tenuity's Purple Writs and the Perfected Record of the Transcendent Taboos* (*Taiwei lingshu ziwen xianji zhenji shangjing* 太微靈書紫文仙忌真記上經, *DZ* 179) as Gong Zhongyang 龔仲陽, who received the text along with his brother Youyang 幼陽. See Bokenkamp 1997, 372 n. 43.
73 The "Two Images" refers to the masculine (qian 乾) and feminine (kun 坤) powers. See *Mr. Zhou's Records of His Communications with the Invisible World* (*Zhoushi mingtong ji* 周氏冥通記, *DZ* 302, 2.2a).
74 A era title from the distant past, in previous world-ages known as the "Former Heavens." Robinet 1984, 1.112–113.

The Perfected Record of Transcendent Taboos states, "If you hope to rise into the heavens, be cautious of the autumnal equinox, for this is when all transgressions great and small are heard on high. It is extremely difficult to seek transcendence when transgressions are associated with one's name. Therefore, study the Dao with fear and trepidation."[71] These are key instructions of Master Zhongyang[72] from Zhuhuo in Danling.

The autumnal equinox has balanced qi and a mild sun, a consonance between earth and the heavens. It is the time when the fiery qi begins to taper off and the dark waters embryonically emerge through metal, when the rays of the sun begin to lessen and the sun cloaks the world in its nourishing power. The rays of the sun begin to change into Lesser Solarity, and the entire world is preserved and nourished. On this day, there is stability between the rigid and the supple, and an equilibrium between the succession of the Two Images.[73] In a flash, all is transformed into light, and yin, yang, and the Three Primes can be clearly distinguished. Truly, this is the most important of the Eight Nodal Days and is a crucial step for seeking the Dao.

Every autumnal equinox, at midday, the Jade Worthy, his highness the Grand Imperial Lord of the Upper Monarch[74] Luminaries reigns, ascends his numinous residence, the Vast Chill Palace in the Supreme Purity heavens. He lives in a jade tower, with long damask drapery, built on a purple terrace atop the cinnabar walls of the Grand Vacuity gate-towers. The Grand Imperial Lord and all the perfected will assemble at the belvedere of Grand Tenuity. Above, he will notify the perfected sovereigns of the Nine Heavens. In the middle, he will summon the Three Venerable Lords on High, the Perfected of the Northern Bourne, and the great spirits of the Eight Seas. Below, he will command adepts who have attained the Dao on the Five Sacred Peaks and famous mountains and the millions of venerated numina, to all meet together at the Yang Distant Basilica.[75]

They will assemble to judge the transgressions and good deeds of all people on earth and will record the relative level of diligence shown by those studying the Dao and seeking transcendence. They will discuss the days and months when infractions were committed, the good and bad efforts at cultivation, the level of punishments to be applied, and the indictments detailing their lives or deaths. Each person shall be listed according to the group and realm they belong to, the root causes of these transgressions will be detailed line by line, then copied to the Director of Destinies and inscribed in the August Record. Every transgression and good deed, how-

---

75 In its earlier appearances, the term "yang-distance" describes any lofty place high in the heavens (*DZ* 1139, 12.7b). By the Tang dynasty, however, the term was used as a proper name for a specific palace in the *Scripture of Jade Purity of the Great Dao Most High* (*Taishang dadao yuqing jing* 太上大道玉清經, *DZ* 1312, 4.1b).

纖芥，刻于丹城之籍。伏匿之犯惡，陰德之細功者，無不一二縷而知之者也。

其夕夜半，當出中庭，北向脫巾。再拜長跪，上啓太上北極天帝太帝君。因密自陳已立身已來，犯罪多少之狀。乞得赦宥，從今自後，改往修來之言。言之必使信。誓于丹心，盟於天地：「不敢復犯惡之行也。」其中言，在意陳之也。

畢云：「願太上皇帝削其罪名，移書三官。使神仙之錄，某厠玉札，長生久視，通真達靈。」畢，又叩齒四下，再拜而還靜室。

深自刻責，并存念三元中神，令上啓太上。如此者三，名上仙籍，罪咎除滅也。三元：泥丸、絳宮、丹田三神也。存令三元三神，上啓天尊求恩赦。助己自陳，令必上聞也。三啓秋分，生籍乃定，死名乃除。

此一法出《經命青圖》，是長生祕法矣。俗人雖存道，未離人間。甚多罪咎，犯之者非一。恐未便可施用秋分首過之法也。

ever small, will be inscribed on the Dancheng registers. They will know every single thing you have done, from faults you have hid to minor merits of your secret virtues that have gone unnoticed.

At midnight on the autumnal equinox, go out into your courtyard, face north, and remove your turban. Bow twice and kneel upright, then send an announcement to the Grand Imperial Lord, the Celestial Emperor of the Northern Bourne Most High. You should meticulously list transgressions you have committed since birth, together with the number of offenses. Beg that you will receive his mercy and forgiveness, and convey to him in word that you will reform your past conduct and never do such things from that time forth. You must say these words so as to inspire confidence. Make a vow with a fervent mind and seal a covenant with Heaven and Earth: "I will not dare commit the same transgression again." While making this speech, make sure you express your intentions.

When finished, say, "I pray that you, August Emperor Most High, will strike my sinful name from the record and send this document to the Three Officials. May you add a jade slip with my name to the Transcendent Register so that I will have an eternal vision of long life and communicate with the perfected and transcendents." After this, click your teeth together four times, bow twice, and return to your oratory.

Maintain a deep sense of self-reproach as you visualize the inner gods of your Three Primes and command them to take your entreaty up to the Most High. If you do this three times, your name will be entered on the Transcendent Register, and your transgressions and faults will be completely removed. The Three Primes refer to the spirits in your Muddy Pellet, Scarlet Palace, and Cinnabar Field. By visualizing and commanding the three spirits of the Three Primes, they will ascend to request grace and amnesty from the Celestial Worthies. They will assist you in explaining your case and will ensure that you are heard on high. When you make three entreaties on the autumnal equinox, your place on the record of life will be settled, and your name upon the death registers will be erased.

This method is taken from *The Azure Chart of Passing through Fate*[76] and is an esoteric method to attain long life. While commoners might meditate on the Dao, they never escape the human world. Their transgressions and offenses are numerous, and they commit them more than once. Such a person, I fear, cannot successfully use the method of absolution practiced on the autumnal equinox.

---

76 A scripture listed in "Zhou's Hagiography" as a text Zhou received from the Lord Director of Destinies (simingjun 司命君) at Mt. Dahuo 大霍山. See *DZ* 303, 10a; Miller 2008, 141.

入山林中，遠去人事，蕭然獨處；不犯萬物者；乃可為之。既有反善之詞，誓有改行之言，言已聞於高上之聽，慎不可復使犯惡遠生之事也。重犯罪十過，天地弗救。身死為驗，非可復改補者矣。以此求道，無所復索也。養生者有如水火之交爾。得其益則白日昇天，犯戒律則身沒三泉也。

　　又此日獨重於七節，趙伯玄所謂「生死門戶者」也。《三九素語》曰：「秋判之日，尊卑盡會。生死之日也。」古人以秋分之日為秋判之日也。所以爾者，秋分之日，乃會九天八地眾真人神、上皇、至尊，三日三夕，共定萬民之命。所聚議者咸多，而神尊並集故也。諸八節日，會天地諸真官，先後及節，凡三日三夕，而各還所司。此是支公之口訣。

　　又別此一事，不離七節之條例也。《候夜神童金根經》曰：「八節之日，求仙極會。天命眾真，皆當集對。未節一日，萬靈詣闕。節日日中，尊卑入謁。節後一日，

77　The "Three Fonts" perhaps refers to deep graves, but is also used a metaphor for death. See Sima Qian 1997, 265.

Go deep into the forest, leave human affairs far behind, and find a remote place where you can live alone without offending any creature; only then can you undertake this. Once you have conveyed your wrongdoings and pledged to change your conduct, and your words have been heard on high, be sure never again to commit evil or depart from life. Once you have committed ten crimes, Heaven and Earth will not save you. As proof of this, your body will die, and there will be no second chance to make amends. Those who seek the Dao in this way can never make a request to the Three Primes again. Self-cultivation is like when water meets fire. One who obtains the benefits of this ritual will ascend to heaven in broad daylight, but whoever violates its precepts and codes will sink into the Three Fonts.[77]

Moreover, the day of the autumnal equinox, which Zhao Boxuan[78] called the "gateway between life and death," stands alone as the most important of the Eight Nodal Days. The Three and Nine Simple Saying states, "The day of autumnal judgment is a time when the venerated gather together. It is the day when life and death are determined." Thus, the ancients thought that the autumnal equinox was the day of autumnal judgment. The reason is that the Grand Imperial Lord convenes the perfected and spirits of the nine heavens and eight directions, the Upper Sovereigns, and the most revered ones on the autumnal equinox for three days and three nights to determine the lifespans of all the people. The discussions are exhaustive because the gods and the divine worthies must all be brought together. So on each of these Eight Nodal Days, he convenes the various perfected officers of Heaven and Earth, taking each node as it comes in turn, using three days and three nights, and then each officer returns to his ministry. This was an oral instruction of Duke Zhi.[79]

Moreover, there is another source still related to the list-making of the other seven nodal days: *The Scripture of the Golden Root Watched at Night by the Divine Lad* states, "Those seeking transcendence will attend lofty meetings on the Eight Nodal Days. Heaven mandates that all the various perfected must gather and compare records. On the day prior to a nodal day, the myriad numina will arrive at the palace. During midday on a nodal day, the superior and inferior gods will pay their respects. The day after a

---

78   A transcendence seeker who died eating dragon embryos. See *DZ* 1016, 14.16b; Strickmann 1979, 131.
79   Zhi Ziyuan.

罪福分別。三日三夕，天事乃畢。子其慎罪，務為功德。名可上真，列編太極。吾不試言，知者深密，急宜謝過。祕而慎泄。」此亦支公所告出，以傳示裴君。

太素真人教裴君二事為真人之法。曰：「旦視日初出之時，臨目閉氣十息。因又咽日光十過，當存令日光霞使入口中，即而吞之。畢，仍存青帝君從日光中來，在我之左。次存赤帝君從日光中來，在我之右。次存白帝君從日光中來，在我之背。次存黑帝君從日光中來，在我之左手上。次存黃帝君從日光中來，在我之右手上。五帝都來，乃又存陽燧絳雲之車，駕九龍，從日光中來到我之前。仍與五君共載而奔日也。」

裴君止於空山之上，修行精思。一年之中，髣髴形象。二年之中，五帝俱乘日形，見在左右。三年之中，終日而言語笑樂。五年之中，五帝日君遂與裴君駢乘飛龍之車。東到日窟之天東蒙長丘大桑之宮八極之城。登明真之臺，坐希琳之殿。

授裴君以《揮神》之章，《九有》之符。食青精日粘，飲雲碧玄腴。

nodal day, the transgressions and good deeds will be determined. These heavenly affairs will conclude after three days and three nights. Beware of your transgressions and devote yourself to doing virtuous deeds. Your name will thus be among the Upper Perfected, and you will be listed on the scrolls at the Grand Bourne Palace. I will say no more, but let those who understand this keep it a deep secret and quickly confess their wrongdoings. Keep this a secret and do not let others know about it." This was also revealed by Zhi Ziyuan, who passed it on to Lord Pei.

The Perfected Being of Grand Simplicity taught Lord Pei two methods leading to perfection. He said, "At daybreak, when you see the sun first appear, nearly close your eyes and stop breathing for a count to ten. Then gulp down the rays of the sun ten times, after which you should visualize sunlight from auroras entering your mouth, which you then swallow. When finished, visualize the Azure Imperial Lord emanating from within the sunlight and taking a position on your left side. Next, visualize the Red Imperial Lord emanating from within the sunlight and taking a position on your right side. Next, visualize the White Imperial Lord emanating from within the sunlight and taking a position behind you. Next, visualize the Black Imperial Lord emanating from within the sunlight and taking a position on top of your left hand. Next, visualize the Yellow Imperial Lord emanating from within the sunlight and taking a position on top of your right hand. Once all Five Emperors have arrived, visualize a carriage with solar-inferno[80] wheels and scarlet-cloud canopy, pulled by nine dragons emerging from the sunlight and coming before you. Mount this carriage with the Five Emperors and ride off to the sun."

Lord Pei stayed at Mt. Kong, where he cultivated his conduct and practiced refined contemplation. Within one year, misty forms of the Emperors began to appear. Within two years, the Five Emperors came streaming in on sunlight and positioned themselves all around him. By the third year, he spent the entire day speaking to them with laughter and cheer. Within five years, the Five Imperial Sun Lords rode the flying dragon chariot with Lord Pei. They traveled eastward to Giant Mulberry Palace in the Eight Bourne City of the Eastern Shroud highlands in the Solar Cavern Heaven. There they ascended the Allying with the Perfected Terrace to take their seats in the Rare Green-Gem Basilica.

They transmitted to Lord Pei the *Marshalling Spirits* petition and a *Nine Realms* talisman. He then ate azure essences of solar viands and drank dark oil skimmed off of nebulous cyan stones. Pei then traveled daily with the

---

80 A mirror that can focus sunlight and start fires. See Zhang Shuangdi 1997, 172; Major et al. 2010, 116.

於是與五帝日君日日而遊。此所謂奔日之道也。

日中亦有五帝,一曰日君。《太上隱書》中篇曰:「子欲為真,當存日君。駕龍驂鳳,乘天景雲。東遊希琳,遂入帝門。精思仍得要道不煩。名上清靈,列位真官,乃執《鬱儀文》。」

「第二事為真人之法。日夕視月,臨目閉氣九息。因又咽月光九過。當存月光使入口中,即而吞之。

畢,仍存青帝夫人從月光中來,在我之左。次又存赤帝夫人從月光中來,在我之右。次又存白帝夫人從月光中來,在我之背。次又存黑帝夫人從月光中來,在我左手上。次又存黃帝夫人從月光中來,在我右手上。五帝夫人都來,乃又存流鈴飛雲之車,駕十龍,從月光中來到我之前。仍存五夫人共載而奔月也。

裴君止於空山之上,修行精思。一年之中,髣髴姿容。二年之中,五夫人遂俱乘月形見在君左右。三年之中,並共笑樂言語。五年之中,五帝月夫人遂與君共乘飛龍之車。西到六嶺之門八絡之丘協晨之宮八景之城。登七靈之臺,坐太和之殿。

授裴君《流星夜光》之章,《十明》之符。食黃琬紫津之粕,飲月華雲膏。

81 In *Supreme Purity Most High Divine Elixir Instructions of Incarnation from the Central Scripture of the Nine Perfected* (*Shangqing taishang jiuzhen zhongjing jiangsheng shendan jue* 上清太上九真中經降生神丹訣, *DZ* 1377, 21a–b), both of these are acquired prior to an adept's ascent to the high heavens, where he would intone sacred stanzas and visualize a carriage to ride with the Lunar Ladies to the moon.

Five Imperial Solar Lords. This is what is called the Dao of Dashing for the Sun.

There are Five Emperors in the sun, who are elsewhere called the Solar Lords. The middle fascicle of *The Hidden Writings of the Most High* states, "If you want to become a perfected being, you must visualize the Solar Lords. You will harness dragons and tether phoenixes so that you can ride with the lords on heavenly phosphors and clouds. Travel east to the Rare Green-Gem Basilica and enter through the gate of the Emperors. Practice refined contemplation and you will succeed; this essential Dao is not complex. You will be appointed to Pure Numinosity, listed among the perfected officials, and given a copy of *The Writs of the Streaming Regalia*."

The Perfected Being of Grand Simplicity also said, "There is yet a second method for becoming a perfected being. At nightfall look at the moon, nearly close your eyes, and stop breathing for a count to nine. After this, gulp down the moonlight nine times. You should visualize the lunar rays entering your mouth and then swallow them.

"When finished, visualize the Azure Imperial Lady emanating from within the moonlight and taking a position on your left. Next, continue by visualizing the Red Imperial Lady emanating from within the moonlight and taking a position on your right. Next, continue by visualizing the White Imperial Lady emanating from within the moonlight and taking a position behind you. Next, continue by visualizing the Black Imperial Lady emanating from within the moonlight and taking a position on your left hand. Next, continue by visualizing the Yellow Imperial Lady emanating from within the moonlight and taking a position on your right hand. After all Five Imperial Ladies have arrived, visualize a carriage with swirling bells and a soaring cloud canopy that is hitched to a team of ten dragons emerging from the moonlight and coming before you. Then visualize your mounting this carriage with the Five Ladies, and ride off to the moon."

Lord Pei then stayed at Mt. Kong, where he put this refined contemplation into practice. Within one year, the faces of the Ladies began to appear. Within two years, the Five Ladies all streamed in on lunar rays and positioned themselves around him. Within three years, they would speak together with laughter and cheer. Within five years, the Five Imperial Lunar Ladies then rode the flying dragon chariot with Lord Pei. They traveled westward to the Harmonious Dawn Palace in the Eight Phosphor City of the Eight-Web Highlands in the Six Ridge Gate. There they ascended the Seven Numina Estrade to take their seats in the Grand Harmony Basilica.

They transmitted to Lord Pei the *Nocturnal Rays of a Comet's Luminescence* petition and a *Ten Purities* talisman.[81] He then ate food made from yellow round jade of the Purple Ford and drank cloudy paste of the lunar

於是與五夫人夕夕共遊。此所謂奔月之道矣。

月中亦有五帝夫人，外經云「日君月夫人」者，是少有髣髴也。《太上隱書》中篇曰：「子欲昇天，當存月夫人，駕十飛龍，乘我流鈴。西到六嶺，遂入帝堂。精思乃見上朝天皇，乃執《結璘章》。」

裴君白日精思，對日存日中五帝君。夜則精思，對月存月中五夫人。五年之中，日月精神並到。共乘飛龍，上遊太玄。

始學則五靈形見，授書賜芝。終成則日月五帝君五夫人驂轡清虛。乘雲太丹，朝謁三元，稽首金闕。乃獲《玉璽金真》，威制群神，役使玉女玉童。北朝四真人，受書為真。佩《神虎》之符，以制嚴六天。授流金之鈴，以命召眾精，仗青旄之節，以周流九宮。

皆由精思微妙，幽感天心。是以靈降扶身，上昇帝庭爾。道士行之者則是耳。不必以已仙人也。若處密室及日月不見時，但心中存而思之可也。不待見日月。

efflorescence.[82] Pei then traveled nightly with the Five Ladies. This was what is called the Dao of Dashing to the Moon.

In the moon are the Five Imperial Ladies, which profane scriptures refer to as the "Lunar Ladies of the Solar Lords," but their descriptions have some minor inconsistencies. The middle fascicle of *The Hidden Writings of the Most High* states, "If you want to ascend into the heavens, you must visualize the Lunar Ladies driving ten flying dragons riding atop your carriage's swirling bells. Proceed west to the Six Ridges and enter into the Emperor's Hall. You can ascend to the heavenly sovereign's court through refined contemplation and will receive *The Stanza on Knotted Spangles*."

During Lord Pei's daytime refined contemplation, he faced the sun to visualize the Five Imperial Lords of the sun. During his nighttime refined contemplation, he faced the moon to visualize the Five Ladies of the moon. Within five years, the spirits of the solar and lunar essences all arrived. They flew together with Pei on dragons, and traveled upward to the Grand Mystery heavens.

Back when Lord Pei started his studies, the Five Numina appeared in physical form and transmitted scriptures and bestowed mushrooms. In the end, when he finished what the Perfected Being of Grand Simplicity taught, the Five Imperial Lords of the Sun and Five Ladies of the Moon drove their team through the Pure Vacuity. They rode atop the clouds to the Grand Cinnabar, called upon the Three Primal Lords, and kowtowed before the Golden Porte. There Pei obtained the *Jade Seal of Golden Perfection*, with which he could wield power over the various spirits and order the jade maidens and jade lads. He had an audience with the Four Perfected Beings in the north and received a document confirming him as perfected. The Four Perfected gave him *Divine Tiger* talismans to wear on his waist so that he could control the Six Heavens. They also bestowed bells of swirling gold that could beckon forth any sprite, and gave him a staff with azure banners allowing him to roam throughout the Nine Palaces.

All of Pei's success stemmed from the subtle miracle of refined contemplation, which causes a mysterious resonance in heavenly minds. With such contemplation, numina will descend to support your body as it ascends into the courts of emperors on high. All Daoist adepts can achieve these same things in their practices. You do not necessarily need to be a transcendent being. If you are in a closed chamber, or the sun and moon are not visible, then you can do this by visualizing the sun and moon in your mind and contemplating them. You do not need to wait until you see the sun and

---

82   For more on the difference between round jade and pointed jade (yan 琰), see Knechtges 1987, 90 n. 199. For more on lunar efflorescence as orpiment, see Bokenkamp 1997, 336–337.

要見視之為至佳。惟精思心盡，無所不通。此言要也。

　　臨目者，令目當閉而不閉之間也。少令得見日月之光景。密而行之；勿令人知。雖雜人同室而止，有密其思者，比肩仍自不覺。每事盡當爾，不但此一條而已。求生養命在於心，三丹田三寸之間耳。是以龍變蟬蛻，皆以一致而成也。

　　《八素經》曰：「仙者心學，心誠則成仙。道者內求，內密則道來。榮者外求，口發則貴至。財者動心，心寂則富集。諸寂動異用，而所攻者一。守之在役用之機也。」

　　太素真人曰：「為真不知道者，亦復多耳。要於乘光揚景，騰雲昇虛，並日月之精，遊九天之表，餐霞飲玄，呼吸太和，乃不可不為此奇道。此道亦易成而速得也。眾真有不知此道者，見吾乘雲而攜日月五帝五夫人，莫不敬親而求請問之也。吾亦復未示之也。」

　　《內視中方》曰：「子欲步空常，當存日月。

83　The Eight Immaculates are the eight goddess counterparts of the gods called the Eight Phosphors (bajing 八景), all of which help an adept ingest the qi associated with the different parts of the year. See Robinet 2011b, 219–220.

moon. But you need to see and examine them for the best result. Everything is possible only if you wholeheartedly engage in refined contemplation. This is the most essential point.

"Nearly closing one's eyes" means that your eyes will nearly be closed, but not completely shut. This will allow you to see only a small amount of light from the sun and moon. Do this in secrecy; do not let others know about it. While other people might be in your chamber sitting right next to you, if you keep your thoughts a secret, they will never perceive what you are doing. Everything you do in your oratory should be done in this way, not simply these particular two methods. Seeking a long life and increasing your years is done through the mind, in spaces three inches under the skin of your Three Cinnabar Fields. Just as dragons transform and cicadas shed their skin, you too can achieve all of this in an instant.

The Scripture of the Eight Immaculates[83] reads, "What we call transcendence is learned with the mind, for one will become transcendent when one's mind is sincere. What we call the Dao is sought from inside, for the Dao will manifest when one is inwardly calm. What we call honor is sought from outside, for high esteem will come to one who speaks up. What we call wealth puts one's mind in motion, yet fortune only accumulates when you still your mind. All these kinds of action and inaction are employed differently, but their goal is the same—the One. Guarding it is at the heart of everything you do."

The Perfected Being of Grand Simplicity said, "There are so many people who want to become perfected, but know nothing about the Dao. The key is that you never neglect to do the following if you are to practice this miraculous Dao: You must ride beams of lights, stir phosphors, ride clouds, ascend vacuity, roam atop the Nine Heavens with the spirits of the sun and moon, sup on auroras, drink mystery, and breathe in the air of Grand Harmony. Nevertheless, this Dao is easy to complete and can be quickly attained. Every perfected being who does not know about this Dao will surely come to me and respectfully ask for it after seeing me riding the clouds with the Five Solar Emperors and Five Lunar Ladies. I have, however, never taught it to them."

The Middle Formula of Inner Vision reads, "If you want to regularly pace Kong and Chang,[84] you should visualize the spirits of the sun and moon. If

---

84 Alternative names for the two invisible stars of the Big Dipper. In the *Supreme Purity Airy and Mysterious Scripture on the Universal Metamorphosis and Ten Thousand Transformations of the Five Permanent Ones* (*Shangqing wuchang biantong wanhua yuming jing* 上清五常變通萬化鬱冥經, *DZ* 324), adepts pace a series of stars leading upward toward the Big Dipper. See Schipper and Verellen 2004, 172–173.

子欲登清泠,當存五星。密室密行,不出宇庭。」此之謂也。

夫守道者及學道求仙者,修行至精,皆可為之。為之既得,便成昇天仙人也。此道不必真人,而當獨行之也。子有真骨真性而密行之,必能含章守慎,不妄傳泄,故以相教耳。

《黃老祕言》曰:「子得《鬱儀》《結璘》,乃成上清之真。子得《大洞真經》,乃能飛行上清。無此三文,不得見三元君。」要道盡此,仙子加勤。中仙都無知此道者。此道相傳惟口訣耳。能知此道,不問賢愚,皆乘雲昇天,役使鬼神,羣仙立盟為約。不得妄宣,泄則滅門。口訣者,《黃老祕言》是也。

裴君受命留在空山之上,精思存修二事。五年之中,得見日月之精五帝夫人。讀《隱書》及《九有》、《十明》之符,積十一年。太素真人來告曰:「子成真矣。」因錫以龍車,給以羽蓋。並日月之遊精,參五帝之同乘。詣太素宮見上清三元君,受《玉璽金真》,給玉女二十四人,玉童三十二人。北遊詣太極宮及太微宮,位為清靈真人。

太素真人曰:「子存日精五帝君,口含《太上

you want to ascend into the clear and chilly heavens, you should visualize the gods of the Five Planets. Do these in secret within a secret chamber; do not go into your courtyard." This basically sums it up.

Any person who guards the Dao, including those who study the Dao to attain transcendence, can do these things if his practice is highly refined. If you do it and attain it, you will ascend to the heavens and become a transcendent being. You do not necessarily have to be perfected to receive this Dao, but all must practice it in solitude. As long as you have perfected bones and a perfected nature, practice this Dao in secret, can embody its fine qualities, can guard it with care, and do not recklessly divulge it, I will teach it to you.

The Secret Words of the Yellow Elder reads, "If you obtain *The Streaming Regalia* and *The Knotted Spangles*, you will become a perfected being of the Supreme Purity. If you obtain *The Perfected Scripture of the Great Cavern*, you can fly up into the Supreme Purity. Without these three writings, it will be impossible to see the three Primal Lords." These three texts are the consummation of the indispensable Dao. So all transcendent beings should work even harder to put them into practice. Even middle transcendents might be unaware of this Dao. This Dao is transmitted only through oral formulas. No matter whether one is a sage or a fool, one can ride up to the heavens on clouds, order demons and spirits, and make oaths and contracts with the various transcendents if one knows about this Dao. You should never carelessly transmit it to others, for this violation will cause the destruction of your lineage. This oral transmission refers to *The Secret Words of the Yellow Elder*.

After receiving these directives, Lord Pei stayed on Mt. Kong to focus on the two practices of refined contemplation and visualization. Within five years, the solar and lunar essences, that is, the Five Emperors and Five Ladies, appeared before him. For a total of eleven years, he read *The Hidden Book*, as well as the *Nine Realms* and *Ten Purities* talismans. Then the Perfected Being of Grand Simplicity came to him and announced, "You have become a perfected being." He was thereupon bestowed a dragon chariot, and supplied with a feathered canopy. He roamed with the solar and lunar essences, and traveled with the Five Emperors. They called upon the Palace of Grand Simplicity, where they had an audience with the Three Primal Lords of the Supreme Purity, who gave Pei the *Jade Seal of Golden Perfection* and supplied him with twenty-four jade maidens and thirty-two jade lads. He then traveled northward to call on the Grand Bourne Palace and the Grand Tenuity Palace, after which he was given the position of Perfected Being of Pure Numinosity.

The Perfected Being of Grand Simplicity said, "If you visualize the solar essences of the Five Imperial Lords and recite *The Most High Writ of*

鬱儀文》，須此道成，乃見日中君。無此徒勞自煩冤。」

太素真人曰：「子存月精五帝月夫人，口含《太上結璘章》，須此道成，乃見月中夫人。無此徒勞自悼傷。」

右二條太素真人受太帝君訣言。

《太上隱書》云：「存時執之。」帝君云：「含之。」太素真人教裴君：「存時含一文，執一文，並行之。」

《太上隱書》曰：「欲行此道，不必愚賢，但地上無此文耳。真官玄法，啟誓乃傳。金丹之信，道乃備焉。青帛之盟，道乃可宣。有得而行，位為真人。乃乘步景雲，晏羽旆瓊輪，遊行九天。上詣太極宮，謁高皇上元君。」

裴君乃先密受《太上鬱儀文》、《太上結璘章》二書，然後齋戒而得存日月之精爾。有仙名骨錄者，乃得見此二書。見之者仙，為之者真。

《鬱儀》、《結璘經》及《大洞真經》，乃太極四真人之所祕，上清天皇之所珍貴也。西玄山下洞臺中有此書；刻以玉簡，書以金字。及王屋清虛洞中，亦見有《鬱儀》、《結璘》之篇目爾，而不盡備具。惟大玄宮高上臺及

Streaming Regalia, then—and only then—when you realize the Dao, you will see the lords in the sun. Without this, you will labor away and be overcome with troubles."

The Perfected Being of Grand Simplicity further said, "If you visualize the lunar essences of the Lunar Ladies of the Five Imperial Lords and recite *The Most High Stanza of Knotted Spangles*, then—and only then—when you realize the Dao, you will see the ladies in the moon. Without this, you will labor away only to be overcome with pain."

These last two quotes were oral instructions that the Perfected Being of Grand Simplicity received from the Grand Imperial Lord.

The Hidden Writings of the Most High states, "When you visualize them, you will hold them." The Imperial Lord said, "Place them in your mouth." The Perfected Being of Grand Simplicity taught Lord Pei, "During visualization, place one text in your mouth while holding the other text; do these things at the same time."

The Hidden Writings of the Most High reads, "While you might wish to practice this Dao, there is no way to attain this text on Earth, regardless of whether you are a fool or a sage. According to the mysterious laws of perfected officials, it is transmitted only to those who first make a request and take an oath. The Dao can be fully revealed only after one makes a pledge of gold and cinnabar. This Dao can be transmitted to others only after they make a covenant of azure silk. Anyone who attains this Dao and puts it into practice will be a perfected being. Thereafter, they will ride on phosphors and clouds as they soar into the Nine Heavens on a chariot with feathered flags and rose-gem wheels. They will visit the Grand Bourne Palace and call upon the high and august Upper Prime Lord."[vi]

Lord Pei first secretly received two texts, *The Most High Writs of the Streaming Regalia* and *The Most High Stanza on Knotted Spangles*, after which he observed the purification precepts and could visualize the solar and lunar essences. Those who have a transcendent name inscribed on the osseous register will be able to view these two texts, and those who view the texts will become transcendents, while those who put them into practice will become perfected.

The Streaming Regalia, *The Knotted Spangles*, and *The Perfected Scripture of the Great Cavern* are the texts that the Grand Bourne's Four Perfected keep secret, and that are cherished by the celestial sovereigns of the Supreme Purity heavens. The grotto terrace beneath Mt. Xixuan contains these two texts, engraved on jade slats and written in gold letters. Although the Pure-Vacuous Grotto beneath Mt. Wangwu has copies of *Streaming Regalia* and *Knotted Spangles*, they contain only the table of contents, not the full text. The only other full copies of these texts can be found in the highest terrace of the Great Mystery heaven and the northern chamber of

蓬萊府北室金柱玉壁刻文，並備具也。精心存念，晝夜為之。十一年而成爾。與修《洞經》者大都等爾。

夫此二文，是《洞經》之祖宗，《素靈經》之園囿爾。凡諸下仙，莫有聞《鬱儀》之篇目，《結璘》之密旨者。得其道，皆速成而無試也。又致神之驗，是為逕疾。得其要道者，但速於《大洞》之祕妙爾。

非有仙名者，皆不得聞此書。聞見此書而敢妄以語一人者，即滅侍真官、玉女、玉童各十人，自然使天火災而失之。語二人已上，不可得以學仙也。按泄《洞經》之科條，即已有輕重之異，減損侍真，便十倍於《大洞》。

地上骨錄有相之道人，而有此書者，皆為師主。男稱「監靈大夫」，女稱「執明大夫」。男稱「左」，女稱「右」。

《素奏丹符》曰：「大哉！《鬱儀》，妙行《結璘》。非上真不見，非上仙不聞。以致日月五精之神，乘龍步空，足躡景雲，遂與五帝，上入天門。有之聞之，慎勿妄言。去世可出，誓金乃傳。要付弟子有心之者，勿道篇目，玉童上言。泄則被考，身終不仙。玉童玉女，去而不還。書文必失，獲刑三官。子其慎之！言為罪先！」

the Penglai Isles bureau, where they are carved in jade on the gold pillars. From morning to night, visualize them with great care. After eleven years, this practice will be completed. The results will be more or less equal to cultivating the techniques of *The Cavern Scripture*.

These two texts are the forebears of *The Cavern Scripture* and the garden out of which grew *The Scripture of the Immaculate Numen*. Not a single lesser transcendent has heard the contents of *The Streaming Regalia* and the secret directives of *The Knotted Spangles*. But those who attain this Dao can quickly complete it without need for testing. Moreover, when they summon gods, the response will come instantly. Those who attain this essential Dao just make faster progress than if they were to rely on the marvelous wonders of *The Great Cavern*.

If someone does not possess a name fated for transcendence, they must not be permitted to hear about these texts. If you hear or see these texts and dare to recklessly divulge them to a single person, you will lose the service of the ten perfected officials, ten jade maidens and ten jade lads, and the texts will spontaneously be consumed by a heavenly conflagration. If you speak of the texts to two or more people, you will no longer be able to learn about transcendence. According to the rules about divulging *The Cavern Scripture*, which rules already provide- punishments of varying degrees, the loss of attendant perfected beings for divulging these two texts will be ten times more than that for *The Great Cavern*.

The osseous register on Earth has a list of marks of people of Dao, and anyone who possesses this document will have the title of master. Men are called "grandees who oversee the numina," and women are called "ladies who cling to luminosity." Men are called "the left," and women are called "the right."

The *Pure Announcement on Cinnabar* talisman reads, "Great indeed is *The Streaming Regalia*, and wondrous are the ways of *The Knotted Spangles*. Only the greater perfected have seen them, and only the greater transcendents have heard about them. With these texts one can summon the gods of the five solar and lunar essences, ride dragons, pace the void, tread atop phosphors and clouds, and ascend to enter Heaven's Gate alongside the Five Emperors. If you possess or have heard of them, you may report this to the heavens, but take care not to recklessly divulge them. If someone has abandoned the world, you can show it to him, but do so only after an oath sealed with gold. It is essential that if you give it to a disciple who 'has a mind,' do not speak of its contents, for jade lads will report this on high. If one leaks its contents and is found out, one will in the end never become a transcendent. Accompanying jade lads and jade maidens will depart and never return. The texts one possesses will certainly disappear, and one will be punished by the Three Officials. Be very careful about this! Speaking of it leads to transgressions!"

峨嵋山北洞中石室戶樞刻石書字曰：「《鬱儀》引日精，《結璘》致月神。得道為上官，位稱大夫真。」凡二十字，下仙讀此，不解其意。仙人自有不見其篇目者多矣。其《金液》、《九丹》蓋小術也，皆不得飛行上清。

《大洞真經》有泄之者，按《玄中科》，即減一紀，玉童玉女各減一人。三泄之身死，不得復成仙人。《太上鬱儀文》、《結璘章》有泄之者，減玉童玉女各十人。天火燒屋，書從火中失而還上天也。再泄身刑，死不復生。學道終不成仙也。泄言妄說篇目，並受考於三官。

師有當因緣去世之日，或歸反陰塗絕迹藏變之時，要當有所授。若無其人，乃自隨身。受之者皆青金丹縷之贐，為誓天地不泄宣之盟約，乃得出之。師隨事上聞，而有奏署日月也。不從科條，皆為妄泄。

《大洞真經》乃中央黃老君之寶書。非至真上士有玉名之者，莫見篇章條目也。真仙亦有不聞此書者矣。初限令一百年乃得一出傳可成，而不得妄說篇目。《太上鬱儀》、《結璘文章》，以致於日月之精神，上奔日月，通天光，飛太空之道也。皆乘雲車羽蓋，

Inside the northern grotto of Mt. Emei is a stone chamber whose door contains the following text carved in stone: "Draw in the solar essences with *The Streaming Regalia*, and cause the lunar spirits to descend with *The Knotted Spangles*. You will attain this Dao and become a high official, with the position of grandee perfected." Generally, when lesser transcendents read these twenty characters, they cannot understand its meaning. And many transcendents have never even seen its title. The Golden Liquor and Nine Tripods are lesser arts insufficient for flying up to the Supreme Purity heavens.

Anyone who divulges *The Perfected Scripture of the Great Cavern*, according to the Mystic Central Code, will lose twelve years from their lifespan in addition to losing one jade lad and one jade maiden. If one leaks it three times, one will die and never become a transcendent being. Anyone who divulges *The Streaming Regalia* and *The Knotted Spangles*, however, will lose ten jade lads and ten jade maidens. Furthermore, a heavenly conflagration will burn one's house down, and the copy of this text will be lost in the fire and returned to Heaven. Anyone who divulges this text yet again will pay the price with his life, and once dead, he will not be reborn. Although one has studied this Dao, one will, in the end, have no chance to become a transcendent. Anyone who leaks these texts or recklessly speaks about their contents will be interrogated by the Three Officers.

Masters have karmic affinities that will determine the day of their death. In some cases, when a master prepares for his return on the Yin Path and erases his traces to hide his transformation, he should designate someone to receive transmission of these texts. But if there is no such person for transmission, these texts should follow him to the grave. All those who receive texts should pledge an offering of lead and cinnabar threads as they make a vow to Heaven and Earth promising to never divulge the texts, at which time the text may be released. A master must then make this known on high and announce his office to the gods of the sun and moon. But if these codes are not followed, transgressions will be treated the same as if one recklessly divulged the text.

The Perfected Scripture of the Great Cavern is the precious book of the Yellow Elder Lord of the Center. If one does not have a jade name of an utmost perfected and superior man, there is no way one can even see its table of contents. Even many perfected and transcendent beings have never even heard of this book. Initially, one is allowed to transmit it a single time every hundred years, but one must never recklessly speak about its contents. *The Streaming Regalia* and *The Knotted Spangles* are a Dao enabling one to summon the solar and lunar spirits, race upward to the sun and moon, penetrate the heavenly radiance, and fly into the Grand Void. All who obtain it will be able to ride on a chariot of clouds with a feathered canopy,

駕命羣龍，而上昇皇天紫庭也。

《大洞真經》以致於朝靈之道，招神成真人之法也。乘雲駕龍，騰躍玄虛。衣繡羽佩，金真玉光。逍遙太霞，上昇九霄矣。

此二書，天帝之祕塗，微妙哉！太素真人猶隱其篇目，但漫云二事者，是祕諱之甚也。況世人而令知其甲乙乎？有相遇而得之者，至誠好事。仍可為之，別有事旨，故不一二。

裴君所受真書篇目，列之于左：

支子元《神訣》五首，蔣先生所祕用。咸陽城南佛圖中曲室密房受之。
青帝君授《紫微始青道經》一卷。
蒼帝君授《蒼元上籙》、《北斗真經》、《中命四旋經》四卷。
白帝君授《太素玉籙》、《寶玄經》三卷。
赤帝君授《龍胎太和丹經》二卷。
黃帝君授《四氣上樞太元黃書》八卷。

85 The realm of burgeoning dawn-light. See Kroll 2003, 177 n. 70.

and command a team of dragons to ascend upward to August Heaven's Purple Court.

The Perfected Scripture of the Great Cavern, by means of its Dao enabling one to summon numina of the divine court, is a method of becoming perfected by beckoning gods. One can ride clouds, drive dragons, and leap up to the mystic void. One will wear finely stitched robes with feathered pendants as they shine with a jade radiance of pure gold. They will stroll across heavens of the Grand Aurora[85] and will ascend into the Nine Empyreans.

How subtle and sublime are these two books, the secret paths of the Heavenly Emperor! Even though the Perfected Being of Grand Simplicity has hidden their contents, he has spoken widely about these two texts, but with the utmost secrecy and discretion. How could an ordinary person be allowed to know about one or the other of these sources? If one were fated to encounter these texts and acquire them, what a truly great thing this would be! What is more, if one can put them into practice, one should not have even a single other worry or matter to concern oneself with.

The titles of the perfected books that Lord Pei received are as follows:

Divine Instructions in five stanzas, bestowed by Zhi Ziyuan and used secretly by Master Jiang. Pei received these in South Xianyang monastery in a sealed chamber in a private room.
Scripture of Purple Tenuity's Inaugural Azure Dao in one fascicle, bestowed by the Azure Imperial Lord.
Upper Register of the Gray-Blue Prime, Perfected Scripture of the Northern Dipper, and *Four Revolutions of the Central Mandate* in four fascicles, bestowed by the Gray-Blue Imperial Lord.
Jade Register of Grand Simplicity and *Perfected Scripture of Precious Mystery* in three fascicles, bestowed by the White Imperial Lord.
Cinnabar Scripture of Grand Harmony of the Dragon Embryo in two fascicles, bestowed by the Red Imperial Lord.
Grand Primal Yellow Book of the Upper Pivot of the Four Qi in eight fascicles, bestowed by the Yellow Imperial Lord.[86]

---

86 A "yellow book" consists of rules or guidelines on the use of sexual intercourse as a macrobiotic regime. See Wang Ka 1997, 72; Zhu Yueli 1998, 167; Kohn 1995, 198. There are two extant yellow books closely associated with Supreme Purity texts—the *Cavernous Perfection Yellow Book* (*Dongzhen huangshu* 洞真黃書, DZ 1343) and *Supreme Purity Yellow Book's Ritual of Passage* (*Shangqing huangshu guoduyi* 上清黃書過度儀, DZ 1294)—but neither uses the vocabulary in this title. See Raz 2008, 90–91 n. 5.

青帝君授《通光陽霞》之符。
蒼帝君授《鬱真簫鳳》之符。
白帝君授《皓靈扶希》之符。
赤帝君授《四明朱碧》之符。
黃帝君授《中元八維玉門》之符。

　　右十書，於太華山西洞玄石室受。

谷希子青帝君授青精日水青華芝，東到青丘受服。
《上皇籙》，司命君於太山授。
太素真人授《太上鬱儀文》，在白水沙洲空山之上授。
太素真人授《太上結璘文》，在白水沙洲空山之上授。
太素真人授《太上隱書》，在白水沙洲空山之上授。
上清三元君授《玉璽金真》，在太素宮金闕下授。
四真人授《神虎》符、流金火鈴，在太極宮授。
日中五帝君授《揮神》之章、《九有》之符、青精日粕、雲碧玄腴。
月中五帝夫人授《流星夜光》章、《十明》之符、黃琬紫津之粕、月華雲膏。

87　In *DZ* 1138, 64.1b, this talisman is also associated with the Azure Lord and used to safeguard one's liver.

Penetrating Solar Auroras talisman, bestowed by the Azure Imperial Lord.[87]

Piping Phoenix of Embellished Perfection talisman, bestowed by the Gray-Blue Imperial Lord.

Hoary Numen That Grasps the Imperceptible talisman, bestowed by the White Imperial Lord.

Four Lights of the Vermillion Discs talisman, bestowed by the Red Imperial Lord.

Central Prime of the Jade Gate's Eight Directions talisman, bestowed by the Yellow Imperial Lord.

Pei received the last ten of these texts when he was in the mysterious stone chamber in the western cave of Mt. Taihua.

Solar water infused with azure essence and azure-blossom mushroom, bestowed by the Azure Imperial Lord, Guxizi, when Pei went east to the Azure Hillocks to consume them.

Register of the Higher Luminaries, bestowed by the Director of Destinies at Mt. Tai.

Most High Writs of the Streaming Regalia, bestowed by Perfected Being of Grand Simplicity when Pei went high atop Mt. Kong at the sandbars of the Baishui River.

Most High Writ on Knotted Spangles, bestowed by the Perfected Being of Grand Simplicity when Pei went high atop Mt. Kong at the sandbars of the Baishui River.

Hidden Writings of the Most High, bestowed by the Perfected Being of Grand Simplicity when Pei went high atop Mt. Kong at the sandbars of the Baishui River.

Jade Seal of Golden Perfection, bestowed by the Three Primal Lords of the Supreme Purity when Pei kneeled beneath the Golden Porte of the Palace of Grand Simplicity.

Divine Tiger talisman and fiery bells of flowing gold, bestowed by the Four Perfected Beings when Pei was at the Palace of the Grand Bourne.

Marshalling Spirits petition, *Nine Realms* talisman, azure essences of solar viands, and dark oil skimmed off of nebulous cyan stones bestowed by the Five Imperial Solar Lords.

Nocturnal Rays of a Comet's Luminescence petition, *Ten Purities* talisman, food made from the yellow pointed jade of the Purple Ford, and cloudy ointment of the lunar efflorescence bestowed by the Five Imperial Lunar Ladies.

右裴君所受眾書符之目。

　　裴君授支子元服茯苓法，焦山蔣先生所傳。茯苓五斤，盛治去外皮，乃擣下細簁。 以漬白蜜三斗中，盛之以銅器（若耐熱曰瓦器）。以此器著大釜中，著水裁半於所盛藥器腹。微火燒釜，令水沸煮藥器。數反側藥，令相和合。

　　良久蜜銷竭煎。出著鐵臼中，擣三萬杵。令可丸。但服三十丸，如梧桐子大。百日百病除。二百日可夜書。二年使鬼神。四年玉女侍衛。十年夜視有光，能隱能彰，長生久視。服此一年，百害不能傷，疾病不復干。色反嬰兒，肌膚充悅。白髮再黑，眼有流光。

　　合藥齋三日。烹之於密盛處。勿令婦人雞犬見，及穢漫之也。五斤茯苓、三斗白蜜為一劑。當作木蓋，蓋之烹藥器上，勿露也。烹之時，反側藥。熟乃開之耳。火以好薪炭，不可用不成樵輩以烹之也。當用意伺候料視，恒以為意，欲并合多少在意。藥成，預作丸，盛之以密器，可經於千歲不敗。

　　裴君受支子元服胡麻法，蔣先生於黃金鼇祖山中授支公也。胡麻三斗肥者。黃黑無拘，在可擇之。使精潔，於微火上熬，令香氣極。令燥，細擣以為散。令沒沒爾；勿下簁。

All the titles above are the entire catalog of Lord Pei's books and talismans.

Lord Pei also received a method for consuming poria from Zhi Ziyuan, which was transmitted by Mr. Jiang at Mt. Jiao. Clean and prepare five catties of poria by peeling its outer coating, pounding it with a pestle, and finely straining it. Infuse it in three pints of white honey; then place this mixture in a bronze receptacle (it only needs to be heat-resistant, so some recipes call for an earthenware receptacle). Place this receptacle inside a large cauldron, which should be filled with water until the water reaches halfway up the side of the inner receptacle. Apply low heat to the cauldron so that the water surrounding the inner receptacle boils. Then tip the inner receptacle from side to side so that the herbs are evenly mixed throughout the mixture.

After a long time, the honey should dry and harden. Scrape out what remains and pound it with a pestle in a mortar thirty thousand times so that it can be made into pills. Each day, consume thirty pills the size of paulownia seeds. After a hundred days, one's illnesses will be cured. After two hundred days, one can write in the dark. After two years, one can command ghosts and spirits. After four years, jade maidens will attend to one's needs. After ten years, a beam of light will appear so that one can see in the dark, can appear and disappear at will, and will attain long life. Even ingesting these pills for only a year will safeguard one from harm and ensure good health. One's complexion will return to a youthful appearance, and one's entire body will feel pleasant. White hair will turn black, and the eyes will have a flashing brilliance.

Compounding this medication requires three days of purification. Boil the mixture in a secret location when preparing it. Do not let women, chickens, or dogs see you do this, and do not let anything unclean sully the mixture. Five catties of poria and three pints of clear honey will yield one portion. Fashion a wooden cover, and place it on top of the receptacle so that the mixture is not exposed. As it boils, occasionally mix it by turning the receptacle around. Open the lid only after the mixture has been thoroughly cooked. Be sure to use high-quality charcoal for the fire; do not use wood that is still green. Pay close attention while preparing this mixture, and remain focused at all times on the quantity being made. When finishing the preparation, make pills, and store them in a sealed container that will allow the pills to stay fresh for a thousand years.

Lord Pei received a method for consuming sesame from Zhi Ziyuan, which Master Jiang had given to Duke Zhi on the golden hills of Mt. Biezu: Obtain three pints of large sesame seeds. It makes no difference whether you select yellow or black seeds. After thoroughly cleaning the seeds, simmer them over low heat, which will bring out their fragrance. Reduce this until dry, and then pound the mixture in a mortar until it becomes a fine powder. Leave everything mixed together; do not sift it.

白蜜三斗，以胡麻散，漬會蜜中。攪令相和，使調巾。安器，著釜水中。乃煑如前煑茯苓法也。

伺候令煎竭可擣。乃出擣之三萬杵。如桐子大，旦服三十丸。盡一劑，腸化為筋，不知寒熱。面反童顏，役使眾靈。

蔣先生惟服此二方。先生已凌煙化升，呼吸立至。出入無間，輿乘羣龍。上朝帝，真位為仙宗者也。

當簸擇胡麻令精。此二方與世方書小異。裴君所祕者，驗而有實也。云：「體先不虛損，及年少之時，當服茯苓。若出三十者，當服胡麻。」蔣先生云：「此二方是大有之要法。長生神仙之祕寶。」

《寶玄經》云：「茯苓治少，胡麻治老。合以齋戒，服以朝畚。卉醴華腴，火精水寶，和以為一，還精歸寶。」此之謂也。卉醴華腴，蜜也。火精，茯苓也。水寶，胡麻也。裴君以年少時所用，故服茯苓，二方同耳。皆長生不死，必仙之奇方也。

若大有資力者，亦可合二物。倍用蜜共煎，擣以

---

88 A common phrase in early medieval China to express the transformation of the body into a transcendent form. See *DZ* 388, 2.11b, where this is one of the bodily processes occurring when an adept begins drinking from fonts of jade.

Steep the sesame powder in three pints of clear honey. Mix the ingredients until the powder completely dissolves. Place this mixture in a receptacle, and put it in a cauldron filled with water. Boil this just as in the aforementioned poria method.

Wait for this mixture to dry and harden so that it can be compounded. Remove it from the receptacle, and pound it a total of thirty thousand times in a mortar. Consume thirty pills per day that are the size of paulownia seeds. After finishing the entire batch, a person's intestines will turn into tendons,[88] and they will no longer feel cold or hot. One's face will revert back to a youthful appearance, and one will be able to command droves of numina.

Master Jiang practiced only these two methods. Yet the master could ascend to the heavens on a wisp of smoke and arrive there in a single breath. He was always disappearing and reappearing on his chariot, which was hitched to a team of dragons. He ascended to the courts of celestial emperors, where his title of being perfected earned him the veneration of transcendent beings.

To make the purest pills, be sure to sift out the chaff when selecting the sesame seeds. These two methods are only slightly different from those commonly circulated. These recipes, which Lord Pei kept secret, really worked for him. Pei said, "One should consume poria while one's body is in its prime and one is young. But if one is thirty years or older, one should consume sesame." Master Jiang said, "These two methods are key rituals of the Great Existence heaven.[89] They are secret treasures for living long as a divine transcendent."

The *Scripture of Precious Mystery* reads, "Poria cures the young, while sesame cures the elderly. Maintain a fast and uphold the precepts before compounding them, and consume the pills each morning. Combine the grassy liquor of flowery oil with fiery essence and aqueous treasure, and one's seminal essence will be restored when all of these are mixed into one." This refers to the recipes above. The grassy liquor of the flowery oil is honey. The fiery essence is poria. The aqueous treasure is sesame. Because Pei was young when he started using them, he consumed poria, but both recipes are essentially the same. They must be miraculous recipes used by transcendents, for they allow one to live forever.

If one is endowed with the powers of Great Existence, one can compound both substances at the same time. It is best if you double the amount of honey and reduce the poria and sesame until it hardens, then pound it

---

89 The name of a lofty Daoist heaven populated by many high gods. Pettit and Chang 2020, vii.

為丸乃佳，亦並治老少矣。茯苓、胡麻，不必別作之也。此二方，蔣先生乃各在一處授支公，不頓之也。是以焦山而茯苓方傳，鼈祖而胡麻方出。明道祕之文，乃不可得一盡其根源也。至於支公授裴君，亦乃頓倒囊笈之奧言。肆傾玄真之祕塗，將以逆鑒察天錄，必當已知應為仙真乎。

into pills. It can cure both the elderly and the young. Poria and sesame do not need to be prepared separately. Master Jiang gave these two methods to Duke Zhi at two different places rather than all at once. Jiang transmitted the poria recipe at Mt. Jiao and gave Zhi the sesame recipe at Mt. Biezu. Usually, all the writs illuminating the secrets of the Dao cannot be obtained from a single source. But in the case of Duke Zhi, he bestowed all of the mysterious words to Lord Pei at once by dumping out his bag of slips. So anyone truly inclined to learn the esoteric path of mystic perfection must first check the heavenly registers, for they must know if they are a transcendent or a perfected being.

Text-Critical Endnotes

i. This sentence is unusual in that it clarifies a term in the previous sentence, which suggests that it may be a commentarial layer embedded in the text.
ii. Reading the first *zhu* 諸 in this sentence as a scribal error for *yi* 詣.
iii. Reading *ruo* 若 as *huo* 或.
iv. Reading *qing* 青 as *qing* 清.
v. Reading *hao* 浩 as *hao* 皓.
vi. Reading *zhu* 諸 as *yi* 詣.

玄洲上卿蘇君傳
周季通集

先師姓蘇諱林字子玄。濮陽曲水人也。少禀異操,獨逸無倫。訪真之志,與日彌篤。

常負擔至趙,師琴高先生。時年二十一受煉氣益命之道。琴高初爲周康王門下舍人,以内行補精術及丹法;能水游飛行。時已九百歲,唯不死而已,飛仙也。後乘赤鯉入水,或出入人間。而林託景丹霄,志不終此。

後改師華山仙人仇先生。仇先生者,湯王時木匠也。服胎食之法,還神守魂之事,大得其益。先生曰:「子真人也,當學真道。我迹不足蹋矣。」乃致林於涓子。涓子者,真人也。

---

1 The city of Puyang is located in modern Hebei and was the burial place of Zhuanxu 顓頊 or Gao Yang 高陽, one of the so-called Five Emperors and grandson of the early mythical emperor Huangdi. See Zang Lihe 1972, 1282.
2 Qin Gao, reported to be from the state of Zhao, lived near the end of the Zhou era and was accomplished in both the zither and techniques of longevity. According to Zhou Yishan's hagiography, he was also called Mister Cen 岑先生 and was the teacher of Zhou Yishan 周義山. King Kang of Zhou was the third sovereign of the Zhou empire and ruled ca. 1020–996 BCE.

Traditions of Lord Su, Upper Chamberlain of the Mysterious Continent
Compiled by Zhou Jitong

My former teacher was surnamed Su, with the taboo name Lin, and was styled Zixuan. He was from Qushui in Puyang County.[1] When young, he was endowed with unusual moral integrity and lived in solitude without a companion. He had an ambition to search for perfected beings, and he became more devoted to this each day.

Su often went to the state of Zhao to work, and that is where he took Master Qin Gao as his teacher. When Su was twenty years old, Qin Gao gave him a Dao for refining his qi and prolonging his life. Formerly, Qin Gao had been a retainer at the court of King Kang of Zhou, where he engaged in internal practices of mending his essence and in alchemical techniques. He could travel on water and move through the air.[2] At this time, Qin Gao was nine hundred years old, but had managed to avoid death only as a flying transcendent. Later in life, he plunged beneath waters by riding a red carp, and only occasionally visited the human world.[3] But while Su could grasp phosphors to rise to the cinnabar empyrean, his ambitions did not end here.

Later, Su changed teachers to follow Master Qiu, a transcendent being at Mt. Hua. Master Qiu was a carpenter in the time of King Tang.[4] He knew a ritual for nourishing his spiritual embryo and a way to return his spirit[5] and guard his cloud-souls, which was of great benefit to him. Master Qiu said, "You are a perfected being, and thus should study a perfected Dao. My tracks are not sufficient for you to follow." So he sent Su Lin to Juanzi, a perfected being.

---

3   For more on this passage and its relation to other early Daoist texts, see Pettit and Chang 2020, 40.
4   The first king of the Shang, ca. 17th c. BCE.
5   In texts written before the Supreme Purity revelations, the term *huanshen* referred to practices that would help restore bodily spirits that had fallen into disarray. Supreme Purity writers claim that an adept must always concentrate on keeping both cloud-souls (*hun*) and white-souls (*po*) fixed in his body, since the former tend to roam to heaven and the latter to earth. See Robinet 1993, 44.

既見之,遂授以真訣。告林曰:
「欲作地上真人,必先服食藥物。除去三尸,殺滅穀蟲。

　　三尸者,一名青古。伐人眼,是故目暗、面皺、口臭、齒落。由是青古之氣穿鑿泥丸也。二名白姑。伐人五臟,是故心耄、氣少、喜忘、荒悶。由白姑貫穿六府之液也。三名血尸。伐人胃管,是故腸輪、煩滿、骨枯、肉燋。志意不開,所思不固。失食則飢,悲愁感欷。精誠昏怠,神爽雜錯。由血尸流噬魂胎之關也。

　　若不去三尸,而服藥者,穀食雖斷,蟲猶不死也。徒絕五味,雖勤吐納,亦無益者。蓋其蟲生,而求人不死,不可得也。是故服食不辟於死生,由青古、白姑、血尸三鬼

6　See *Traditions of Lord Pei* (p. 11 above).
7　Our translation of this passage was aided by Michael Stanley-Baker's translation in "Daoists and Doctors" (2013, 197).
8　See *DZ* 303, 4a; Kubo Noritada 1956, 171; Raz 2004, 372; Pettit and Chang 2020, 289 n. 23.

Upon meeting, Juanzi provided Lin with perfected formulas. Juanzi said to Lin,

"If you desire to become a terrestrial perfected, you must first take medicine. This will eliminate the three corpses and exterminate the grain worms.[6]

"The first of the three corpses is called the Azure Ancient.[7] It attacks one's eyes, causing one's vision to become dim, one's face to wrinkle, one's breath to become foul, and one's teeth to fall out. These are signs that the Azure Ancient's qi has bored a hole in one's Muddy Pellet. The second is called the White Maid.[8] It attacks one's five viscera, which causes cognitive decline, a decrease in one's qi, a loss of happiness, and an onset of melancholy. These are signs that the White Maid has penetrated the fluid of the six organs.[9] The third is called the Bloody Corpse. It attacks one's guts, which causes one's bowels to churn, ailments to abound, one's bones to wither, and one's flesh to become emaciated. One loses willpower and cannot think straight. One loses appetite and becomes emaciated, as melancholy causes one to sigh. One's zeal fades away, and one's spirit rattles all about. These are signs that the Bloody Corpse has gnawed at the pass of one's cloud-soul embryo.[10]

"If one does not first expel the Three Corpses but still takes medicine, even though one has stopped eating grain, these worms will not die. And if one cuts out the five flavors from one's diet, even though one has adhered to breathing exercises, one will still receive no benefit. If these worms are still living, a person looking to stave off death will never succeed. Thus, eating a certain way will never allow one to overcome the cycle of life and death, for the three demons—the Azure Ancient, the White Maid, and the

---

9   Or the six bowels, namely, the gallbladder, stomach, large intestine, small intestine, bladder, and "triple burner" (sanjiao 三焦) of the thorax. See Chen Guying 1994, 845–848.
10 Many forms of Supreme Purity practice focus on the transformation of an adept (or his ancestors) as he gives life to a spiritual embryo, often achieved through breathing techniques (see Robinet 1993, 84–85; Pregadio 2004, 126–127). The cloud-soul embryo is mentioned in the *Cavernous Perfection Supreme Purity Purple Book of the Green Waist, with the Combined Scriptures of the Golden Root* (*Dongzhen shangqing qingyao zishu jin'gen zhongjing* 洞真上清青要紫書金根眾經, DZ 1315, 11b) as the essence of an adept's embryo, nourished by the qi of the Nine Heavens, which one must protect or guard. The pass refers to the nine heavenly points that an adept passes through during his embryonic transformation. See the *Cavernous Perfection Supreme Purity Scripture on Dipper Transfer, with Three Limits for Opening Heaven* (*Dongzhen shangqing kaitian santu qixing yidu jing* 洞真上清開天三圖七星移度經, DZ 1317, 1a); Robinet 1993, 216.

不去所致爾。雖復斷穀，人體重滯奄奄淡悶。又所夢非真，顛倒翻錯，邪淫不除。由蟲在内搖動五神故也。

凡欲求真，當先服制蟲丸。制蟲丸者，一名初神去本丸也。欲作真人，當先服制仙丸。制仙丸者，太上八瓊飛精之丹也。夫求長生不死仙真之初，罔不先服制蟲丸。以除尸蟲，建長生之根矣。若人腹中有蟲，寧得仙乎？形中饒鬼，安得真乎？其蟲凶惡，速人之死，故當除之。」

涓子後告林曰：「我被帝召，上補中黃四司大夫領北海公。去世無復日也。」

後林詣涓子寢靜之室，得書一幅，以遺林也。其文曰：

《五斗三一》，太帝所祕。精思二十年，三一相見，授子書矣。但有三一，長生不滅；況復守之乎？能存三一，名刊玉札，況與三一相見乎？加存洞房爲上清公。加知三元爲五帝君。

---

11 See *Great Cavern's Jade Scripture* (*Dadong yujing* 大洞玉經, *DZ* 7, 2.5a), in which an adept is "given the transcendent title of a Supreme Purity Duke" (*wei wei Shangqinggong xianwei* 位为上清公仙位) once he has produced a baby through alchemical meditation.

Bloody Corpse—have yet to be expelled. Although one might repeatedly stop eating grains, one's body will become heavy and sluggish, frail and failing, weak and downcast. And since one's dreams are not directed toward perfection, one will topple over in a state of confusion and never eradicate what is evil and lewd. These are signs that the worms are jolting one's five visceral spirits within.

"When one starts to seek perfection, one should first take the Commanding-Worms Pill. The Commanding-Worms Pill is also called the Pill of Initiating Godhood by Cutting Off the Root. But when one is about to become a perfected being, one should first take the Commanding-Transcendence Pill. The Commanding-Transcendence Pill is also called the Elixir of the Flying Essences of the Eight Rose-Gems Most High. Now, everyone who seeks a long life as a new transcendent or perfected must first take a Commanding-Worms Pill. By expelling the corpses and worms, one can establish the basis for a long life. If one has worms in one's chest, how can one achieve transcendence? If one's body is rife with demons, how can one achieve perfection? The worms are ferocious and hasten death. So one must expel them."

Juanzi later told Su Lin, "I have been summoned by imperial command and promoted to fill a position in the Central Directorate of Circuit Supervisors as the Duke of the Northern Seas. Once I leave this realm, I will have no occasion to return here."

After this, Su Lin went to Juanzi's meditation chamber and found a text scroll that had been left for him. The document read,

> *The Three Ones of the Five Dipper Stars* is a secret of the Grand Emperor. I concentrated my thoughts for twenty years and received this text during an audience with the Three Ones. Those who have the Three Ones will gain long life and not perish. Wouldn't it be so much better to guard them? Those who can visualize the Three Ones will have their name inscribed on the jade slats. Wouldn't it be so much better to have an audience with them? To this add visualizing the Grotto-Room, which will manifest the Supreme Purity Duke.[11] To this add knowing the Three Primes, which will manifest the Five Imperial Lords.[12] The Dao of the Three Primal Perfected Ones of the

---

12 See the description of the techniques of the Five Imperial Lords in the *Traditions of Lord Pei* (p. 43 above).

後聖金闕帝君所以乘景迅雷，周行十天，寔由洞房三元真一之道。

吾餌朮精三百年，服氣五百年。精思六百年，守三一三百年。守洞房六百年，守玄丹五百年。中間復周遊名山，看望八海。廻翔五嶽，休息洞室。樂林草之垂條，與鳥獸之相激。川瀆吐精，丘陵蓊鬱。萬物之秀，寒暑之節。

弋釣長流，遨遊玄瀨。靜心山岫，念真養氣。呼召六丁玉女，見衛展轉六合，無所羈束。守形思真二千八百餘年，寔樂中仙，不求聞達。今卒被召，上補天位。徘徊世澤，惆悵絕氣，吾其去矣。請從此別，子勤勗之，相望飆室也。

林省書流涕，徬徨拜空。涓師之迹，於是絕迹矣。

Grotto-Room is how the Later-Age Sage, that is, the Imperial Lord of the Golden Porte, rode phosphors and thunderclaps to circle the ten heavens.[13]

I consumed essence of atractylodes for three hundred years, and ingested qi for five hundred years.[i] I remained in refined contemplation for six hundred years, and guarded the Three Ones for three hundred years. Then I guarded the Grotto-Room for six hundred years, and guarded the Mysterious Elixir for five hundred years. During that time, I repeatedly roamed famous peaks, and gazed out over the Eight Seas. I encircled the Five Sacred Peaks, where I rested in grotto chambers. I delighted in the drooping branches of flora, and was moved by the calls of birds and beasts. The streams and rivers disgorged their essences, while the hills and knolls were overgrown with plants. The beauty of all creation was moderated by the seasons.

I fished in long streams and roamed mystic rapids.[14] I stilled my heart-mind in source-monts,[15] concentrating on perfection and nourishing my qi. I beckoned the Six Ding jade maidens, and watched over the unfolding and revolving Six Harmonies.[16] There was nothing to restrain me. I have guarded my form and meditated on perfection for more than 2,800 years, and I have delighted in becoming a middle transcendent without thought of fame or gain. Now I have finally been summoned to fill a celestial position above. I have roamed across the marshlands of this world and sadly have breathed my last breath, so I must now go. While we must now part, if you apply yourself with the utmost diligence, we will see each other again in the Gale Chamber.[17]

Upon reading the document, Lin shed tears and then lingered there as he saluted the sky. These traces of Master Juan were the last he left behind.

---

14 In addition to the verbatim passage in Zhou's hagiography (*DZ* 303, 14a), mystic rapids also appear in the *Inner Traditions of Han Emperor Wu* (see p. 169 below). But the term is not mentioned elsewhere and does not seem to refer to a particular place.
15 A word for mountains whose rocky exteriors hide traces of the heavens trapped in the earth at creation. These peaks were thought to be the sources of clouds and medicinal springs. See Bokenkamp 1986, 271.
16 These jade maidens are protective spirits associated with the goddesses of the six *ding* days. See the *Numinous Treasure Secret Procedure Concerning the Six Ding* (*Lingbao liuding bifa* 靈寶六丁祕法, *DZ* 581, 1b–2a). Also see Andersen 1990, 33–34; Schipper 1993, 142–144; Bokenkamp 1997, 328–329. "Six Harmonies" refers to the entire world. See Chen Guying 1994, 74; Watson 1968, 44.
17 A palace on Fangzhu. See Smith 2013, 96 n. 65.

夫玄丹者，泥丸之神也。其法出《太上素靈訣》。守三一爲地真，守洞房爲真人，守玄丹爲太微官也。林謹奉法術，施行道成。周觀天下，遊眺名山，分形散影。寢息丹陵，賣履市巷。醜形試真，得意而栖遯化不倫。時人莫能識也。

以漢元帝神爵二年三月六日告季通曰：「我乍被玄洲召爲真命上卿，領太極中候大夫。與汝別。」

比明旦，有雲車羽蓋，驂龍駕虎。侍從數千人迎林。即日登天，冉冉西北而去。良久，雲氣覆之遂絕。林未去之時，先是太極遣使者下拜爲中嶽真人。後又太上遣王郎，下拜爲五嶽地真人，宮在丹陵。

予見先師得道爲仙。已三被拜授，而乃登昇。蓋洪德高妙，玄韻宿感。靈化虛源，神澄八方。龍昇鳳逐，飛步真門。隱顯津梁，

18　The tonal shift and content of this paragraph suggest that it is in the voice of Zhou Jitong.
19　For more on the formation of this scripture, see Pettit and Chang 2020, 77–98.
20　This may refer to esoteric practices for replicating and multiplying one's form, or dissolving and hiding it. Pregadio (2004, 116) provides an exhaustive discussion of this concept.

Now, the Mysterious Cinnabar mentioned above is the god of the Muddy Pellet.[18] The ritual associated with it is found in the *Instructions of the Immaculate Numen Most High*.[19] Guarding the Three Ones will make one a terrestrial perfected, guarding the Grotto-Room will make one a perfected being, while guarding Mysterious Cinnabar will make one an officer of the Grand Tenuity. Su Lin vigilantly observed these ritual methods, for by putting them into practice he would complete this Dao. He looked out across the entire world, gazed in wonder upon famous peaks, divided his form, and scattered his shadows.[20] Then he rested in Danling, selling grass sandals in the market alleyways. With an uncouth appearance, he underwent tests for perfection, and achieved all he wanted, for his skills as a recluse were unparalleled. No one at that time could recognize him.

On the sixth day of the third month of the second year of the Shenjue era of Han Emperor Yuan,[21] Su Lin said to me, Jitong, "I have just been summoned to the Mysterious Continent, where I will receive an appointment as a perfected upper chamberlain of fate, who oversees the middle-watch grandees of the Grand Ultimate heaven.[ii] I must now leave you."

The next morning, there appeared a cloud chariot with a feathered canopy flanked by dragons and driven by tigers. An entourage of many thousands of beings welcomed Lin. They immediately ascended to the heavens, gradually veering to the northwest as they went. After a while, the cloudy air hid them from view until they disappeared. Just before Su Lin departed, an envoy from the Grand Ultimate heaven descended to formally appoint him as a perfected of the Central Sacred Peak. After this, the Lord of the Dao Most High dispatched a jade gentleman to descend and formally appoint Lin as a terrestrial perfected being of the Five Sacred Peaks, with a palace in Danling.[iii]

I witnessed my former teacher attain the Dao and become a transcendent.[22] He received three appointments before rising to the heavens. This is surely because his vast virtue was of the highest quality, and his mysterious manners were ever present. During his numinous transformation in the vacuous source, Lin's spirit was cleansed across the Eight Directions. He ascended to the skies on dragons, with phoenixes trailing behind, and he flew to the Perfected Gate. By means of the imperceptible bridges and

---

21 Curiously, Han Emperor Yuan (Liu Shi 劉奭, r. 49–33 BCE) did not have such an era, but his father, Han Emperor Xuan (Liu Bingyi 劉病已, r. 74–49 BCE), did, from 61 to 58 BCE.

22 A note in Li Yongcheng 2012, 2247, points to fascicle 7 of the *Transcendent Mirror* (*Xianjian* 仙鑑), which indicates that this is Zhou Jitong speaking.

觀試風塵。其道神矣！其法珍矣！非紙札麤意所能述宣。今聊撰本師之標略爾。將來有道之士，以遊目也。

fords of his mind, he was able to judge this dusty realm. Truly, his Dao is divine! Truly, his ritual methods are precious! All this is not something one could describe by writing rough ideas on slips and paper. Here I have merely pieced together a rough sketch of my master's life. I hope that future masters of the Dao will be able to see it.

Text-Critical Endnotes

i. Reading *shu* 术 as *zhu* 朮. A parallel passage of these few paragraphs is found in *DZ* 303, 13b–14a. See Miller 2008, 158–159.
ii. Reading *zuo* 昨 as *zha* 乍.
iii. A note in Li Yongcheng 2012, 2247, states that 玉郎 was originally written as 王郎, but was changed to accord with editions in the *Sibu congkan* and *Daozang jiyao*.

清虛真人王君內傳
弟子南嶽夫人魏華存撰

華存師清虛真人王君。諱襃字子登。范陽襄平人也,安國侯七世之孫。君以漢元帝建昭三年九月二十七日誕焉。

洪基大業,世籍貴盛。君父諱楷,以德行懿美。比州所稱,舉茂才。除議郎轉中壘大夫、上黨太守、黃門侍郎、侍中、左將軍、鴈門太守。楷正色彤管,坦誠獻替。納言推謀,披衿拔領。率職蒞民,政以禮成。捨刑寬賦,不肅而敬。

天子賢之,遷殿上三老。使賓皇太子,講《春秋》、《尚書》、《論語》、《禮》、《易》。恢恢仁長,循循善誘。微言旣甄,搢紳乘其範。大義已陳,百王格其准。遷光祿大夫,謚曰文侯。

---

1 Xiangping was a county bordering Korea in present-day Liaoning Province, but here the author claims that this town was in Fanyang, a county in present-day Hebei Province. See Zang Lihe 1972, 1298.

2 Gentleman consultant was an honorary position in the Bureau of Consultation for people who lacked a regular appointment. Hucker 1985, 267; Loewe 2000, 763. The director of the capital garrison served in the command structure of the capital army. Hucker 1985, 191; Loewe 2000, 764. Shangdang was in the commandery of Bing Province 并州, which is near present-day Changzhi, Shanxi Province (Rogers 1968, 330). A gentleman in attendance was a person who oversaw the protection of the palace gates. Hucker 1985, 262; Loewe 2000, 760.

Inner Tradition of Lord Wang, Perfected Being of Pure Vacuity
Compiled by his disciple Wei Huacun, Lady of the Southern Sacred Peak

My teacher was Lord Wang, Perfected of Pure Vacuity. His taboo name was Bao, and he was styled Zideng. He was from Xiangping in Fanyang County,[1] and was a seventh-generation descendant of a Sogdian marquis. He was born in the third year of the Jianzhao era [36 BCE] of Han Emperor Yuan on the twenty-seventh day of the ninth month.

The vast achievements and great service of his family are attested in numerous records. Lord Wang's father, whose taboo name was Kai, conducted himself virtuously and had a striking appearance. Following the recommendation of his province, Kai was appointed as a Flourishing Talent. He was appointed as a gentleman consultant and then transferred to the following positions: director of the Capital Garrison, prefect of Shangdang, gentleman in attendance at the Palace Gates, palace attendant, general of the left, and prefect of Yanmen.[2] Kai delivered his reports with gravity,[3] and remonstrated the emperor with candor. As an imperial official, he put forth strategies and made impartial appointments.[i] He always fulfilled his duties to govern with the utmost decorum. He eliminated punishments, relaxed taxes, was never severe, and was always respectful.

The emperor held Zideng's father in high regard, and promoted Kai as one of the Three Elders at court.[4] Kai was commissioned as a retainer of the crown prince to lecture on the *Spring and Autumn Annals*, the *Documents*, the *Analects*, the *Rituals*, and the *Changes*. Kai's respect for his elders was broad and boundless, and his good guidance was patient and prudent. Once his subtle words were selected, scholars holding official titles followed his example. Once he expounded the key principles, all the noblemen took what he advocated as their standard. He then was promoted to imperial household grandee,[5] and was posthumously named Marquis of Letters.

---

3   "Delivered his reports" is literally submitted "vermillion pipes," a term in early Chinese poetry used to refer to a gift from a woman to a man (Cheng Junying and Jiang Jianyuan 1999, 116). By the time of this text, this term described the brush that an official uses. See Fang Xuanling 1997, 1491.

4   "Three Elders" was an honorary title, usually bestowed at the local level, for people who provided moral leadership and discipline (Hucker 1985, 399).

5   An imperial household grandee was an intimate imperial advisor who lived in the palace (Hucker 1985, 288; Loewe 2000, 759).

夫人司馬遷之孫，淑愼沈博。德配母儀，蓋以清源高流，圓潁遠映，靈根散條，芳華朗曜。是用忠孝啓於上葉，善誘彰於文德。世載英旄，斯人有焉。

　　君體六和之妙炁，挺天然之嘉質。含嶽秀以植韻，秉靈符而標貴。暉灼煥於三晨，峻逸超於玄風。少讀五經，傍看百子，綜箏象緯，通探陰陽，及風炁律呂。靡有不覽也。

　　父爲娉丞相孔光女。娶婦在室以和人倫，而君凝形淳觀。明德獨徃，高期真全，絶不內盼。

　　峨峨焉若望慶雲之沓軫；浩浩焉似汎滄溟之無極。神棲萬物之嶺，炁邁霄漢之津。鴻漸鄧林，

6　One's numinous root is one's innate potential to practice Daoist cultivation. Closely related to the "root of life" (minggen 命根), it is the potential or energy one has, to live a long life.

Zideng's mother, a descendent of Sima Qian, was gentle, cautious, calm, and knowledgeable. She was a virtuous wife and a paragon of motherhood, for she was like a clear spring flowing down from on high, a heavenly intellect shining from afar, a numinous root sprouting in every direction,[6] and a fragrant blossom sparkling in resplendence. As such, her loyalty and filial piety drew upon her ancestors, and her good guidance was displayed in her moral character. She was most certainly one of the distinguished talents of her generation.

Lord Wang embodied the sublime qi of the Six Harmonies,[7] and assumed the finest disposition endowed by heaven. He contained the elegance of the Sacred Peaks to manifest harmony, and grasped numinous talismans to manifest his noble status. His brilliant radiance outshone the Three Twinklers, and his uninhibited freedom took him beyond the Mystic Wind.[8] In his youth, he read the Five Classics and the Hundred Philosophers in his spare time, calculated the position of the stars, knew all about yin-yang operations, and could decipher the notes the wind blew. There was nothing he did not read.

His father wanted Zideng to marry the daughter of Prime Minister Kong Guang.[9] To abide by social norms, Lord Wang took this young woman as his wife, but he fixed his attention on his own body and maintained a pure mind. With his radiant virtues he walked alone with high hopes of complete perfection, but never ceased to look inward.[10]

Towering tall, he gazed out over billowing swirls of auspicious clouds; vast and limitless, he seemed to sail over a never-ending Gray-Blue Sea. His spirit roosted atop the peak of all creation, and his qi crossed the ford over the empyrean Han River.[11] He was like a goose skimming over Deng Grove,

---

7   The "sublime qi of the Six Harmonies" referred to desirable aspects of human character, resonating with the finest qualities of Buddhist practice. In particular, the term was used to describe a person as being respectful in body, words, thoughts, views, successes, and adherence to precepts. See Xingyundashi 2003, 1269.
8   "Three Twinklers" here refers to the sun, moon, and stars. "Mystic Wind" refers to the Daoist arts of longevity in a general sense. See Shen Yue 1974, 1778.
9   Kong Guang (65 BCE–5 CE), a descendant of Confucius, held many different titles in the palace, culminating in his 7 BCE appointment as prime minister during the reign of Han Emperor Ai. Ban Gu 1997, 3357; Loewe 2000, 208.
10 That is, to carry out meditative rituals. The term "look inwardly" (*nei pan*) appears in *DZ* 331, 43b–44a, to describe an adept looking introspectively inward during meditation.
11 A metonym for the heavens.

展翮東園。將藏鳳羽以翳於南風,匿龍華以沈於幽源。是乃夜光潛躍,映耀於難掩。遂名沸絶圃,聲馳京夏,四府交辟。

君即閑夜之感,喟然悲嘆曰:「人間塵藹!趣競得失,利害相攻。有踰鶵鷚之視老燕矣!」遂決志辭親,入華山中九年。契闊備至,精感昊穹。神映幽人,體期冥靈。心唱至真爾。

一日夜半,忽聞林澤中有人馬之聲,簫鼓之音。須臾之間,漸近此山,仰而望之,見千騎萬乘,浮虛空而至。神人乘三素雲輦,手把虎符。朱鉞啓途,握節執旄。曲晨傾蔭,錦旆蔽虛。

神人暫停駕而言曰:「吾太極真人西梁子文也。聞子好道,劬勞山林。未該真要,誠可愍也。勤企長生,實爲至矣!」

12 The goose metaphor is based on a line from the late third-century "Rhapsody on a Westward Journey" ("Xizheng fu" 西征賦), by Pan Yue 潘岳 (247–300), in which "cormorants dive and geese skim the waters" 鳧躍鴻漸. Cf. Knechtges 1987, 231 n. 675. According to the *Classic of the Mountains and Seas* (*Shanhai jing* 山海經), Deng Grove was a mythical place where Kuafu 夸父 died on his long journey to quench his thirst after racing the sun. See Yuan Ke 1995, 238; Birrell 1999, 123.
13 In *DZ* 1138, 11.3b, phoenix feathers were markers of being a god. Dragon blossoms adorned the sashes of gods and goddesses and served as a marker of their status. See *DZ* 1138, 61.2a.

spreading its wings in the Eastern Garden.¹² He concealed his phoenix feathers to hide in the southern wind, and submerged his dragon blossoms to sink into the dark springs.¹³ Indeed, Wang was like a flickering light shining in the night sky, for his luminescence was difficult to conceal. His name was known in the farthest field, his fame spread throughout every city, and every government agency solicited his service.¹⁴

Feeling melancholy one lonesome night, Lord Wang sighed deeply and mournfully said, "How abundant is the dust of this profane world! People clamor over success and failure, and gains are soon followed by losses. It even exceeds the phoenix who saw the old swallow!"¹⁵ After this, Wang became determined to leave his family and went to live on Mt. Hua for nine years. Enduring utmost hardships, his sincere devotion moved the vast heavens. His spirit remained undercover among the recluses, while his body rendezvoused with unseen numina. His heart sang out for ultimate perfection.

One day at midnight, he suddenly heard the sound of men on horseback riding through the forests and marshes, along with the melody of flutes and drums. Moments later, as they quickly approached the mountain, Wang looked up and saw a thousand riders and ten thousand chariots floating on thin air toward him. Divine beings rode in cloudy palanquins of three elemental colors,¹⁶ and held tiger talismans in their hands. They cleared the way with vermillion battle-axes, grasping staves and holding up pennants.¹⁷ Their winding dawn carriages blocked the moonlight as their brocade flags hid the sky.

A divine being halted his carriage saying, "I am Ziwen of Xiliang, a perfected being of the Grand Ultimate heaven. I have heard that you are fond of the Dao and are hardworking and assiduous in this mountain grove. But you have yet to secure the key perfected teachings, and this is truly pitiable. If you harbor earnest intentions to live a long life, surely this is your highest aspiration!"

---

14 "Every government agency" is literally "the four bureaus," that is, the four most prominent offices of the imperial bureaucracy, a list that varied according to time period to include various civil and military offices.
15 In the *Zhuangzi* chapter "Autumn Floods," the lofty *yuanchu* phoenix flies over lesser birds and their inferior appetites with indifference, a reference to Zhuang Zhou's own indifference to power and success. See Chen Guying 1994, 442; Watson 1968, 188.
16 Understood by Yang Xi as the three colors of clouds, either purple, azure, or scarlet (*DZ* 1016, 9.11b), though later texts reinterpreted the colors as cinnabar, green, or blue (Smith 2013, 155 n. 10). "Of three elemental colors" was a common adjective used to describe the chariots and phaetons of gods and goddesses.
17 The Chinese here can also be translated as tally, rod, or staff borne as a credential of one's office and authority. See Durrant et al. 2016, 511.

君乃馳詣輪轂之下，叩頭自搏而言曰：「褒以肉人，愚頑庸賤。體染風塵，恣躁亂性。然少好生道，莫知以度。」

真人曰：「夫學道無師無緣自解。我太極真人，神仙之司主。試校學者，領舉正真爾。子玄錄上清，金書東華，名編清虛，位登小有。必當掌括寶籍，爲天王之任爾。但注心四景，勤慕上業，道自成也。」

後隱陽洛山中，感南極夫人、西城真人並降。南極夫人乃指西城曰：「君當爲王子登之師，子登亦佳弟子也。」

良久，西城真人長歎而謂君曰：

「夫學道者諒不可以倉卒期，求生者不可以立爾綜。故冥術棲於玄元而高偕，太妙凌重霄以纍抗矣！

夫道雖無形，其實有焉。妙雖昧昧，其實坦然。

---

18 The practice of using both hands to slap one's face as a sign of humility. See Chen Shou 1997, 1463.
19 In the *Inner Chapters of the Master Embracing Simplicity*, a life of leisure, sweet wines, and fragrances erodes one's nature in this way. See Ge Hong 1996, 1.

Lord Wang ran over to kowtow before the wheels of the god's carriage and slapped himself in the face,[18] saying, "I am but a mortal human being who is both ignorant and mediocre. My body is sullied by the windy dust, and I have the befuddled nature of one who is impetuous and impulsive.[19] Even though I have been fond of the Dao of life since I was young, I am not sure how I could ever be saved."

The perfected being said, "You have studied the Dao without a master and released yourself without any karmic connections. I am a perfected being of the Grand Ultimate, and the head director for all divine transcendents. I test and evaluate adepts, and appoint and promote those who are bona fide perfected. Your name is now written in the mystic register of Supreme Purity, inscribed in gold in the Eastern Efflorescence Palace, and listed among the Pure Vacuity perfected beings, and your rank has been elevated to the level of Lesser Existence. You will surely be given the precious writs and then assume the duties of a celestial king. You need only focus your mind on the four phosphors[20] and work diligently at this high calling, and this Dao will fall into place."

After this, Wang went into reclusion in Mt. Yangluo, which moved the Lady of the Southern Culmen and the Perfected Being of the Western Citadel[21] to descend unto him. The Lady of the Southern Culmen then gestured to the Perfected Being of the Western Citadel and said, "You, sir, should be Wang Zideng's teacher, for Zideng will make a fine disciple."

After a while, the Perfected Being of the Western Citadel let out a long sigh and addressed Lord Wang, saying,

"Those who study the Dao cannot expect to hurry it along, and those who seek a longer life cannot expect to quickly arrange it. Thus, even if you were to dwell in the Mystic Prime with secret arts and reach great heights, you will find it exceedingly difficult to pass through the layers of heaven unto the grand marvel!

"Now, the Dao, while formless, has a substance that exists. While the marvelous is dim and dusky, it is nevertheless perceptible. You should strive

---

20 In Supreme Purity practice, the eight phosphors is a common term (see p. 46, n. 83 above), but four phosphors also occasionally appears to describe the chariots upon which an adept travels. See *Supreme Purity Most High Cavernous Perfection Golden Prime Eight Phosphors Jade Record of the High Sage Lord of the Great Dao* (*Shangqing gaosheng taishang dadao jun dongzhen jinyuan bajing yulu* 上清高聖太上大道君洞真金元八景玉錄, *DZ* 1389, 12b); Robinet 1983, 416; Schipper and Verellen 2004, 140.
21 For more on Mt. Yangluo 陽洛山, see *Traditions of Lord Pei*, p. 20, n. 46 above. "Xicheng" appears in *Traditions of the Director of Destinies* (Lord Mao) (p. 118 below) as a place near Ankang 安康. But in this hagiography, it is likely a distant mountain or cosmic place in which this Perfected Being lives. Hence our translation "Western Citadel."

子當勤求其無，然後見其至有。子廣延諸妙，然後究其坦大。得有則有生；得妙則年全也。

子求生雖篤，而未見其涯。慕道雖勤，而未啓其門。殆猶沿湧波以索鳥巢，尋長木而訪淵鱗爾。

是故子心疲於導引，而朱宮爲之喪潰。肺弊於理炁，故神華爲之凋落。肝勞於視盻，而魂精爲之遼索。脾竭於守神，而丹田爲之閡滯。腎困於經緯，而津液爲之不澤。膽銳於趣競，故四肢爲之亂作。

五臟相攻，六府顛覆。三焦滯而不瀉，八關絕而無續。賴餌飯以勁汝身，恃丹青以固汝内爾。正可却衰白之凋折，猶不免必死之期會。徒有萬年之壽，豈足貴乎？」

西城真人遂以即日授君：《太上寶文》、《八素隱書》、《大洞真經》、《靈書八道》、《紫度炎光》、《石精

22　Here "Vermillion Palace" means the heart, though the term typically refers to the place that a human spirit would go to after death to be refined for rebirth. Robinet 1984, 2.209; Bokenkamp 1997, 411.

23　Divine blossoms were markers of an adept's divine appearance. See *Cavernous Perfection Most High Wondrous Scripture of the Immaculate Numen Celestial Palace and Penetrating Mystery of the Great Existence Heaven* (*Dongzhen taishang suling dongyuan dayou miaojing* 洞真太上素靈洞元大有妙經, *DZ* 1314, 40b); Pettit and Chang 2020, 214.

to find the emptiness of the Dao, for only then can you see its ultimate existence. You must invite its various marvels, for only then can you apprehend its immense size. If you obtain the existence of the Dao, you will gain life; if you comprehend the marvelous, you will live out all of your years.

"Although you seek life earnestly enough, you have not yet seen its other shore; although you revere the Dao diligently enough, you have not yet opened the door. Surely this is just like surfing surging waves in search of a bird's nest or climbing a tall tree to find a circling school of fish.

"For this reason, your heart is exhausted from guiding your qi, and your Vermillion Palace crumbles away because of it.[22] Your lungs are beleaguered by regulating qi, causing the divine blossoms of your spirits to wither away.[23] Your liver is weary from prolonged visualization, causing cloud-soul essences to be cast off afar. Your spleen is overtaxed with guarding the spirits, and your cinnabar field has become clogged. Your kidneys are weary from maintaining your metabolism, causing your saliva to stop flowing. Your gallbladder is pierced by your constant struggles, making your four limbs flail.

"Your five viscera attack one another, and your six repositories are turned upside down. Your Triple Heater is blocked up and will not drain, and your Eight Passes are cut off and are not linked together.[24] You rely on easy rice to strengthen your body, and depend on cinnabar-azure writings to fortify your interior.[25] You have surely staved off the dismal demise of your weakening, graying body, but you still cannot avoid the appointed hour of your death. You will merely enjoy a lifespan of ten thousand years. How could that be worth treasuring compared to immortality?"

The Perfected Being of the Western Citadel that very day bestowed the following on Lord Wang: *Precious Writs of the Most High, Hidden Book of the Eight Immaculates, Perfected Scripture of the Great Grotto, Numinous Book of the Eight Paths, Purple Crossing and Blazing Radiance, Lithic Essence*

---

24 The "Triple Heater" refers to the thorax and other spaces in the upper torso associated with breathing. Ge Hong 1996, 274.
25 Easy rice was an esoteric recipe prepared by adepts working toward arts of longevity. See Stanley-Baker 2013, 193–194. *Danqing* (cinnabar-azure writings) typically refers to the cinnabar and malachite pigments used in painting canvases and buildings; here, however, it is likely used as a synonym for *dance* 丹冊 (Morohashi Tetsuji 1955–1960, 1.324d) or *danshu* 丹書 (Morohashi Tetsuji 1955–1960, 1.325c), which are auspicious writings, sometimes given to humans by miraculous animals.

玉馬》、《神真虎文》、《高仙羽玄》。凡三十一卷,依科立盟結誓而付。

乃將君觀玄洲,須臾而至。四面大海,懸濤千丈。洲上宮闕、朱閣、樓觀、瓊室、瑤房,不可稱記。西城真人曰:「此儴都之府,太上丈人處之。」

乃將君入紫桂宮。見丈人著流霞羽袍,冠芙蓉之冠。腰帶神光,手把火鈴。侍女數百,龍虎衛階。太上丈人與西城真人相禮而已,相攜共坐。君時侍側焉。太上丈人曰:「彼所謂王子登乎?學道遭逢良師,將得之矣。」

西城真人笑,因命君拜。拜畢,太上丈人使坐北向。丈人乃設廚膳,呼吸立具。靈肴千種,丹醴湛溢。燔煙震檀,飛節玄香。陳鈞天之大樂,擊金璈於七芒。崆峒啓音,徹朗天丘。

於是
龍騰雲崖
飛鳳鳴嘯
山阜洪鯨

26 The same set of texts appears in *Inner Tradition of the Lady of the Southern Sacred Peak* (Lady Wei), p. 109 below. For more on this passage and its relation to early Supreme Purity catalogs of scriptures, see Pettit and Chang 2020, 21–25.

27 The Elder Most High is a figure who appears in dozens of early Daoist scriptures. He is often listed alongside Lord Lao Most High, which has caused some commentators to see them as alternative names for the same high god, though he may be a separate god who ruled over the Mysterious Continent. See *Cavernous Mystery Numinous Treasure Table of the Ranks and Functions in the Pantheon* (*Dongxuan lingbao zhenling weiye tu* 洞玄靈寶真靈位業圖, DZ 167, 7a).

of the Jade Horse, Tiger Writs of Divine Perfection, and *Winged Mystery of High Transcendence.*[26] In all, there were thirty-one fascicles, which were handed over only after he pledged according to the code.

Then the perfected being took Lord Wang to see the Mysterious Continent, and in mere seconds they arrived. There, he saw great oceans all round with towering waves ten thousand feet high. On the island, there were so many palaces, vermillion galleries, lofty towers, jasper rooms, and rose-gem chambers that it was impossible to recount. The Perfected Being of the Western Citadel said, "This is the administrative district of Transcendent Metropolis; the Elder Most High lives here."[27]

Then he led Lord Wang to enter the Purple Cassia Palace. There Wang saw the Elder wearing a long-feathered robe of purling auroras and a crown with lotus flowers. The Elder tied a sash of divine light at his waist and held fiery bells. He was attended by hundreds of servant maids, and dragons and tigers flanked the steps of his dais. The Elder Most High and the Perfected Being of the Western Citadel just bowed to one another and went arm in arm as they sat down. At this time, Lord Wang took up a position standing by their side. The Elder Most High said, "Is that the one they call Wang Zideng? He has encountered a fine master while studying the Dao; he will surely attain it."

The Perfected Being of the Western Citadel laughed and then commanded Lord Wang to bow down. When Wang finished, the Elder Most High instructed him to sit facing north. In the space of single breath, the Elder had laid out a succulent feast. There were numinous roasts of a thousand kinds, and cinnabar ales overflowed. The food was roasted and smoked over crackling sandalwood with soaring plumes of mysterious fragrance. The Elder marshaled forth the great music of Midmost Heaven, striking golden chime-stones from the Seven Awns.[28] The cavernous void produced tones that resounded through the hills of heaven.

After this,
Dragons soared over cliffs of clouds,
And flying phoenixes warbled.
Whales as massive as mountains and bluffs

---

28 In some Supreme Purity texts, we find the term "Seven Awns with seven tails," perhaps referring to dust propelled by solar radiation, streaming from Venus. Daoist adepts visualized the Seven Awns and consumed them, which enabled them to arrive in the starry palaces of Venus. See the *Most High Instructions of the Five Planets, the Seven Original Ones, and Kong-Chang* (*Taishang wuxing qiyuan kongchang jue* 太上五星七元空常訣, DZ 876, 7b). Elsewhere, the Seven Awns are said to be seven gates (men 門) on Venus.

湧波淩濤
雲起太虛
風生廣遼
靈歌九真
雅吟空無
玉華作唱
西妃折腰

爾乃
衆仙揮袂
萬神遷延
羽童拊節
慶雲纏綿

於是太上丈人會二十九真人，皆玄洲之太真公也。其第一真人自稱主仙道君，指 君而向西城真人言曰：「彼悠悠者，將西城之室客，上宰之賓友耶！視此子心眸澄邈，神淳形凝。圓晨不煥，六景發華。殆真人之美者，小有之賢王也。夫彼果何人哉？」

於是西城真人笑而答曰：「道君今何清音之不妙？曲問之陋碎哉。請粗陳其歸要焉。

蓋夫聖匠剖太混之一朴，分爲億萬之體。發大蘊之一包，散爲無窮之物。是故 立三光呼天而置晷儀。封區域呼地而

---

29 In Supreme Purity literature, there are nine palaces in the human brain where nine perfected beings live. Adepts could open portals in the brain to access these beings (Pettit and Chang 2020, 81). As these practices developed, the Nine Perfected were associated with the nine months of gestation when an adept creates a divine embryo in his body through inner alchemical methods. Miller 2008, 27.
30 The Western Consort is a goddess who, along with celestial maidens, performed music in primordial times when the scriptures first emerged in the heavens.

Crested over the top of surging swells.
Clouds appeared in the Grand Void
As wind arose in the Broad Expanse.
The numinous song of the Nine Perfected[29]
Rang out harmoniously across empty nothingness.[ii]
Jade blossom maidens sang in unison,
While the Western Consort bowed at the waist.[30]

At this time,
The assembly of transcendents waved their sleeves
As the myriad spirits moved as they pleased.
The feathered lads beat their staffs in time,
While auspicious clouds weaved through the scene.

Then the Elder Most High convened twenty-nine perfected beings who were all grand perfected dukes of the Mysterious Continent. The first of these perfected beings was called the Lord Who Governs over the Transcendent Dao. He pointed at Lord Wang and said to the Perfected Being of the Western Citadel, "Is this carefree fellow perhaps a disciple of the Western Citadel, your cherished guest? I can see that his mind is clairvoyant, his spirit untainted, and his bodily form focused. Even though his round dawn[31] has yet to shine, his six phosphors are already aglow. Surely, he seems to be one of the most beautiful of the perfected, or a virtuous prince of Lesser Existence heaven. But who is he, in the end?"[iii]

The Perfected Being of the Western Citadel laughed and replied, "How is it that your clear voice now sounds amiss? Why are your elaborate questions so base and incoherent?[iv] Allow me to give a quick overview of some key facts to clear this up.

"Now, the Sage Carpenter carved out the singular unhewn block of grand chaos and split it into ten million forms. He broke open the single envelope of the great cluster and sent out infinite phenomena. For this reason, he hung up the three luminaries in heaven and then installed a sundial.[32] He

---

31 Perhaps a synonym for "round blossoms" (yuanhua 圓華) or "round light" (yuanguang 圓光), which are halos of light that appears behind people that have attained godhood (Daoism) or enlightenment (Buddhism).
32 The three luminaries are the sun, moon, and stars. See Chen Guying 1994, 812; Watson 1968, 342.

制五服。制漏刻以分日夜，正四時以財歲月。五位以正方面，山川以定險阻。 城郭以自居焉，兵械以自衛焉。旌旗輿服以自表，用九穀以自養。凡此之類，象玄乎天而形存乎地。

日月有幽明之分，寒暑有生殺之炁。震雷有出入之期，風雨有動靜之節。類炁浮乎上而衆精流乎下。廢興之數，治亂之運，賢愚之質，善惡之性，剛柔之炁，壽夭之命，貴賤之位，尊卑之班，吉凶之徵，窮達之期普陳矣。

性發乎天而命成乎人也。故立之者天，而行之者道受焉。性合神同，混而爲一。流通並行，不可細得分別也。」

於是主仙道君命侍女范運華、趙峻珠、王抱臺等，發瓊笈，披緑蘊，出《上清隱書龍文八靈眞經》二卷。授子登。又

---

33 The five concentric realms of submission to the Son of Heaven. See Qu Wanli and Wang Yunwu 2009, 34.
34 In ancient texts, "the five positions" referred to various astral or terrestrial objects correlated with the Five Phases. Here, however, it seems simply to mean the four cardinal directions along with the center.
35 The "nine grains" refers to the nine major crops, such as millet, rice, and soybeans, but the term is often used to refer to agricultural products more generally.

demarcated all the regions of the earth and instituted the five realms of submission.[33] He created a water clock to divide day and night and rectified the four seasons, thus sequencing the months of the year. He calibrated the cardinal directions according to the five positions,[34] and he delineated where dangers and impasses lie within the mountains and rivers. He built inner and outer city walls within which to make his home, and trained soldiers and fashioned weapons with which to defend himself. He created banners, flags, chariots, and regalia to identify himself, and used the nine grains to nourish himself.[35] All such things had signs that mysteriously appeared in heaven before their forms were present on earth.

"The sun and the moon manifested the division of darkness and light, and the winter and summer manifested the qi of being born and killing. Quakes and thunderclaps came and went, while the wind and rain raged and calmed. The various kinds of qi floated on high as the multitude of essences flowed below. The calculation of decay and growth, the cycle of order and chaos, the basic substance of worthies and fools, the nature of good and bad, the qi of hard and pliant, lifespans both long and short, the positions of the weak and the poor, the ranking of superior and inferior, the presages of the auspicious and ominous, and the expectations of the weak and the capable—all were established.

"A person's nature first emanates in heaven, but his fate is determined by his own actions. Thus, what establishes them is Heaven, and what moves them is received from the Dao. Their nature has the same substance as their body spirits; they are joined together as one. They proceed together side by side, and there is no way to isolate and distinguish them."

Then the Lord Who Governs the Transcendent Dao ordered his servant maidens Fan Yunhua, Zhao Junzhu, and Wang Baotai to bring forth together the rose-gem bookbox and open a green bag containing the *Perfected Scripture of the Supreme Purity Hidden Book of the Eight Numina of Dragon Writs* in two fascicles.[36] These were given to Zideng. In addition, Wang also

36 The three female attendants are grouped together in many Daoist scriptures. The title of this scripture is also mentioned in the *Sworn Code of the Four Bournes of the Grand Perfected Jade Emperor* (*Taizhen yudi siji mingke jing* 太真玉帝四極明科經, DZ 184, 2.4a), but is described as two oral instructions (erjue 二訣), rather than as a scripture. According to this codebook, this scripture was possessed by a vast array of deities, including the Queen Mother of the West and the Azure Lad.

以雲碧陽水晨飛丹腴二升賜君。君拜服之。

真人遂將君還西城。九年道成。給飛飆之車，東行渡啓明滄海。登廣桑山，入始暉庭。詣太帝君，稽首再拜。太帝授以《龍景九文》、《紫鳳赤書》、《上清神圖》、《八道玉籙》。

次南行渡渤海丹海登長離山。詣南極紫元夫人，一號南極元君。授以《九道廻玄太丹綠書》。又詣赤臺童子華蓋上公。授以五雲夜光、雲琅、水霜。南極夫人曰：「昔日之言，豈負舉哉？」君稽首，謝恩辭退。

次西行渡庚丘巨海沈羽之津。登麗農山，詣紫蓋晨夫人景真三皇道君。授以《玉道綠字廻曜太真隱書》。

次北遊渡彫柔玄海，濟飲龍上河匏瓜津，登廣野山。詣高上虛皇大道玉君。會其出遊，駕日月之晨，乘紫始之光。

---

37 A speedy chariot of wild wind used to take adepts to the far reaches of the cosmos. See Robinet 1993, 113.
38 According to *DZ* 184, 2.2b–3a, this is one of the two texts transmitted by the Celestial King of Primordial Commencement (Yuanshi tianwang 元始天王) to the perfected kings. The passage details protocols for receiving and transmitting the text, including the grave dangers one faces for improper transmission.

received two liters of dawn flight cinnabar oil in solar water of cloudy jade. He bowed and then drank it.

The Perfected Being then led Lord Wang back to the Western Citadel. After nine years he attained the Dao. He received a flying-whirlwind chariot,[37] in which he traveled eastward across the gray-blue seas of Enlightened Brilliance. He then ascended Mt. Guangsang and entered the Court of Incipient Radiance. There he called on the Grand Imperial Lord, kowtowing and bowing twice. The Grand Imperial Lord gave Lord Wang *Nine Writs of the Dragon Phosphors*, the *Red Book of the Purple Phoenix*, as well as the *Divine Chart of Supreme Purity* and the *Jade Register of the Eight Paths*.

Later Wang headed south and crossed the Bohai Sea and the Dan Sea[v] and then ascended Mt. Changli. He called upon the Lady of the Purple Prime in the Southern Culmen, also known as the Primal Lord of the Southern Culmen. She bestowed upon him the *Grand Cinnabar Green Book of the Encircling Mystery of Nine Paths*.[38] He also called upon the Lad of the Red Tower,[39] a Floral Canopy upper duke. He gave Wang five-colored-cloud nocturnal radiance, cloudy gems, and water frost.[40] The Lady of the Southern Culmen remarked, "Considering what I said to you in the past, how could I fail to recommend you?" Lord Wang kowtowed and expressed his gratitude as he left.

Wang later headed west, crossing the giant Yuqiu Sea via the Chenyu Ford. He ascended Mt. Linong to call upon the Lady of the Purple Canopy Dawn and the Lord of the Dao for the Phosphorically Perfected Three Sovereigns. She gave Wang the *Grand Perfected Hidden Book of the Encircling Starlight in the Jade Dao's Green Register*.[41]

After this, Wang headed north and passed over the dark Diaorou Sea, crossed the upper reaches of the Yinlong River at Paogua Ford, and ascended Mt. Guangye.[42] There he paid his respects to the Jade Lord of the Great Dao, also known as the Vacuous Sovereign Most High. It so happened that the Jade Lord was about to go off on an excursion, harnessing the dawning light of the sun and moon and riding light beams of purple incipience.

---

39 The Lad of the Red Tower appears in various Daoist scriptures as a god who dwells in the sun. See *DZ* 435, 13b.
40 Cloudy gems and jade frost (yushuang 玉霜) appear in *DZ* 1016, 6.2b, as alchemical ingredients used in elixirs. See Strickmann 1979, 154–155. Smith (2020, 94 n. 35) identifies the substances as malachite and pearl-like chalcedony.
41 According to *DZ* 184, 2.2b–3a, this is the other text transmitted to the perfected kings.
42 By the turn of the tenth century, this mountain is listed as a peak in the distant north where the Black Emperor lives. See the *Record of Cavern-Heavens, Auspicious Sites, Holy Mountains, and Conduits, as Well as of Famous Mountains* (*Dongtian fudi yuedu mingshan ji* 洞天福地嶽瀆名山記, *DZ* 599, 3b).

鬱藹黃素之雲，勃蔚八景之曜，飛真萬億；不可稱數。君再拜，道側唱者曰：「聞 ……」。

君乃詣上清玉晨帝君、玄清六微元君。二君授以《寶洞飛霄絶玄金章》及賜《太極隱書》、龍明珠、絳和雲芝。君拜而飲之。即身金色，項映圓光。七曜散華，流煥映形。

又退登閬風之野玄圃之宮。詣中皇玉帝，受《解形遞變流景玉經》。

乃越鬱絶，濟弱河，西詣龜臺，謁九靈太真上清夫人。退更清齋三月，受《三華寶曜瓊文琅書》、《靈暉上籙》、《七晨素經》。

退又清齋三年。浮浩汗之河，登白空虞山。山周廻三萬里遊行。翌日趨詣紫清太素瓊闕，即太素三元上道君所治焉，處丹靈白玉宮。飛映絶曜，紫霞落煥。七光交陳，結於雲宇之上，奇麗玄黃，不可名字。

43 The "Seven Sparklers" usually refers to the sun, moon, and five planets, but in some Daoist texts this term refers to the seven stars of the Big Dipper. It is unclear which meaning the author of this text has in mind.
44 The Mysterious Bower is the name of one of the peaks in the mythical Kunlun Mountains. One who ascends it gains the ability to control the wind and rain. See Knechtges 1982, 298 n. 604.

Soaring on billowing clouds of yellow and white, rising on the luxuriant dazzle of the eight phosphors, the flying perfected numbered in the billions; there were far too many to count. Lord Wang bowed twice on the side of the road, and the singers sang, "Hear, hear . . ."[vi]

Lord Wang then called upon the Jade Dawn Imperial Lord of Supreme Purity, as well as the Primal Lord of Mystic Purity's Six Subtleties. These two lords gave Wang *Treasure Grotto's Golden Stanzas on Flying into the Empyrean's Farthest Mystery* and the *Hidden Book of the Grand Ultimate*, as well as dragon-bright pearls and nebulous mushrooms of scarlet harmony. Lord Wang bowed and consumed the latter. His body then glowed with a golden hue, and there was a round halo emanating atop his head. The Seven Sparklers blossomed all around him with a swirling radiance that outlined his bodily form.[43]

He also returned to ascend to the palace on the Mysterious Bower of the wilds of Lofty Winds.[44] He called on the Jade Emperor of Central Sovereignty and received the *Jade Scripture on the Coursing Phosphors for Unraveling Forms and Hidden Transformations*.[45]

Then he traversed Mt. Yujue, crossed the Ruo River,[46] and went west to the Gui Terrace, where he sought an audience with the Supreme Purity Lady of the Nine Numinous Grand Perfected. Retiring, he fasted for three months, then received the *Rose-Gem Writs in the Gem Book of the Three Efflorescences' Precious Starlight*, the *Upper Register of Numinous Starlight*, and the *Immaculate Scripture of the Seven Stars*.[47]

After withdrawing, Lord Wang fasted for three more years. He drifted across raging rivers before ascending into the bright skies of Mt. Yu. He roamed about the peak's thirty-thousand-mile circumference. The next day, he suddenly went to visit Grand Simplicity's Rose-Gem Tower of Purple Purity, which was governed by the Grand Simplicity Lord of the Three Primes' High Dao, who ruled from his White Jade Palace of Cinnabar Numinosity. There were soaring beams that infinitely dazzled and purple auroras that cast down bright flashes. Seven rays of light intertwined and wrapped around the highest echelons of clouds, creating an indescribable, beautiful

---

45 Mentioned in *DZ* 1138, 38.11b, as a text used in a hundred-day fast. *DZ* 184, 2.12b–13a, also has many details on the dozens of gods and goddesses who received this text. A copy is stored in a cave in the Kunlun Mountains and is permitted to be transmitted once every ten thousand eons.

46 "Ruo River" is a name applied to many different rivers, but here it likely refers to the river in distant Central Asia or India where medieval Chinese imagined a religious utopia to exist. See Schafer 1981–1983, 336 n. 116. On Mt. Yujue, see *Traditions of Lord Pei*, p. 27 above, where the mountain is called Mt. Yujuegen.

47 In *DZ* 1138, 9b, these three texts can be used to conduct a thirty- or sixty-day fast.

仙童玉女，侍右天尊，蓋無數也。君旣至，稽首再拜，詣瓊闕之下。

久時，太素三元上道君乃使繡衣命者西林藻，授君《金真玉光》、《流金火鈴》、《豁落七元》、《八景飛晨》。又使清真左夫人郭靈蓋、右陽玉華仲飛姬，齎神策、玉璽，授君以爲太素清虛真人，領小有天王、三元四司右保上公。治王屋山洞天之中，給玉童玉女各三百人。

主領《上清玉章》、《太素寶玄》、《太極上品九天靈文》、《六合祕籍》、《山海妙經》，悉主之焉。又總括《洞內明景三寶》。得乘虎斾龍輦，金蓋瓊輪，八景飛輿，出入上清。受事太素，寢宴太極也。

後歸西城，清齋三月，授書爲太素清虛真人矣。

Text-Critical Endnotes

i. Reading *mo* 謨 as *mou* 謀.
ii. *Wu* 無 must be a scribal error here because it does not rhyme with the rest of the verse. It is possible that the character was once *yao* 遙 (distant) or *xiao* 霄 (empyrean).
iii. Reading *wei* 未 as a scribal error for *fu* 夫.
iv. Reading *jian* 間 as *wen* 問.
v. "Bohai" is a common name for the sea between present-day Shandong and Liaoning provinces. Since Lord Wang is traveling to the distant south, this is likely a scribal error. Other quotations of this passage read *boyang danhai* 渤陽丹海 (DZ 783, 2.16b).
vi. Li Yongcheng (2012, 2293) suggests that these last five characters are extraneous.
vii. This last sentence is possibly a later editorial insertion into the text. Wang already returned to Western Citadel in the text and had just been confirmed as a perfected being in the preceding paragraph. This last statement contradicts this earlier timeline.

vision of the world.⁴⁸ Countless transcendent lads and jade maidens waited on the celestial worthy. When Wang finally arrived, he knocked his head twice on the ground to call on the lord from the lower entry of the Rose-Gem Watchtower.

After a long while, the Grand Simplicity Lord of the Three Primes' High Dao then dispatched a damask-clad messenger named Xi Linzao to give Lord Wang the talismans of *Jade Brilliance of the Golden Perfected*, *Fiery Bells of Flowing Gold*, *Seven Primes of Unobstructed Descent*, and *Eight Phosphors of Soaring Dawn*.⁴⁹ He also sent the Pure Perfected Lady on the left, Guo Linggai, and the Solar Jade Blossom Lady on the right, Zhong Feiji, to present him with divine slips and a jade seal, and to confer on Lord Wang the title of Grand Simplicity's Perfected Being of Pure Vacuity, concurrently appointing him as Celestial King of Lesser Existence and as an Upper Duke of the Protectorate of the Right to the Four Ministries of the Three Primes. He ruled from within the grotto heaven beneath Mt. Wangwu and was given three hundred jade maidens and three hundred jade lads.

Now he oversees the transmission of the *Jade Emblem of Supreme Purity*, *Precious Mystery of Grand Simplicity*, *Numinous Writs of the Nine Heavens from the Upper Grade of the Grand Ultimate*, *Secret Records of Six Harmonies*, and *Miraculous Scripture of the Mountains and Seas*. He also has overall jurisdiction over the Three Treasures of the Grotto's Inner Bright Phosphors. He acquired a dragon palanquin with tiger flags, a golden canopy, and rose-gem wheels, loaded on a flying chassis of eight phosphors, which he uses to leave and enter the Supreme Purity heavens. He gets his assignments from Grand Simplicity, and takes rest and respite in the Grand Ultimate heavens.

Later he returned to the Western Citadel and performed a three-month pure fast and then received an appointment letter making him the Perfected Being of Pure Vacuity in Grand Simplicity.ⁿⁱⁱ

---

48 Black and yellow (xuan huang) is another term for the world, black being the color of the sky, and yellow being the color of the earth.
49 All four titles appear in medieval Supreme Purity literature as names of talismans (Pettit and Chang 2020, 246).

紫虛元君南嶽夫人內傳

逮乎晉武皇帝時任城魏華存，字賢安。乃魏陽元之女也。陽元仕至滎陽、宜陽二郡太守，散騎常侍冀州刺史。其父乃嫁賢安於南陽劉乂，字幻彥。乂妻時，除爲修武縣令，賢安隨焉。

　賢安自少爲女，處乎內室，性好至道。雖未得仙，而真人屢降。及其長也，女子有夫之義，修尚之事。有時而廢及至兒女成立，告誡子曰：「我願終尋真之志。」於是離群獨處，不交人事。深託隱疴，還修曩尚，入室百日。所期仙靈，積思希感。爾乃獨節應神，丹心潛會。精苦仰徹，天真遐降。

　於是季冬之月，夜半清朗，忽聞空中有鍾鼓之響，笳簫之聲，音韻嘈嗜。出戶望之，見從東方虛空而來。旍旗鬱勃，羽

1　Rencheng is in present-day Jining, Shandong (Zang Lihe 1972, 282). Emperor Wu (Sima Yan 司馬炎) reigned from 266 to 290.
2　The style name of Wei Shu 魏舒 (209–290) (Fang Xuanling 1997, 1185).

Inner Tradition of the Lady of the Southern Sacred Peak, Primal Lord of Purple Vacuity

In the time of Emperor Wu of the Jin dynasty there was one Wei Huacun, styled Xian'an, of Rencheng.[1] She was the daughter of Wei Yangyuan.[2] Yangyuan had been assigned as the governor of two commanderies, Rongyang and Yiyang,[3] and was also the cavalier attendant in ordinary for the prefect of Jizhou. Her father arranged for Xian'an to marry Liu Yi, styled Youyan, of Nanyang.[4] When he was to be married, Yi was appointed as a county magistrate in Xiuwu, and Xian'an followed him there.[5]

From the time Xian'an was a young girl, she remained in her inner quarters, yet by nature she was inclined toward the highest Dao.[6] Even though she had not attained transcendence, perfected beings would frequently descend to her. When she grew up, she attended to her duties as a wife and cultivated an upstanding character. Yet she would sometimes neglect these duties, so when her children became adults, she informed her son, "I plan to fulfill my ultimate wish to search for Perfection." She then left to live alone where she would be unfettered by human affairs. Feigning a serious illness, she resumed the cultivation she esteemed in the past and remained in her chamber for one hundred days. The idea of rendezvousing with transcendent spirits dominated her thoughts, for she had high hopes of eliciting a response. Thereafter, she steadfastly welcomed spirits, awaiting a secret meeting with a fervent mind. With painstaking devotion, she gazed upward until the heavenly perfected descended to her chamber.

Later during the last month of winter, in the middle of the night when the sky was crisp and clear, Lady Wei suddenly heard the reverberation of bells and drums, as well as the melody of reed pipes and flutes blaring forth. She went outside, looked up, and saw something coming down from the eastern sky. Flags and banners waved in profusion amid a multitude of feathered

---

3   Both commanderies were located in present-day Henan Province. See Zang Lihe 1972, 1096, 456.
4   Nanyang is in present-day Henan Province. See Zang Lihe 1972, 595.
5   Xiuwu County is in present-day Henan Province. See Zang Lihe 1972, 679.
6   *Extensive Records of the Taiping Era* (Li Fang 2003, 356) states that in her youth, Lady Wei read broadly in classical texts and practiced macrobiotic techniques such as consuming sesame and circulating breath.

蓋紛紜。光輝幽藹,煥爛太虛。他人莫之見也。

須臾有虎輦、玉輿、隱輪之車,並頓駕來,降夫人之靜室。凡四真人,並年可二十餘。容貌偉朗,天資秀穎。同著紫花蓮冠,飛錦衣裳。瓊藥寶帶,體佩虎文。項有圓光,手把華旛。

其一人自稱曰:「我太極真人安度明也。」其一人曰:「我東華大神、方諸青童君也。」其一人曰:「我榑桑碧海賜谷神王、景林真人也。」其一人曰:「我清虛真人、小有仙人王子登也。」於是夫人匍匐再拜,叩頭自搏:「不期今日,道君降下。唯乞神仙,長生度世。」

四人乃坐良久,王子登告夫人曰:「聞子曩日念善,展轉求生。密練真氣,魂和體清。丹懷遠邁,錄字上清。高契真人,抱信期靈。幽感啓微,潛曜赤城。遂金書紫極,藏簡玉庭。故感高晨,玄唱齊并。是以太帝君勑我今來,教授於子神真之道焉。」

---

7   See *Traditions of Lord Pei*, p. 21, n. 46 above.
8   We are reading this appellation as a somewhat generic title for all higher Daoist gods, rather than as Most High Lord of the Dao (Taishang daojun), based on its use to refer to many different deities in the *Inner Tradition of Lord Wang*.

canopies. A beam of bright light shone from the endless darkness with a brilliance that lit up the Grand Void. No one else saw any of these things.

An instant later, a tiger palanquin, a jade carriage, and a coach with invisible wheels all simultaneously halted, and the group descended unto Lady Wei's oratory. In total, there were four perfected beings, who appeared a little over twenty years old. They had bright and imposing features, and looked as though they were gifted with refined intelligence. They all wore caps adorned with interlaced purple flowers, and jackets and robes made from flying brocade. They had belts inlaid with rose-gem pistils from which they hung tiger-writ talismans. Round halos radiated behind their heads, and they grasped floral pennants.

One of them introduced himself, saying, "I am An Duming, a perfected being of the Grand Bourne." Another said, "I am the great spirit of Eastern Efflorescence, the Lord Azure Lad of Fangzhu." Another said, "I am the Divine King of the Sunlight Vale[7] from the cyan seas of Fusang, the Perfected Being of the Phosphor Forest." Another said, "I am Wang Zideng, a transcendent being of Lesser Existence and a perfected being of Pure Vacuity." After this, Lady Wei prostrated herself, bowed twice, kowtowed, and slapped herself in the face saying, "I never expected the day would arrive when you, lords of the Dao,[8] would descend unto me. I wanted simply to be a divine transcendent who might attain a long life and be saved from this world."

After the four beings sat for a long while, Wang Zideng announced to Lady Wei, "I have heard that you have been mindful of goodness for a long time, and have time and time again sought to lengthen your life. You refined perfected qi in private, and your cloud-soul became harmonious and your body pure. You had a heartfelt longing to go to distant places, and your name was recorded in Supreme Purity. You made a lofty contract with the perfected and kept your pledge to rendezvous with numina. Your responsiveness to shrouded spirits helps you perceive subtle ideas, and you have submerged yourself in the sparkle of the Red City.[9] As such, your name has been written in gold up in the Purple Bourne Palace on slips hidden away in a jade hall.[10] This is why you resonate with high dawn, and sing in union with the mysterious. Hence, the Grand Imperial Lord commanded me to come now, to transmit a Dao of divine perfection to you."

---

9 The Red City here refers to the place in the far south where the souls of people go upon death.
10 The Purple Bourne Palace is one of the many heavenly dwelling places of transcendents (Ge Hong 1996, 123).

其東華青童君曰:「此清虛真人者,爾之師也。當受業焉。」

其安度明曰:「子因緣上業,積感求道。苦心久矣,用思至也。道今來矣,子得之焉。」

其景林真人曰:

「子勤感累世,積念真靈。將積應之所期,乃明挺之標會也。虛皇早鑒爾之用思,太極已注子名於玉札,錄字紫虛之宮。金書東華之閣刻名上清丹文錦籍。應爲紫虛元君、上真司命,又加名山之號,封南嶽夫人。

今視子之質實:霄景高煥,圓精重照,鳳骨龍姿,腦色寶曜,五藏紫絡,心有羽文。形棲晨霞,神友靈肆。天人之任良不虛矣。帝誨王褒相爲盟師。故遣太極真人,鑒子之精。子其勖哉!」

---

11 According to Tao Hongjing, Vacuous Sovereign and Vacuous Sovereign Lord of the Dao (Xuhuang Daojun 虛皇道君) are alternate names for the Celestial Worthy of Primordial Commencement (Yuanshi tianzun 元始天尊). *DZ* 167, 3a.

The Lord Azure Lad of the Eastern Efflorescence said, "Here is a perfected being of Pure Vacuity, who will be your master. You will receive instructions from him."

Then An Duming said, "You are karmically destined to take on this endeavor, for you have time and time again sought the Dao. You have been long suffering, yet have reached this point by honing your mind. Now the Dao has come to you, and you will acquire it."

Then the Perfected Being of the Phosphor Forest said,

"You have diligently sought a response from perfected numen for many lifetimes by continually being mindful of them. Your constant desire for a divine response has made this lofty meeting of brilliantly appointed gods possible. The Vacuous Sovereign[11] has long been inspecting your thoughts, and now the Grand Bourne perfected have recorded your name on jade slats and inscribed these characters in the palace of Purple Vacuity. Your name is also found in the golden books stored in the gallery of Eastern Efflorescence, where the cinnabar writs of Supreme Purity are kept in a brocade register. Accordingly, you have been made Primal Lord of Purple Vacuity, an upper perfected director of destinies, and have also been given a position at a famed peak and will be enfeoffed as Lady of the Southern Sacred Peak.

"Now we have witnessed your true qualities: You have phosphors that flash high in the empyrean, a perfect essence that shines on, the bones of a phoenix, the face of a dragon, a brain whose hues shine with a precious radiance, five viscera aligned in a purple web, and a mind full of eloquent words.[12] Your body dwells atop the auroras of dawn, as your spirit finds companions among the top numina. We have full confidence in your appointment as a celestial being. The celestial emperors have decreed that Wang Bao will assist you as your covenant master. So your case has been passed on to the Grand Bourne perfected beings, who will examine your essences. You must do your utmost from this point on!"

---

12 *DZ* 1139, 8.23, continues with the following: "Because of this, your body can now rest in dawn auroras, and you can interact with spirits and be a channel for numina. Accordingly, your harmonious virtues render great peace, and you rank transcendent beings and govern over them. Your excellence has been deemed useful, and your talents are magnificent and splendid" 是以形棲晨霞，神交靈津也。方協德太平，理仙佐治。挺應稱用，才亦偉鑠。

四真各有辭致。言畢，夫人叩頭自搏而言曰：
「華存卑賤，枯骨之餘。自處塵垢，久染濁穢。天地寥邈，高下懸隔。縱恣五濁，翻錯臭穢。滯塞靈衹，沈淪凡俗。無冀日月，廻曜幽宄。

　　不謂天尊下交凡肆，所以割心斷意，取同螻蚓自顧。少好神仙，貪樂長生，心之所詣，出於自然，志之所期，誓以三光。而值季世俱忌，禮度制置，無從脫免，良願不遂。

　　今形非顧影，體氣臭惡。久爲垢穢所逼者，徒勵節無益。自入劉門，修道日廢，須者少閑。內外乖隔，容得齋思。謹按道法，尋求經方。入室之制，爲欲靜護五藏，辟諸疾病耳？豈圖上願？

　　惟在今日今夕，道君並降，慶出分外，光照幽谷。荷戴天眷，不勝惶懼。此是婢子有幸，當得度世。唯乞哀矜賜以性命。」

The four perfected each conveyed their words. When they finished speaking, Lady Wei kowtowed and slapped her face, saying,

"I am mean and lowly, a mere remnant of shriveled bones. I have dwelled in dust and dirt, and have long been polluted by sullied filth. Heaven and Earth are separated by a vast distance, and superior and inferior are remote from one another. I have given free rein to the Five Defilements,[13] which have multiplied into many blunders most foul. I have stifled the numina and spirits, which has caused me to be mired in common customs. I no longer have any hope that the sun or moon will return and cast light onto my dark and idle mind.

"If not for you, heavenly worthies, who have come down to pardon all those things that break my heart and fracture my thoughts, I would be no different than a cricket or an earthworm.[14] It is true that I have been fond of divine transcendence from a young age, avidly sought a long life, set my mind's purpose to act with spontaneity, and aimed my hopes to make a pledge to the three luminaries. But I live in a decadent age, when all is detestable and ritual decorum is so rigid that decadence cannot be avoided, so my good intentions have gone unrealized.

"My present body is nothing to be proud of, for my bodily qi is sluggish and repulsive. I have long been drawn to the despicable and filthy, and have focused on principles to no benefit. But when I entered my dilapidated compound, I cultivated the Dao by abandoning the world each day and reduced my needs as much as possible. Life within my quarters was cut off from the outside, and I could fast and meditate. I earnestly followed the techniques of the Dao and sought scriptures and formulas. But are the protocols for entering an oratory really done to protect one's five viscera through tranquility, and to ward off disease? Would this really encompass my highest desire?

"Yet now, on this day at twilight, the lords of the Dao have descended to afford me favors undeserved and shine a light in this obscure valley. You have come bearing your heavenly generosity so that I will no longer be overwhelmed with fearful anxiety. All of this is most fortunate for me, a mere maidservant, who can now transcend this world. I beg simply for your compassion, that grant me renewed life."

---

13 See the *Inner Tradition of Han Emperor Wu*, p. 179 below.
14 That is, a petty person.

自陳畢,東華小童指招而告之曰:
「子少好道真,至誠窅感。是故因緣世生,胎鍊五神。寄慧齊見,超度八難。氣適靈輝,挺會真筭。
　　自當爲紫虛之宮上真司命,勤精彌綸,太極所斿。又加名嶽之封,位均諸侯。然不受聞《上道内法晨景玉經》者,仙道衆妙,無緣得成也,子其勉哉。我後日當更期會於陽洛山中。汝勤之矣。」
　　於是清虛真人王君乃命侍女華散條、李明允等,使披雲蘊,開玉笈,出《太上寶文》、《八素隱書》、《大洞真經》、《靈書紫文八道》、《紫度炎光》、《石精玉馬》、《神真虎文》、《高仙羽玄》等經三十一卷。是王君昔於陽洛山,遇南極真人、西城,王君所授者也。今於汲郡修武縣中,授夫人焉。
　　暘谷神王,又別授夫人《黃庭内景經》。正一真人張君又別授《治精制鬼法》。夫人前後所授,非但此三十一卷而已。其篇卷悉在傳中,不能一一書之。

When she had finished speaking, the Lesser Lad of the Eastern Efflorescence pointed at her and said,

"From an early age you have been fond of the Dao and perfection with complete sincerity and intimate feeling. So on the basis of your karma and birth in this world, you have been able to refine the five spirits of your embryo. You have found refuge in your wisdom and pious sight, and have saved yourself from the Eight Difficulties.[15] Your qi exudes a numinous shine, and so you have been selected for a chance to meet the perfected.

"You shall be appointed director of destinies for the Upper Perfected in the Purple Vacuity Palace, where your diligent essence will be known to all under the Grand Bourne Palace banner. Additionally, you have been enfeoffed with a famous peak and given a title equal to that of marquis. Even though you have not heard about the Inner Rituals of the Highest Way of the Jade Scripture of Dawn Phosphors, you have been able to achieve the various wonders of the Transcendent Dao, not through karma, but by your diligence. We shall meet again at a later date when we rendezvous at Mt. Yangluo. Please be vigilant."

After this, the Perfected Being of Pure Vacuity, Lord Wang, ordered his attendant maidens—Hua Santiao, Li Mingyun, and others—to unfurl the cloudy bookcase and open the jade bookbag and take out thirty-one fascicles of scriptures, for instance *Precious Writs of the Most High*, *Hidden Book of the Eight Immaculates*, *Perfected Scripture of the Great Grotto*, *Numinous Book and Purple Writs of the Eight Paths*, *Purple Crossing and Blazing Radiance*, *Lithic Essence of the Jade Horse*, *Tiger Writs of Divine Perfection*, and *Winged Mystery of High Transcendence*. These were the scriptures that Lord Wang received long ago when he encountered the Perfected Being of the Southern Bourne and the Perfected Being of the Western Citadel at Mt. Yangluo. In this age, in Xiuwu County of Ji Prefecture, these texts were transmitted to Lady Wei.

On a separate occasion, the divine king of the Sunlight Vale transmitted to Lady Wei the *Scriptures of the Inner Phosphors in the Yellow Court*. On another occasion, Lord Zhang, the Perfected Being of Correct Unity, transmitted the *Method for Controlling Demons by Ordering Essences*. All the scriptures she received from start to finish were not just the thirty-one fascicles mentioned above. These chapters and fascicles are all detailed in the full version of her hagiography; there are far too many to enumerate here.

---

15 See Pettit and Chang 2020, 323 n. 37.

太元真人東嶽上卿司命真君傳

弟子中候仙人李道，字安林撰

真人姓茅諱盈字叔申，咸陽南關人也。姬胄分根，氏族於茅。積德累仁，祚流百世。誕縱明賢，繼踵相承。

高祖父諱濛字初成。深識玄遠，察覽興亡。知周之衰，不仕諸侯。乃師於北郭北阿鬼谷先生。遂隱遁華山，盤桓靈峯。逍遥幽岫，靜念神仙。高抗蕭寥，絕塵人間也。

盈曾祖父諱偃字泰能，濛之第四子也。仕秦昭王之世，位爲舍人，稍遷車騎校尉、長平恭侯。毗弼霸正，有功業於時焉。

盈祖父諱嘉字正倫。仕秦莊王爲廣信侯。始皇即位，嘉輔帝室，當莊襄王時也。秦地漸以并巴、蜀、漢中、宛、郢，置南郡矣。北收上郡以東爲河東、太原、上黨。

---

1 Xianyang was the capital of the state of Qin and later the Qin dynasty (221–207 BCE).
2 Perhaps after the brutal Qin conquest of Changping in 260 BCE. See Sima Qian 1997, 2373. King Zhao ruled from 306 to 251 BCE.

Traditions of the Perfected Director of Destinies, Grand Prime Perfected Being and Upper Chamberlain of the Eastern Sacred Peak

Compiled by his disciple the Middle Marquis Transcendent Being Li Dao, styled Anlin

The Perfected Being surnamed Mao with the taboo name Ying, styled Shushen, was from Nanguan of Xianyang.[1] He was a descendant of a branch of the Ji family line whose clan was named Mao. His accumulated virtues and amassed humane acts brought blessings upon a hundred generations.[i] From birth he was known as a bright worthy who would set an example for others to follow.

Ying's paternal great-great-grandfather had the taboo name Meng and was styled Chucheng. Meng had a deep understanding of profound mysteries and could perceive when kingdoms would rise and fall. He knew that the Zhou dynasty was in decline and chose not to serve any feudal lords. Instead, Meng studied at the fortifications north of Xianyang under Master Guigu of the northern ridge. Thereafter, he lived in reclusion atop Mt. Hua, where he roamed among its numinous peaks. Meng roamed free and easy among the dark Sacred Peaks, and peacefully pondered divine transcendence. He was upright and unyielding in his solitude, and rejected the sullied human world.

Ying's great-grandfather, whose taboo name was Yan and was styled Taineng, was Meng's fourth son. Yan served under King Zhao of Qin, and held the position of palace secretary before being promoted to commandant of the cavalry and then honored as marquis of Changping.[2] He supported and strengthened the campaigns against the hegemons and had many meritorious exploits during this period.

Ying's grandfather had the taboo name Jia and was styled Zhenglun. He served King Zhuang of Qin as the marquis of Broad Faithfulness.[3] When the First Emperor took the throne as King of Qin [246 BCE], Jia became a minister of the royal house, just as he had during the time of King Zhuangxiang. The Qin realm gradually incorporated the lands of Ba, Shu, Hanzhong, Wan, and Ying, making them part of the Southern Commandery. It conquered the Upper Commandery to its north and incorporated the commandery into its eastern lands of Hedong, Taiyuan, and Shangdang. It then went

---

3   King Zhuang reigned from 250 to 247 BCE.

東至滎陽，滅二周，置三川郡。以呂不韋爲丞相，號文信侯。以嘉爲德信侯，使招置賓客游士，欲并天下。

始皇六年，韓、魏、趙、衛、楚共擊秦，取壽陵。始皇使嘉將兵攻之，有功焉。衛迫東都，嘉又尅討，皆平之。始皇壯嘉志節，賜金五千斤。二十五年，秦大興兵，使嘉攻燕、遼東。得燕王而還。

又遣嘉定荊，江南地皆降。是年置會稽郡，嘉將兵於會稽而亡。始皇哀其忠，因以相國禮葬之於長安龍首山西南。

嘉有六子，並知名於時。始皇皆官爵承先，並各賜姓。其第六子諱祚字彥英。不仕不學，志願農巷。即盈之父也。

祚有三子：長子諱盈字叔申，次子諱固字季偉，小子諱衷字思和。盈少秉異操，天才頴爍，矯志蕭抗。行邁遠逸，不營聞達，不交非類。獨味清虛，恬心玄漠。

4   The two kingdoms of Zhou refers to the final partition of Zhou during the reign of the final Zhou king, King Nan 周赧王 (r. 314–256 BCE).
5   The description of Qin's territory up to Lu Buwei's enfeoffment is drawn almost verbatim from fascicle 6 of *Records of the Historian* (Sima Qian 1997, 223). The only change from that account is the insertion of Ying's grandfather into the events.
6   This passage also parallels *Records of the Historian*, fascicle 6, but names Jia as the general who leads the counterstrike. Interestingly, Sima Qian states that Qin seized the Wei capital and pressed on Dongjun 東郡, whereas the author of this text identifies Wei as pressing on Dongdu 東都, suggesting that the author may have altered the events to insert Jia into the action. See Sima Qian 1997, 224.

east to Xingyang, destroyed the two kingdoms of Zhou, and established the Three Rivers Commandery.⁴ When the emperor made Lü Buwei his prime minister, Lü was given the title Marquis of Lettered Faithfulness. Jia was given the title Marquis of Virtuous Integrity and was charged with recruiting retainers and wandering knights who could help unify the empire.⁵

In the sixth year of the First Emperor's reign as king [240 BCE], the states of Han, Wei, Zhao, Wei, and Chu simultaneously attacked Qin and seized Shouling. The First Emperor sent Jia with an army to attack them, and he was successful. When Wei pressed upon the eastern capital, Jia launched a punitive expedition and pacified them.⁶ The First Emperor praised Jia's ambition and integrity, and rewarded him with five thousand catties of gold. In the twenty-fifth year, the First Emperor amassed a large army and sent Jia to lead an attack on Yan and Liaodong. After Jia captured the king of Yan, he returned home.

Jia was then dispatched to quell unrest in Jingzhou, after which all the lands south of the Yangzi River fell. That year, the Guiji Commandery was established, and Jia perished while commanding the army in Guiji.⁷ The First Emperor mourned the loss of Jia's loyalty, and he buried him with the pomp of a prime minister southwest of the Longshou Hills near Chang'an.⁸

Jia had six sons, all of whom were well known in their day. The First Emperor made them legacy officers on account of the service of their forebears and bestowed upon each of them a surname. Jia's sixth son had the taboo name Zuo and was styled Yanying. He did not serve as a minister, nor did he study. Rather, he desired only to live in a country village. This was Ying's father.

Zuo had three sons: the eldest had the taboo name Ying and was styled Shushen, the second eldest had the taboo name Gu and was styled Jiwei, and the youngest had the taboo name Zhong and was styled Sihe.⁹ When young, Ying had high moral principles, was a genius sharp and bright, and possessed a strong will that would not bend to others. He would often venture off to distant places, would never mingle with people with influence, and never interacted with those who did not meet his standards. He relished only the ways of Pure Vacuity, for there his mind was calm and peaceful.

---

7   According to *Records of the Historian* (Sima Qian 1997, 234), in 222 BCE the First Emperor dispatched multiple armies. In the south, Wang Jian 王翦 pacified Jing 荊 territory south of the Yangzi River, forcing the Lord of Yue 越君 to capitulate. Jia would have served under Wang Jian when he fell.
8   The Longshuo Hills were a chain of small hills extending from the Wei River through Chang'an to the Fan 樊 River. A portion of the hills was leveled to build imperial structures.
9   *DZ* 304, 5.2a, has more specific information about the birthdates of the three brothers.

盈時年十八，遂棄家委親。入于恒山，讀老子《道德經》及《周易》傳。採取山朮而餌服之。潛景絕崖，素挺靈岫。仰希標玄，與世永違。

　　始皇三十年九月庚子，盈高祖父濛，於華山之中，乘雲駕龍，白日昇天。先是時其邑謠曰：

神仙得者茅初成
駕龍上昇入太清
時下玄洲戲赤城
繼世而往在我盈
帝若學之臘嘉平

　　始皇聞謠歌而問其故，父老具對曰：「此仙人之謠，勸帝求長生之事」。於是始皇忻然，乃有尋仙之志，因改臘曰嘉平。

　　盈於恒山積六年，思念至道。誠感寄應，寢興妙論。通于神夢，髣髴見太玄玉女。把玉札而攜之曰：「西城有王君，得真道，可爲君師。子奚不尋而受教乎？」

10　Mt. Heng is one of the Five Sacred Peaks, located in modern Shanxi Province.
11　According to the dates above, this would make Meng roughly 150 years old.
12　"Bounty" (ying) is a pun for Mao Ying's name.

When Ying was eighteen, he left his family and entrusted his affairs to relatives. He then moved to Mt. Heng[10] where he read Laozi's *Daodejing* and the commentaries to the *Classic of Changes*. He plucked wild atractylis and made it into pills that he consumed. He hid his light among the steep cliffs, where his plain virtues were lauded throughout the numinous Sacred Peaks. He would gaze up and yearn for the lofty mysteries, and was forever running counter to social mores.

On a *gengzi* day in the ninth month of the thirtieth year of the First Emperor of Qin's reign [216 BCE], Ying's great-great-grandfather Meng ascended to heaven at Mt. Blossom on a cloud chariot pulled by dragons in broad daylight.[11] At the time, people of a nearby village sang a ballad about Meng that went,

> Of all the divine transcendents, Mao was the first
> To ride dragons and ascend to the Grand Purity heavens.
> Sometimes he descended to the Mystic Continent to have fun in Red City,
> And gave us a bounty passed down through generations.[12]
> If the emperor studies this, the twelfth-month festival will be felicitous and equitable.[13]

The First Emperor heard the ballad and inquired about its origins. The elders replied, "This is a ballad about a transcendent being, and it urges the emperor to pursue the matter of longevity." This pleased the First Emperor, and from that time forth he sought transcendence. As a result, he changed the name of the twelfth-month festival to "Felicitous and Equable."[ii]

Altogether, Ying lived on Mt. Heng for six years while contemplating the ultimate Dao. His sincerity induced the gods to secretly respond to Ying with sublime ideas when he was awake or asleep. During his divine dreams, it was as if he laid eyes upon the jade maidens of Grand Mystery heaven. They took up jade tallies and held them in their hands, saying, "In the Western Citadel, there is one Lord Wang who has attained a perfected Dao and can serve as milord's master. Should you not seek him and receive these teachings?"

---

13 Our translation of *jiaping* is borrowed from Derk Bodde (1975, 50 n. 5), who has extensively studied this pre-Han celebration. Schipper (1965, 80 n. 2) believes that this passage is corrupted because its meaning is so confusing.

心豁靈暢，啓徒內爽。覺悟流光之騰曄，自謂已得之於千載矣。明辰植暉，東盼霄邁。登嶺陟峻，徑到西城。齋戒三月，沐浴向望，遂超榛冒險。稽首靈域，卒見王君。

後二十年，從王君西至龜山見王母。盈乃叩頭再拜，自陳於王母曰：

「盈，小醜賤生，枯骨之餘。敢以不肖之軀，而慕龍鳳之年？欲以朝菌之質，竊求積朔之期？雖仰遠流，莫以知濟。津塗堅塞，所要無寄。常恐一旦死於鑽放之難，取笑於世俗之夫。

是以昔日負笈幽林，貪師所生。遂遇王君，哀盈丹苦。見授治身之要、服氣之法。於是靜齋深室，造行其事。師重見告，以盈身非玉石，而無主於恒。氣非四時，常生於內。正當率御出入，呼吸中適，和液得修，形神靡錯。感應思積，則魂魄不滯。理合其分，氣甄其適，乃可形精不枯，宅不可廢也。

若使精神疲於徃反，津液勞於出入。則形當日凋，神亦枯落。歲減其始，月虧其昔矣。宜便妙訪，求其長易之益。」

---

14 See the *Inner Tradition of Han Emperor Wu*, p. 161 below, for a parallel passage.

Ying's mind was opened up and his spirits lifted, giving him inner joy. His awakening was like a flashing brilliance of swirling light, and yet he felt as if he had had this realization a thousand years before. A bright star shone high as he looked eastward into the endless empyrean. He climbed high ridges and scaled high peaks until he arrived at the Western Citadel. He fasted, kept the precepts for three months, and made ablutions in the proper direction so that he could avert any of the various dangers.[iii] He kowtowed on these sacred grounds, at which point he finally saw Lord Wang.

Twenty years later, Ying followed Lord Wang west to Mt. Gui to see the Queen Mother of the West. Ying kowtowed, bowed twice, and then said the following to the Queen Mother of the West:

"I, Ying, am a wretch and a lowlife, a pile of dried bones. How could a person with a worthless body dare aspire to the long life of a dragon or a phoenix? And how could one hope to live for many moons if he is but a mushroom that grows and dies in a single morning? While I look up at the distant current of the Milky Way, I know of no way to cross it. Ferries and roads are blocked, and I have nothing to rely on. I have a constant fear that I will one day die from the hardships of this search, and will become the laughing stock of even the most vulgar of men.[iv]

"This is why I carried my bookbags into the dark forest in my early years, for I yearned to study with a master. It was then that I encountered Lord Wang, who pitied my heartfelt pain. From him, I received the essentials for regulating the body and techniques for ingesting qi. Later I went into a quiet retreat in an isolated chamber, where I put these instructions into practice. My master has given me constant encouragement, since my body is still not like rock or jade and is always changing. My qi is not regular like the four seasons, but is constantly rising within. From here on, I must regulate the movement of my qi, breathe in a steady fashion, and harmonize my fluids as they move along, so that my body and spirit will never falter.[v] I can thus stir a response and sustain concentration, and my cloud-souls and white-souls will never be impeded. And if I can properly separate these souls and differentiate my qi appropriately, I will prevent my entire being from shriveling up and my bodily dwelling from rotting.

"But even if I did, it would only cause my vital spirits to tire as they go every which way, and my bodily fluids to be taxed by constant production. My body would then decay daily and my spirit would wither away. My remaining years continue to decrease, just like a moon that is ever waning.[14] It is so opportune to be graced by your presence, so that I might at last seek the benefits of an everlasting transformation."

西王母曰:「子心至矣!吾昔先師元始天王、及皇天扶桑太帝君,見遺以要言。汝願聞之邪?」於是,口告盈以《玉珮金璫》之道、《太極玄真》之經。盈拜受所言,稽首而立。

又告盈曰:

「夫《金璫》者,上清之華蓋,陰景之內真。《玉珮》者,太上之隱玄,洞飛之寶章。得其道者,皆上陟霄霞,登遨太極,寢晏高空,游行紫虛也。向說元始天王、太帝君言,是《太霄二景隱書玉珮金璫》之文章也。又有《陰陽二景內真符》,與本文相隨。太上法惟令授諸司命。

子玉札玄挺,錄字刊金。黃映內曜,素書上清。似當為上卿之君,司命之任矣。此道後別當付於子也。然不先聞《明堂玄真之道》,亦無由得《太霄隱書》也。」

盈於是辭師,乃歸帶索混俗,亦不矯於世。自說入恒山北谷學儒俗之業,時年四十九也。盈父母尚存,父見大怒,

---

15 The yin phosphors are the corporeal spirits, usually eight or three groups of eight, that play a key role in helping an adept to release the mortal knots affecting his body (Robinet 2011a, 210–211).

16 We take *Grotto Flight* (*dongfei* 洞飛) to be a contraction of *Treasure Grotto's Golden Stanzas on Flying into the Empyrean's Farthest Mystery* (*Baodong feixiao juexuan jinzhang* 寶洞飛霄絕玄金章) (Pettit and Chang 2020, 243).

The Queen Mother of the West said, "Your mind is exceptional! Long ago, my former master, the Celestial King of Primordial Commencement, along with the Great Imperial Lord of Fusang of August Heaven, presented me with essential instructions. Would you like to hear them?" She then revealed to Ying the Dao of *Jade Pendant and Gold Rings*, as well as the scripture *Mysterious Perfection of the Grand Ultimate*. Ying gratefully accepted her instructions, kowtowed to her, and stood up.

Then she told Ying,

"Now, the Gold Rings is the floriate canopy of Supreme Purity and the yin phosphors of Inner Perfected.[15] The Jade Pendant is the hidden mystery of the Most High and the precious emblem *Grotto Flight*.[16] Those who attain this Dao can ascend into the auroras of the empyrean, climb with ease into Grand Ultimate heavens, take their leisure in the lofty sky, and roam out across the purple void. The instructions of the Celestial King of Primordial Commencement and the Great Imperial Lord that I just mentioned are in the text called *Jade Pendant and Gold Rings of the Grand Empyrean's Hidden Book of Two Phosphors*. There is also the *Inner Perfected Talisman of the Two Phosphors Yin and Yang*, which accompanies this text. According to the laws of the gods on high, all directors of destinies shall receive this text.

"Sir, you have the mysterious talents found on jade slats with a name carved in gold.[vi] The yellow glint of the characters sparkle from within the immaculate books of Supreme Purity. It appears that you are destined to be an upper chamberlain who will assume the responsibilities of a director of destinies. This Dao will be separately transmitted to you at a later time. But there is no way to acquire the *Hidden Writings of the Grand Empyrean* without first knowing the *Dao of the Mysterious Perfected Being of the Bright Hall*."[17]

Ying thereupon took leave of his master to live in poverty among commoners, yet he did not engage in the affairs of the world.[vii] When Ying was forty-nine years old, he returned home, telling everyone that he had moved to the northern valley of Mt. Heng to train in the classics. Ying's parents were still alive at this time, and his father bitterly told Ying, "You

---

17 This scripture, at least in part, was revealed to humans by the Queen Mother of the West. It details the life-giving energies of the sun and the moon. See Schafer 1978, 390. The Bright Hall (mingtang 明堂) is space between the eyebrows one inch beneath the skin. See Pettit and Chang 2020, 58–59.

「爲子不孝,不親供養。尋逐妖妄,流走四方。吾當喻汝爲不生之子也。」

欲杖罰之。盈長跪謝曰:「盈受命應當得道,道法世事,兩不相濟。雖違遠供養,無旦夕之益,能使家門平安,父母老壽。盈已受聖師符籙。見營助者以天丁之兵,見侍衛者以仙童玉女。今道已成,不可打擊,恐三官考察,非小故也。」

父外信禮度,未該內秀。道德玄域,意有未釋。故驗盈情狀,俾衆不惑。於是操杖向盈。適欲舉杖,杖即摧折成數十段。段皆飛揚,如弓矢之發,中壁壁穿,中柱柱陷。父悟不凡瞋意乃止。

盈曰:「向所啓正慮如此,邂逅中人則有所傷故耳。」

至漢宣帝時,二弟俱貴。哀爲五官大夫西河太守,固爲執金吾,並當之官。鄉里相送者數百人。時盈亦在座,謂賓曰:「吾雖不作二千石,亦有仙靈之職矣。來年四月三日當之官,能如今日之集會不?」衆許之。

---

18   Emperor Xuan reigned from 74 to 48 BCE.

have not been a filial son, nor have you taken care of your family.^{viii} Rather, you have pursued wanton ways, and ambled about in every direction.^{ix} It is almost as if we never had a son at all."

Ying's father was about to strike him with his cane. Ying knelt down to apologize, saying, "I have received an order that I should attain the Dao, but the ways of the Dao and those of the world are not compatible. Although I have neglected my duties to provide for you day and night, I have nevertheless been able to bring peace to the family, and you and my mother have lived long lives. I have already received talismans and registers from sage masters. They have provided me with the assistance of armies of heavenly soldiers and offered the protection of transcendent lads and jade maidens. Now that I have attained this Dao, you should not strike me, for I fear the Three Officials would investigate this matter and not treat it lightly."^x

His father externally placed his faith in rules of propriety, but he had never refined himself within. He had yet to understand the meaning of the Dao, its virtues, and the spiritual world. Thus, he wished to test Ying's claims, so that no one would doubt the matter.^{xi} He thereupon grasped his cane and pointed it at Ying. But just when he raised the cane to strike, it splintered into several dozen pieces. These pieces flew out as if they were arrows shot from a bow, penetrating the walls and lodging themselves into the columns. Once Ying's father realized how extraordinary this was, he was content and no longer angry.

Ying said, "This is what I imagined would happen if you thought about hitting me, and the splinters might have unexpectedly hit and injured someone."

During the time of Emperor Xuan,[18] Ying's two brothers grew in prominence. Mao Zhong was appointed as one of the directors of the Five Offices and the prefect of Xihe, while Mao Gu was appointed a bearer of the gilded mace, and they both served in these capacities.[19, xii] Several hundred men of their district turned out to send them off. At this time, when Ying was seated at the feast, he addressed the guests, "Although I may not have a two-thousand-bushel salary, I have been appointed as a transcendent numen. When I assume this post next year on the third day of the fourth month, will we be able to gather as we have done today?" Everyone expected this would happen.

---

19 According to Hucker (1985, 571), the director of the Five Offices dates from the Tang, which would make Mao Ai's position a potential anachronism. The bearer of the gilded mace was commander of an army responsible for policing the capital (Hucker 1985, 157). Berkowitz (1996, 455) places Xihe at the northeastern border of Shaanxi, adjacent to Inner Mongolia.

至期日，盈門前數頃地忽自平，治無復寸芥，皆青縑幄屋。屋下鋪數重白氈，容數百人坐。遠近僉赫相語，來者塞道。客乃有數倍於送弟時。

衆賓並集，爾乃大作主人。不見使人，但見金槃玉杯自至人前，奇餚異果不可名字。酒又美好，又有妓樂，絲竹金石，聲動天地。香麝之芳，達于數里。飲食隨益，六百餘人莫不醉飽。

明日，迎官來至。文官則朱衣素帶數百人，武官則甲兵牙旗，器杖曜日。盈與家人及親族辭決，而語宗族子弟曰：「夫真仙道隱，貴在跡翳。不應表光曲飾，動耀視聽。吾所以不得默遁藏景，潛舉空同者，蓋欲以此道誘勸二弟之追慕也。亦何但固、衷之返迷耶？天下有心者盡當注向神仙之冀獲爾！」

言訖，遂歸句曲，邦人因改句曲爲茅君之山。時二弟在官，聞盈玄跡眇邁，白日神仙。乘飛步虛，越波凌津，靈官奉從。著於民口。節蓋旌旗，光耀天下。

始乃信仙化可學，神靈可致。然後明松喬

---

20 *Supreme Purity Golden Transcendent Annals of the Jade Seal of the Supreme One's Golden Porte* (*Shangqing taiyi jinque yuxi jinzhen ji* 上清太一金闕玉璽金真紀, *DZ* 394, 6b) reads "all his relatives, sons, and brothers," rather than "members of the royal family, sons, and brothers" (zongshi zidi 宗室子弟). We have followed the *DZ* 394 reading, as the royal family was not mentioned in connection with the feast.

When that day arrived, the hectares before Ying's front door suddenly became flat, and every inch of space was covered by a tent embroidered in azure thread. Many layers of white felt mats were laid out on the floor of the tent, so that hundreds of people could take their seats. Far and near, the grand sumptuousness of this event was talked about, and the roads were clogged with those who came to see. The number of guests far outnumbered those who had gathered to send off his younger brothers.

When the guests assembled, Ying presided as their host. No servants could be seen, yet golden platters and jade cups were set before each person with rare meats and strange fruits beyond description. There was liquor most fine, as well as singing courtesans accompanied by an orchestra of strings and bells that shook heaven and earth. A perfume musk scent spread out many miles. The banquet was so plentiful that more than six hundred guests had their fill of food and drink.

The next day, Ying welcomed the officials who arrived. There were hundreds of civil officials in vermillion robes with white sashes, and military officials in standard-bearing armor whose weaponry sparkled in the sunlight. Ying then took leave of his family and kin as he addressed these relatives, sons, and brothers, saying, "The Dao of Perfection and Transcendence is concealed; it is necessary to hide its traces.[20] One should not cast light upon what is hidden by dangling shining objects for all to behold. I cannot remain in reclusion cloaked in phosphors, nor can I float atop an unending emptiness, for I must use this Dao to lead and guide my two younger brothers to follow my example. How could I possibly let Gu and Zhong be led astray? May anyone in this world with a mind to become a divine transcendent receive assistance if they have such aspirations!"

When he finished speaking, he returned to Mt. Gouqu, after which the villagers there changed the name of Gouqu to Mt. Maojun.[21] His two brothers were serving as officials when they heard of Ying's mysterious traces and sublime steps, such as rising in broad daylight as a divine transcendent. Ying flew up to pace the void, surfed waves to traverse the celestial ford, and was served by numinous officials. Everyone was talking about these happenings. The covered staffs, pennants, and banners of his office shone brightly over the world.

Gu and Zhong began to have faith that one could transform into a transcendent through study, and that divine numina could be summoned. And so they knew that the legends about Master Red Pine and Wang Ziqiao

---

21 Lord Mao's Mountain.

不虛，鼎湖實有。於是並各棄官還家。以日仄之年，方修盈糟粕遺事。不得口訣，未爲補益。

乃相與共歎而相謂曰：「家兄得道，非他人也。曷不徃從親稟問密訣，而留此按云云方書，以規度世乎？縱徃而不達，兄之神仙，終不使吾等死於非所也。」

遂共棄家，扶輿自載，以尋斯舉。以漢元帝永光五年三月六日渡江，求兄於東山。遂與相見，悲忻流涕告二弟曰：「悟何晚矣！」

二弟跪曰：「固衷頑下，不達道德。願賜長生，濟弟元元。」

盈曰：「卿已老矣！欲難可補復。縱得真訣，適可成地上仙耳。其上清昇霄大術，非老夫所學。今且當漸階其易行，以自支住。」

於是並教二弟服青牙始生咽氣液之道。以住血斷、補焦枯、攝筋骨之益。亦停年不死之法也。因以長齋三年，授以上道，使存明堂玄真之氣。以攝運生精，理和魂神。三年之內，竭誠精思，神光乃見。於是六丁奉侍，天兵衛護。

22 Tripod Lake was where the Yellow Emperor ascended to heaven on the back of a dragon. See Sima Qian 1997, 468.
23 We benefited from the translation by Thomas Smith (1992, 242) of a similar passage in *DZ* 304, 5.8a.
24 For more on this meditative practice, see Raz 2012a, 92–93.

were true, and that the Yellow Emperor's apotheosis at Tripod Lake really happened.[22] They both thus resigned from their posts and returned home. They wanted to spend their last years engaged in spiritual cultivation using the tidbits known about Ying's practice. But since they did not have esoteric oral instructions, they never benefited from these practices.

Together they lamented and remarked to one another, "Our elder brother, who is no stranger to us, has attained the Dao. Why don't we head off to our kin and petition him for secret instruction, and if he imparts it to us, we will have a step-by-step formula that will guide us to transcend the world? Even if we seek him without finding him, our brother's transcendent status will forever save us from dying inauspiciously."

They then left home and pulled a cart with their belongings so they might pursue this plan. On the sixth day of the third month in the fifth year of the Yongguang era [39 BCE] of Han Emperor Yuan, the brothers crossed the Yangzi River to find their brother in the eastern mountains. When they saw him, Ying broke down in tears of both sorrow and joy and told his younger brothers, "It took you so long to come to this realization!"

The two brothers knelt down and said, "Gu and Zhong are crude and slow, and could never comprehend the Dao and its virtues. We hope you might bestow long life upon us, to save your brothers, mere commoners."

Ying said, "Oh, you have already aged so much! Your desire to restore life will be difficult. Even if you could obtain perfected instructions, this would only suffice to make you a terrestrial upper transcendent. These great Supreme Purity techniques for ascending to the empyrean cannot be learned by old men.[23] At this point, it is best for you to take gradual steps toward transformation, for that can help you."

He then taught his two brothers a Dao for ingesting the initial vitality of the azure sprout by gulping breath and saliva.[24] This regulated their blood flow and strengthened withered tissues, thereby restoring their tendons and bones. He also taught them the ritual of stopping time and never dying. After this, they engaged in a three-year retreat where they received a high Dao for visualizing the qi of the Mysterious Perfected Being of the Bright Hall. With this, they could manipulate the circulation of their living essence and bring order to their cloud-soul spirits. After three years of devotion to refined contemplation, a divine glow appeared around them.[xiii] Then the six *ding* came to serve them,[25] and celestial soldiers came to protect them.

---

25   Within the sexagenary system of ten celestial stems and twelve earthly branches, Daoists considered the twelve times marked with *jia* 甲 or *ding* 丁 as times especially marked with yang and yin energies, respectively (Mugitani Kunio 2011b, 695–696). Both sets of six times became associated in medieval Daoism with spirits who would carry out commands and orders. See Pettit and Chang 2020, 210.

盈又各賜九轉還丹一劑，并神方一首。各拜而服之，仙道成矣。

後授紫素之書各百字，以付固衷。固衷拜受。其時亦有執儀者以啟正之。

《紫素文》曰：

太上有命，天載真書言：

咸陽茅固
家于南關
厥字季偉
受名當仙
位為定錄
兼統地真

使
保舉有道
年命相關
勤恭所蒞
四極法令

宮館洞臺，治丹陽句曲之山。固其勗之動靜察聞。

又曰：

盈固弟衷
挺業該清

26 This alchemical formula was bestowed to the Xu family by Mao Gu. The contents of this elixir and its transmission are discussed in detail by Strickmann 1979, 146–150.

27 The early (or perhaps proto–) Supreme Purity text *Most High Jade Classic of the Yellow Court's Inner Phosphors* (*DZ* 331, 1.4a) asserts there are three primal qi (yuanqi 元氣) that look like clouds of the three elemental colors (sansu yun 三素雲). These vapors are

Ying then gave each of them a single dose of the Reverted Elixir in Nine Cycles,[26] along with one divine recipe. Each brother bowed and swallowed them, and their path to transcendence was complete.

Ying then gave Gu and Zhong Purple-Elemental books made from purple silk, each one hundred characters long.[27] Gu and Zhong bowed and accepted them. Then an officer in charge of investiture came to make an official statement.

The *Purple Elemental Writs* read,

> The Most High has decreed that Heaven record a perfected document. This document reads,
>
>> Mao Gu of Xianyang,
>> Whose family is from the Southern Pass,
>> And who is styled Jiwei,
>> Has been bestowed a transcendent name.
>> He now has the title of Lord of Certifying Registers,
>> And will oversee the terrestrial perfected.
>>
>> He is charged
>> With sponsoring appointments of those with the Dao
>> And making their lifespan consistent with their fate.
>> With zeal and reverence, he takes up his office,
>> Using the decrees and statutes of the Four Extremities.[28]
>
> From his palace lodge within the grotto terrace, Mao Gu will govern Mt. Gouqu in Danyang. He will put every last ounce of his energy into investigating affairs.

It further read,

> Ying and Gu's younger brother Zhong
> Upholds his work with complete purity.

---

in a vertical formation in the body and their alignment determines one's lifespan. Later writers claimed that these qi were the Yellow-Elemental (huangsu 黃素), the White-Elemental (baisu 白素), and the Purple-Elemental, and these three primal qi correspond to the three divine daughters of the Primal Lord of Grand Simplicity (Taisu yuanjun 太素元君). See the *Supreme Purity Three Primes' Jade Rule and the Three Female Primes' Promulgated Scripture* (*Shangqing sanyuan yujian sanyuan bujing* 上清三元玉檢三元布經, *DZ* 354, 42a).

28 For more on the *Illustrious Code of the Four Extremities* (*Siji mingke* 四極明科), see Pettit and Chang 2020, 227.

雖晚反正
思微徹誠
斷馘六天
才穎標明

今
屈司三官
保命建名
總括岱宗
領死記生
位爲地仙
九宮之英
勸教童蒙
開道方成
教訓女官
授諸妙靈
蒞治百鬼
典崇校精
開察水源
江海流傾

封掌金谷
藏錄玉漿
監植龍芝
洞草夜光

Though he was late in returning to what is correct,
His thoughts are rarefied, and his conduct sincere.
Heads of recalcitrants will roll in the Six Heavens
Once the extent of his genius is known.

Now
He is appointed as supervisor of the Three Officials,
Who together safeguard fate and determine names.
He will rule over the ancestral peak of Mt. Tai
To direct the dead and make records of the living.
He has the title of terrestrial transcendent[29]
And the blossoming talent of the Nine Palaces.
He advises and teaches the naive and benighted,
Explaining how all things manifest in the Dao.
He now teaches and instructs the female officers,
Giving them all the wondrous numina.
He oversees and controls the hundred demons,
Ranking their essences by means of his eminent authority.
He seeks to know everything from the tiny bubbling spring
To where rivers pour out into oceans.

He is enfeoffed and rules over Golden Valley,
Where he stores and keeps track of jade nectar.
He oversees where dragon mushrooms will be planted,
As well as luminescent grotto grasses.

---

29 Lower officials in the celestial bureaucracy. For more on their relation to other kinds of transcendent beings, see Pettit and Chang 2020, 36.

治于良常之山，帶北洞之口，鎮陰官之門也。

使者授書，訖而去。
　　至漢平帝元壽二年八月巳酉，五帝各乘方面色車。從羣官來下，受太帝之命。授盈爲司命、東卿、
上真君，文以紫玉爲板，黃金刻之。其文曰：

> 惟盈
> 虛挺遠朗
> 幽耽妙玄
> 爰自童蒙
> 散髮北山
> 靜心林澤
> 積思求神
> 登峻履谷
> 艱尋師門
> 擲形絶崿
> 投軀萬津
> 丹誠率徃
> 肆其天然
>
> 遂造明匠
> 乃授靈篇

He governs Mt. Liangchang and is responsible for the entryway to the northern cavern, where he guards the Yin Palace gate.

After the messenger bestowed these books, he departed.

Many years later, on the *siyou* day of the eighth month of the second year of the Yuanshou era of Han Emperor Ping,[30] the Five Emperors came riding chariots colored according to their respective directions. A bevy of officials followed them down, with orders from the Grand Emperor. They bestowed upon Ying the titles of Director of Destinies, East Chamberlain, and Upper Perfected Lord, in words inscribed in bright gold on a placard of purple jade. The words read,

> Yea, Mao Ying
> Is like a distantly shining light thrusting from the void
> And a sublime mystery emerging from the dimness.
> He went from being a naive boy to one who
> Let his hair down in the mountains of the north.
> He quieted his mind in the forested swamps
> And constantly thought about seeking spirits.
> He climbed pinnacles and walked across valleys
> And went through great pains to find a master
> He threw his body from steep cliffs
> And flung himself atop myriad riverbanks.
> He displayed heartfelt sincerity time and time again,
> Manifesting his heavenly nature.
>
> In the end, he called upon the Luminous Craftsman,
> Who transmitted numinous chapters.[xiv]

---

30 Likely a scribal error, as this should be the second year of the Yuanshou 元壽 era of Emperor Ai 哀帝 (1 BCE) or the Yuanshi 元始 era of Emperor Ping 平帝 (2 CE). *DZ* 304, 5.10a, records that the date is the Yuanshou era of Emperor Ai. Regardless, the dates provided in the text suggest that more than thirty years have passed since the brothers came to be instructed by Mao Ying.

剪髮祝骴
殘首截身
帶索自樂
不恥飢寒
所適惟道
所保以真
情昭上帝
感激太玄

今敬授盈位爲太元真人，領東嶽上卿、司命神君。

君
平心正格
秉操金石
丹心矯衆
栖神高映

故報盈以
玉鉞綠旌
八威之策
使盈
征伐源澤
折衝萬神

> Ying cut his hair and made incantations for aid
> As one about to be decapitated and dismembered.
> He was at ease in his poverty[31]
> And was not ashamed of being hungry or cold.[xv]
> He sought only the Dao,
> And all his protection came from the perfected.
> With feeling he called out to the Upper Emperor
> With emotions that surged up into Grand Mystery.

Now we respectfully install Mao Ying as the Grand Prime Perfected Being, appointed as upper chamberlain of the Eastern Sacred Peak and divine lord director of destinies.

> Lord Mao
> Has a fair mind, engages in upright conduct,
> And possesses integrity firm as metal and stone.
> His fervent heart stands out among all the rest;
> He lodges his spirits in what is lofty and bright.

> Therefore, we reward Mao Ying[32]
> With a jade broadaxe and green ensign
> And the tablet of the eight mighty ones.[33]
> May Ying
> Lead an expedition to fonts and marshes[xvi]
> To repulse and subdue the myriad spirits.

---

31 Literally, wore a rope as a belt.
32 For more on rewarding adepts for the fruits of mental cultivation, see Xie Conghui 1999, 155–157.
33 See *Traditions of Lord Pei*, p. 31 above.

君
寒凍林谷
味玄仰真
思激窮岫
啓心精誠

今故報盈以
紫毛之節
藕敷華冠
使盈
招驅萬靈
封山召雲

君
棄家獨往
離親樂仙
契闊險巇
冬祖山川

今故報盈
繡羽紫帔
丹青飛羣
使盈
從容霄階
攜命玉真

君
步驟深藪
足履危仞
心耽志尚
曾不怨憚

Lord Mao,
With a mind as cold as a forest valley,
Savors mysteries and admires perfection.
His thoughts surge to the farthest Sacred Peak
And inspire his mind with utmost zeal.

Therefore, we now reward Mao Ying
With a staff with purple tassels
And a crown of flowers strewn with lotus roots.
May Ying
Seek out and expel the myriad numina[xvii]
In order to seal off the mountains and beckon the clouds.

Lord Mao
Abandoned his family and struck out on his own,
Leaving his kin to revel in transcendence.
Now he is isolated in distant places of danger and peril
And lies naked in the winter wilderness.

Therefore, we now reward Mao Ying
With a purple cloak embroidered with feathers
Depicting groups of flying gods in cinnabar and azure.
May Ying
Travel as he pleases high in the empyrean,
Taking command of the jade perfected.

Lord Mao
Walks with haste through deep cesspools,[xviii]
Where each step poses a deadly hazard.
His mind is ever focused on excellence,
And not once does he err or fear.

今故報盈以
斑龍之輿
素虎之軿
使盈
浮晏太空
飛輪帝庭

君
披榛併景
寒凌霜雪
心求明真
不戰不慄

今故報盈以
曲晨寶蓋
瓊幢綠室
使盈
遊盼九宮
靜神溫密

君
遠秀遁榮
無疲於心
潛形幽嶽
靜思萬林

Therefore, we now reward Mao Ying
With a chariot pulled by striped dragons
And a phaeton pulled by white tigers.
May Ying
Rise into the tranquil Grand Void,
Riding soaring wheels to the [Celestial] Emperor's court.

Lord Mao
Clears away obstructions[34] to align his phosphors,
To make a frigid climb over frost and snow.
His mind seeks only illumination through perfection
And he never falters nor quavers.

Therefore, we now reward Mao Ying
With a winding dawn carriage and a jeweled canopy,
And a green coach with rose-gem curtains.
May Ying
Roam and gaze into the Nine Palaces,
Where he can still his spirits and ponder over secrets.

Lord Mao
Hides his vast accomplishments from view
And never worries if others are unaware.
He disappears into dark Sacred Peaks,
To quiet his thoughts among myriad groves.

---

34 Literally, pulls back weeds.

今故報盈以
流金火鈴
雙珠月明
可以
上聞太極
通音上清

君
貞心高靜
淫累不經
素挺浩映
內外坦平

今故報盈以
錦旌繡幡
白羽玄竿
可以
呼召六陰
玉女侍軒

君
慈向觸物
陰德萬生
蠢動之毛
皆念經營

Therefore, we now reward Mao Ying
With fire bells of liquid gold
And a pair of moonbeam pearls,
So that he can
Send up reports to be heard in the Grand Ultimate
And communicate tidings to Supreme Purity.

Lord Mao
Is pure of mind and calm with lofty thoughts.
He never experiences fatigue from licentious ways.
His plain virtues are as conspicuous as a floodlight[xix]
And he is frank and fair both in private and in public.

Therefore, we now reward Ying
With brocade banners and embroidered pennants
Made of white feathers atop black poles,
So that he can
Summon the Six Yin Spirits,
While jade maidens serve in his antechamber.

Lord Mao
Shows compassion for all beings he encounters
And enacts secret virtues for the myriad beings.
Even the swaying of an insect's setae
Cause him to act on its behalf.

今故報盈以
鳳鸞之簫
金鐘玉磬
可以
和神虛館
樂真舞靈

君
飢渴養神
艱辛求真
萬物不能致其惑
千邪不能毀其淳

今故賜盈
紫琳之腴
玉漿金醴
可以
壽同三光
刻簡丹瓊也

盈
標領清玄
紫瑋八映
心暉重離
神曜太霞

Therefore, we now reward Mao Ying
With pipes that sound like phoenixes and simurghs,
And golden bells and jade chimestones,
So that he can
Harmonize with spirits within the vacuous hall
And delight in the perfected and dancing numina.

Lord Mao
Endures hunger and thirst while nourishing his spirits,
And encounters hardships while seeking perfection.
The myriad beings cannot bring calamity upon him
And the thousand evils cannot corrupt his integrity.

Therefore, we now give Mao Ying
A paste[35] of purple gems
And jade liquor in a golden pitcher,
So that he can
Live as long as the three luminaries,
With his name inscribed on cinnabar and rose-gem slats.

Mao Ying's
Elegant demeanor is both pure and abstruse,
Like a purple glowing gem shining its eight radiances.
His mind shines out like the brilliant sun;
His spirit dazzles across Grand Auroras.

---

35 In medical contexts, *yu* could be either a paste or an oil. See Stanley-Baker 2013, 189, 275.

實真人之長者，故以太元爲號

君
九德既備
感積太微
天人虛白
不期同歸
今酬九事

以報徃懷盈
心神方朗
四靈所栖
丹神啓煥
秉直不廻
正任全固
監無照微

　　今屈宰上卿，總括東嶽。又加司命之任，以領錄、圖、籍。給玉童玉女各四十人，以出入太微，受事太極也。治宮赤城玉洞之府。盈其涖之，動靜以聞。

　　於是盈與二弟決別，而與王君俱去，到赤城玉洞之府。道次，諸山川神靈有司迎啓。引者將以千萬矣。臨去告二弟曰：「吾今去矣，便有局任。不得復數相徃來，旦夕相見。要當一年再過來於此山，三月十八日，十二月二日。期要吾師及南

36　In early texts, carrying out the nine virtues results in acquiring Heaven's rewards. See *Zuo Tradition*, Duke Zhao 28 (Durrant et al. 2016, 1691).

Truly, he is chief among the perfected beings, and this is why he is called the Grand Prime Perfected Being.

> In Lord Mao
> The nine virtues are all fully realized,[36]
> Arousing many responses from Grand Tenuity.
> The heavenly beings of the vacuous whiteness
> Have spontaneously returned with him,
> To report on the nine affairs.[37]
>
> All of these gifts to Mao Ying will help
> His mind and spirit to remain ever bright,
> And the four numinous beasts to rest beside him.[38]
> His fervent spirit will be inspired with brilliance,
> And he will be straightforward and stay the course.
> He will be upright in his duties and always resolute,
> And inspect those things that have yet to be explained.

Now he will humbly serve as an upper chamberlain and will take command of the Eastern Sacred Peak. He has also been appointed as a director of destinies who will oversee registers, charts, and records. We have given him forty jade lads and forty jade maidens, who will come and go from the Grand Tenuity heaven to accept duties from the Grand Ultimate. He will also rule over the Jade Grotto bureau of the Red City from his palace. Mao Ying will be in charge of all of these places and will have an intimate knowledge of all of their affairs.

Ying then bid farewell to his two brothers and departed with Lord Wang for the Jade Grotto bureau of the Red City. Along the way, all the divine officials of the mountains and rivers came out to welcome Mao. In all, ten million beings were in attendance. Right before he left, Ying told his two younger brothers, "I must leave now, as I am required to take up my posts right away. I will not be able to come back often, let alone to see you every day. I am permitted to come back to this mountain two times per year, once on the eighteenth day of the third lunar month, and the other on the second day of the twelfth lunar month. I will arrange for my master Lord Wang and the Grand Vacuity Red Perfected Being of the Southern Sacred

---

37 "The nine affairs" is a term appearing in various contexts in Han texts to refer to aspects of governance. Here it reinforces the idea that Lord Mao will occupy a position of authority.
38 The four numinous beasts are the phoenix, dragon, kirin, and turtle (Wang Wenjin 2001, 302).

嶽太虛赤真人遊盼於二弟之處也。將可記識之，及有好道者，待我於是乎。吾自當料理之，以相教訓未悟。」

於是季偉、思和遂留治此山。洞內立宮結構於外。將道著萬物，流潤蒼生。德加鳥獸，各獲其情。神驗禍福，罪惡必明。內法旣融，外教坦平。爾乃風雨以時，五禾成熟。疾癘不起，暴害不行。父老謳曰：

茅山連金陵
江湖攄下流
三神乘白鵠
各治一山頭
召雨灌旱稻
陸田苗亦柔
妻子咸保室
使我無百憂
白鵠翔青天
何時復來遊

---

39 "Golden hills" is a translation of Jinling, a city north of Mt. Mao. In Yang Xi's revelations, it refers to the fecund lands of the whole region. *DZ* 1016, 11.1b; Pettit 2013a, 255.

Peak to travel to where you are to see you. You should make a note of these dates, and let those who are fond of the Dao wait for me right here. I will make arrangements for them and give instructions to the unenlightened."

After this, Jiwei and Sihe remained behind to govern over Mt. Mao. They constructed palaces in the grotto, including a structure at the entryway. They made the Dao known to all beings, so that it reached even the most common creature. With their virtue, they reached out to all birds and beasts, so that every animal realized its dispositions. With their spirits, they examined calamities and fortune and cast light on all transgressions and evils. Inwardly, their rituals were fully harmonious, while outwardly, their teachings were straightforward. After this, the wind and rains remained constant, so that the five grains could be harvested.[xx] All disease and illness disappeared, and no one was threatened by disaster.[xxi] There was a song among the village elders that went,

> Mt. Mao is connected to golden hills,[39]
> For the downflow of rivers and lakes is controlled here.[xxii]
> The three Mao spirits rode upon white swans
> To each take control of one of the peaks of Mt. Mao.
> They call for rain to fall and irrigate the dry rice paddies,
> And to spread over fields so that the soil around sprouts will soften.[xxiii]
> Our wives and children are protected within chambers,
> Which helps us avert the hundred sorrows.
> The white swans take flight into the azure heavens.
> When will they come here once again?

Text-Critical Endnotes

i. The *Monograph on Mt. Mao* reads *shi* 氏 for *shi* 世 (*DZ* 304, 5.1b; Wang Gang 2016, 121).

ii. Reading *gai* 改 for *yi* 改.

iii. The *Monograph on Mt. Mao* reads *xin* 新 for *wang* 望 (*DZ* 304, 5.2b; Wang Gang 2016, 122).

iv. The *Monograph on Mt. Mao* reads *fang* 訪 for *fang* 放 (*DZ* 304, 3a; Wang Gang 2016, 123). *DZ* 292 (6a) reads this character as *ying* 仰.

v. *DZ* 292 (5a) reads *zheng* 政 for *zheng* 正, and *xun* 循 for *xiu* 修.

vi. The *Monograph on Mt. Mao* writes *wang* 王 for *yu* 玉 (*DZ* 304, 5.3b). We follow Wang Gang (2016, 133 n. 3) and keep jade in the translation.
vii. *DZ* 304, 5.4a, reads *ji* 迹 for *su* 俗.
viii. The *Monograph on Mt. Mao* reads *yang* 養 for *shan* 善 (*DZ* 304, 5.4b; Wang Gang 2016, 123).
ix. The *Monograph on Mt. Mao* reads *you* 游 for *liu* 流 (*DZ* 304, 5.4b; Wang Gang 2016, 123).
x. Reading *si* 巳 as *yi* 已.
xi. The *Monograph on Mt. Mao* reads shi 示 for *bi* 俾 (*DZ* 304, 5.4b; Wang Gang 2016, 124).
xii. The *Monograph on Mt. Mao* reads *geng* 更 for *guan* 官 (*DZ* 304, 5.6a; Wang Gang 2016, 125).
xiii. The *Monograph on Mt. Mao* reads *xian* 現 for *jian* 見 (*DZ* 304, 5.8b; Wang Gang 2016, 126). We follow Alan Berkowitz's translation of *jingsi* 精思 as "refined contemplation."
xiv. The *Monograph on Mt. Mao* reads *shou* 受 for *shou* 授 (*DZ* 304, 1a; Wang Gang 2016, 42).
xv. The *Monograph on Mt. Mao* reads *chi* 耻 for *chi* 恥 (*DZ* 304, 1b; Wang Gang 2016, 42).
xvi. The *Monograph on Mt. Mao* reads *xieyuan* 邪源 (evil fonts) for *yuanze* 源澤 (fonts and marshes) (*DZ* 304, 1b; Wang Gang 2016, 42).
xvii. The *Monograph on Mt. Mao* reads *qian* 千 for *wan* 萬 (*DZ* 304, 1b; Wang Gang 2016, 42).
xviii. The *Monograph on Mt. Mao* reads *lin* 林 for *shen* 深 (*DZ* 304, 2a; Wang Gang 2016, 43).
xix. The *Monograph on Mt. Mao* reads *hao* 晧 for *hao* 浩 (*DZ* 304, 2a; Wang Gang 2016, 43).
xx. *DZ* 304, 5.15b, reads *shucheng* 熟成 for *chengshu* 成熟, which would help maintain the rhyme.
xxi. *DZ* 304, 5.15b, reads *chao* 超 for *qi* 起.
xxii. *DZ* 304, 5.15b, reads graphic variant *ju* 據 for *ju* 擄.
xxiii. *DZ* 304, 5.15b, reads this line as "going across fields to make them soft again" 陸田亦復柔.

漢武帝內傳

孝武皇帝好長生之術。常祭名山大澤，以求神仙。元封元年甲子，祭嵩山，起神宮。帝齋七日，祠訖廻還。

至四月戊辰，帝夜閒居承華殿，東方朔、董仲舒侍。忽見一女子著青衣，美麗非常。帝愕然問之。女對曰：「我墉宮玉女王子登也。向爲王母所使，從昆山來，語帝曰：『聞子輕四海之尊，尋道求生。降帝王之位而屢禱山嶽。勤哉有似可教者也。從今百日清齋，不閑人事。至七月七日，王母暫來也。』」

帝下席跪諾。言訖，女忽然不知所在。帝問東方朔：「此何人？」朔曰：「是西王母紫蘭室玉女，常傳使命。往來榑桑，出入靈州。交關常陽，傳言玄都。阿母昔以出配北燭仙人。近又召還，使領命錄。真靈官也。」

1   Emperor Wu's complete posthumous name was the Filial and Martial August Emperor.
2   The biographies of Emperor Wu from the *History of the Former Han* and *Records of the Historian* both mention sacrifices at Mt. Song in 110 BCE, but do not mention the spirit palace. See Ban Gu 1997, 85; Sima Qian 1997, 474.
3   This Wang Zideng has the same name as Lord Wang, but here is a female attendant of the Queen Mother of the West. Smith (1992, 231) observes that other versions of the story—such as the *Story of the Emperor Wu of Han* (*Han Wu gushi* 漢武故事)—use figures besides Wang to announce the imminent arrival of the Queen Mother of the West. Yong Palace is possibly one of the peaks of Kunlun (Schipper 1965, 68 n. 9).

Inner Tradition of Han Emperor Wu

Emperor Wu was fond of the arts of longevity.[1] He often made sacrifices at famous mountains and great lakes in his search for divine transcendence. On a *jiazi* day in the first year of the Yuanfeng era [110 BCE], he conducted a sacrifice at Mt. Song and erected a spirit palace.[2] The emperor fasted there for seven days then returned home once the offerings were complete.[i]

Weeks later, at night on a *wuchen* day in the fourth lunar month, the emperor was relaxing in the Chenghua Basilica with Dongfang Shuo and Dong Zhongshu by his side.[ii] Suddenly they saw an exceedingly beautiful maiden dressed in an azure gown. Astonished, the emperor asked her name. "I am Wang Zideng," she replied, "a jade maiden from Yong Palace.[3] I have been dispatched from Mt. Kunlun by the Queen Mother of the West to convey to Your Highness this message: 'I have heard that you care not for the honors of this world, but seek the Dao to extend your life. You often come down from your throne to beseech the gods at Sacred Peaks. Truly, you work hard and seem like someone who can be taught. From today, you must conduct a pure fast for a hundred days and never involve yourself in human affairs.[4] When the seventh day of the seventh month arrives, I, the Queen Mother of the West, will come visit you.'"

The emperor moved off his mat and knelt down, promising to do so. When he finished, the maiden was nowhere to be found. The emperor asked Dongfang Shuo, "Who was that?" and Shuo replied, "That was a jade maiden from the Queen Mother of the West's Purple Orchid Chamber, often sent on missions. She travels to the far reaches of Fusang, and comes and goes all over the Numinous Continent.[5] She has a strong connection to Mt. Changyang,[6] and transmits reports to the Mysterious Metropolis. Long ago, Amah betrothed her to the Northern Torch Transcendent Being. But more recently Zideng was summoned back to oversee the registers of lifespans. Truly, she is a numinous officer."

---

4   The commentary glosses "do not involve yourself in human affairs" as "do not govern" (bu zhi 不治), implying that the emperor should delegate his affairs while he steps away.
5   Or possibly "the numinous isle" (Schipper 1965, 69 n. 6).
6   A mountain in the *Classic of Mountains and Seas* where the sun and moon rest (Yuan Ke 1995, 409).

帝於是登延靈之臺，盛齊存道。其四方之事權委於冢宰焉。至七月七日，迺脩除宮掖之內，設座殿上。以紫羅薦地，燔百和之香。張雲錦之帳，然九光之燈。設玉門之棗，蒲桃之酒。躬監肴物，爲天官之饌。帝迺盛服立于陛下。敕端門之內不得妄有窺者。內外寂謐，以俟雲駕。

至二唱之後，忽天西南如白雲起，鬱然直來，遙趨宮庭間。雲中有簫鼓之聲、人馬之響。復半食頃，王母至也。懸投殿前，有似鳥集。或駕龍虎，或乘獅子。或御白虎，或騎白麖。或控白鶴，或乘科車。羣仙數萬，光耀庭宇。

既至，從官不復所在，唯見王母。乘紫雲之輦，駕九色斑龍。別有五十天仙側近鸞輿，皆身長一丈。同執綵毛之節，金剛靈璽，帶天策。咸住殿前，王母唯扶二侍女上殿。侍女年可十六七，服青綾之袿。容眸流盼，神姿清發。真美人也。

王母上殿，東向坐。着黃錦袷襡，文采鮮明，光儀淑穆。帶靈飛大綬，

---

7   The Duan (Meridional) Gate is the main gate in the city wall due south of the palace (Kroll 2015, 94).
8   The second watch ran from 9 to 11 p.m.
9   Literally, in half the time it takes to eat a meal.

The emperor ascended the Yanling Terrace, where he fasted and visualized the Dao. He committed his worldly duties to his prime minister. When the seventh day of the seventh month arrived, he had fully prepared the private quarters of the palace and arranged the seating in the basilica for a banquet. He used purple silk to make the mats and burned hundred-harmony incense. He hung curtains of cloudy brocade and lit a lamp of nine lights. He laid out jujubes and grape wine of Yumen. He personally oversaw the making of sacrificial meats to ensure that it was a feast fit for heavenly officials. The emperor dressed in his finest clothes and stood at the bottom of the steps leading to the palace. He decreed that everyone inside the Duan Gate could not look inside the hall.[7] Everyone in and around the palace was still and silent as he waited for the Queen Mother's cloud chariot to arrive.

After the second watch of the night,[8] something resembling a white cloud arose in the southwest sky and billowed straight toward them as it spread across the courtyard. Within the cloud, one could hear the sounds of pipes and drums, as well the noise of men and horses. A moment later,[9] the Queen Mother of the West arrived. Her [retinue] hovered in front of the basilica just like a flock of birds.[iii] Some drove dragons and tigers, while some sat astride lions.[iv] Some steered white tigers, while others rode white kirins.[10] Some took the reins of white cranes, while others drove chariots without canopies.[v] The glow from the tens of thousands of transcendents in attendance spread throughout the palace halls and courtyard.

By the time she arrived, her officials were no longer with her, and only the Queen Mother of the West remained. She rode atop a palanquin of purple clouds pulled by dragons with stripes of nine colors. There were also fifty heavenly transcendents, all ten feet tall, who flanked her imperial chariot. Each transcendent held a tipstaff with multicolored feathers, had a numinous diamond seal, and had a heavenly bamboo slip at the waist. They all remained in front of the basilica, while the Queen Mother of the West and her two attendant girls entered. The attendant girls were about sixteen or seventeen years old and wore azure twill gowns. They made sidelong glances at the emperor, their divine bodies both pure and striking. They were truly beautiful women.

Upon entering, the Queen Mother of the West found a seat that faced east. She wore a lined overcoat made of yellow brocade with an elegant design in distinctive bright colors. She wore long Numinous Flight ribbons[11]

---

10 Rather than the typical male kirin (qilin 麒麟), lin refers to a female kirin. Morohashi Tetsuji 1955–1960, 12.914d.
11 See p. 191 below for more information on Numinous Flight Maiden talismans and ritual techniques.

腰分頭之劍。頭上大華結，戴太真晨嬰之冠。履玄璃鳳文之
舄。际之可年卅許，脩短得中。天姿菴藹，雲顏絕世。真靈
人也。

　　下車登牀，帝拜跪，問寒溫。畢，立如也。因呼帝共
坐，帝南面向王母。母自設膳，膳精非常。豐珍之肴，芳華
百果，紫芝萎蕤，紛若填楪。清香之酒，非地上所有。甘氣
殊絕，帝不能名也。

　　又命侍女索桃。須臾以鎜盛桃七枚，大如鴨子，形色
青。以呈王母，母以四枚與帝，自食三桃。桃之甘美，口有
盈味。帝食輒錄核。母曰：「何謂？」帝曰：「欲種之耳。」
母曰：「此桃三千歲一生實耳，中夏地薄。種之不生，如
何？」帝乃止。

　　於坐上酒觴數過，王母乃命侍女王子登彈八琅之璈。又
命侍女董雙成吹雲龢之笙。又命侍女石公子擊昆庭之鐘。又
命侍女許飛瓊鼓震靈之簧，侍女阮靈華拊五靈之石。侍女范
成君擊洞庭之磬，侍女段安香作九天之鈞。

12　Literally, hot or cold. We follow Smith's translation (1992, 484) of this phrase here and below.
13　Mt. Yunhe is perhaps located in present-day Zhejiang Province (Schipper 1965, 75 n. 1). Smith (1992, 238–241) includes further information on the identities of the Queen Mother of the West's maids and their appearances as recorded in *DZ* 304.

at her waist and a head-severing sword in a scabbard. Her hair was braided with flower blossoms, and atop that she wore a Dawn Infant of Grand Perfection crown. Her shoes were adorned with phoenixes inlaid in dark curved nephrite. She looked to be about thirty years old and was of average height. She possessed a celestial beauty and a cloud-like countenance not of this world. Truly, she was a numinous being.

Once the Queen Mother of the West had gotten down from her palanquin and sat atop a raised dais, the emperor bowed and knelt, asking the Queen Mother of the West if she was comfortable.[12] Then he stood up. The Queen Mother of the West called for the emperor to sit beside her, so he sat facing south toward her. She laid out an entire feast of the most exceptional and exquisite dishes. There were succulent meats, a hundred kinds of fragrant fruit, and an assortment of purple mushrooms and polygonum, which were served one after the other on overflowing platters. There was fragrant wine unlike anything found in this world. Its sweet aroma was so extraordinary that the emperor could not find words to describe it.

Next the Queen Mother of the West ordered an attendant girl to bring forth the peaches. Seconds later, the girl reappeared with a tray filled with seven azure peaches as big as duck eggs. She presented them to the Queen Mother of the West, who gave four peaches to the emperor and ate three herself. The luscious sweetness of the peaches filled his mouth. Each time the emperor ate one, he set the pit aside. The Queen Mother of the West asked, "Why are you doing that?" "I want to plant these," the emperor replied. The Queen Mother of the West said, "These peach trees give fruit only once every three thousand years and the soil found on earth is not fertile enough. If you plant them, they will not grow. So why would you?" The emperor thereupon abandoned the idea.

After they toasted one another many times, the Queen Mother of the West ordered her attendant girl Wang Zideng to perform on her chime-stones, made from eight gems. Then she ordered another attendant girl, Dong Shuangcheng, to play her reed-organ from Mt. Yunhe.[13] Then she ordered another attendant girl, Shi Gongzi, to strike the bells of the Mt. Kunlun halls. And then she ordered another, Xu Feiqiong,[14] to strike a bell that shook the spirits, while another, Ruan Linghua, accompanied on the stones of the Five Numina.[vi] Then she ordered another attendant girl, Fan Chengjun, to strike the chime-stones of Dongting Lake,[15] while another attendant girl, Duan Anxiang, performed a melody of the Nine Heavens.

---

14 *Extensive Records of the Taiping Era* contains a brief hagiography of Xu (Li Fang 2003, 433).
15 In Hunan Province. See Zang Lihe 1972, 642.

於是衆聲澈朗,靈音駭空。又命侍女安法嬰歌《玄靈之曲》,其詞曰:

大象雖寥廓
我把天地戶
披雲沉靈輿
儵忽適下土
空洞成玄音
至靈不容冶
太真嘘中唱
始知風塵苦
頤神三田中
納精六闕下
遂乘萬龍蹻
馳騁眄九野

二曲曰:

玄圃遏北臺
五城煥嵯峨
啓彼無涯津
汎此織女河
仰上升絳庭
下遊月窟阿

16 For *liaokuo*, see Kroll 1984, 17 n. 77.
17 An empty region where the primal qi is produced. This entity was mapped onto the body of a Supreme Purity adept whose soul (*shen* 神) would condense into a Hollow of Space, at which time it would serve as a formless source of being in the same place. See Schafer 1981–1983, 333 n. 108.
18 According to Smith (1992, 487 n. 35), the Six Gatetowers are the gallbladder, stomach, bladder, small intestine, large intestine, and the navel.
19 A term for nine regions of the heavens (Knoblock and Riegel 2000, 279).

The sounds from the orchestra were penetrating and clear; its divine tones filled the air. After this, she ordered an attendant girl, An Faying, to sing the *Mysterious Numen Melody*. The lyrics went,

> Although the Great Image goes on for an unimaginable infinity,[16]
> I hold onto the gateway between heaven and earth.
> Draped in clouds, I descend in my numinous carriage,
> And in an instant, I arrive in this lower realm.
> Once the Hollow of Space[17] produces mysterious tones,
> The ultimate numen is beyond superficial beauty.
> Once grand perfected beings sigh and sing out,
> You begin to realize the hardships of this windy, dusty world.
> Nourishing the spirits within your Three Cinnabar Fields,
> Drawing your essences in together beneath the Six Gatetowers,[18]
> You then ride a myriad dragons in the other direction,[vii]
> Galloping in haste as you look out across the Nine Wilds.[19]

The second song went,

> Within the Mysterious Bower,[20] you pause at the Northern Terrace,
> And see the Five Cities[21] glowing atop towering peaks.
> Then you set out to ford the river with no other shore
> And set adrift on the Weaver Maiden's River.[22]
> Looking up, you ascend to the Scarlet Court,[23]
> Then travel downward to the cliffs of the lunar cave.

---

20 According to Smith (1992, 487 n. 37), the home of the Queen Mother of the West on Mt. Kunlun.
21 Correlated with the Five Directions and Five Emperors. For more, see *Lord Lao Most High's Book of the Center* (*Taishang Laojun zhongjing* 太上老君中經, DZ 1168, 1.11b).
22 See Pettit 2004, 1–21.
23 "Scarlet Court" refers to the heart of an adept's body. See Pettit and Chang 2020, 58–61. It likely means the same as Scarlet Repository, mentioned below on p. 159.

顧眄八落外
指招九雲遐
忽已不覺勞
豈寤少與多
撫璈命衆女
詠發感中和
妙暢自然樂
爲此玄雲歌
韶盡至韻存
真音辭無邪

歌畢,帝乃下地叩頭。自陳曰:
「徹受質不才,沉淪流俗。承禪先業,遂覊世累。政事多闕,兆民不和。風雨失節,五穀無實。德澤不建,寇盜四海。黔首勞斃,戶口滅半。當非其主,積皋丘山?

然少好道,仰慕靈仙。未能棄祿委榮,棲跡山林。思絕塵餌,罔知攸向。且捨世尋真,鑽啓無師。歲月見及,恒慮奄忽。不圖天顏頓集今日。下臣有幸,得瞻上聖。是臣宿命合得度世,願垂哀憐。賜諸不悟,得以奉承切己之教。」

24 In *Conversations of the States*, "Central Harmony" refers to any music that has a moderating influence (Xu Yuangao 1998, 109).
25 Perhaps a reference to the ousting of Liu Rong 劉榮 (d. 148 BCE) as heir apparent in favor of Liu Che in 150 BCE. See Twitchett and Loewe 1995, 153.

Gazing askance beyond the Eight Directions,
I point and beckon to the Nine Clouds scattered afar.
Suddenly finding you are no longer weary,
For how could I have possibly known what is great or small?
We tap a cloud jade and order all the jade maidens
To chant out and sing "Central Harmony" in unison.[24]
The music of spontaneity is wondrously expansive,
As we play this song of the mysterious clouds.
Once this hymn ends, its fine melody lingers,
For it has perfected tones and words without flaw.

When she finished the songs, the emperor got down on the ground and kowtowed. He then told [the Queen Mother of the West],

"By birth, I lack talent and have sunk into vice and prevailing customs. I took up this family enterprise after an abdication and have been burdened by worldly matters ever since.[25] In the affairs of governance, I have many flaws, and the commoners are never at peace. The wind and rain have been relentless, and the Five Grains no longer bear fruit. Those who are virtuous and charitable are not selected for office, while robbers and thieves are everywhere. Commoners labor themselves to death, and the population has decreased by half. Is it not because my, their ruler's, faults pile up like hills and mountains?

"Nevertheless, since I was young, I have been fond of the Dao and have admired the holy transcendents. But I cannot now give up my position, responsibilities, and honors in order to live in seclusion in the mountain forests. I wish that I could remove myself from the lures of the dusty world, but I do not know where I might turn. How I have wanted to cast off the world and seek perfection, but I have never had a teacher to enlighten me. As the years fly by, I have become increasingly anxious about my death. I never thought that I might meet your heavenly face here today. I, your humble servant, am so fortunate to be able to gaze upon such a lofty sage. If my karmic deeds befit one who might transcend this world, I would hope you would shower me with your pity. May you grant these things to such an unenlightened person, so that I can gladly uphold a teaching so dear to me."[26]

---

26 This paragraph is modeled on the speech by Liu An 劉安 (ca. 179–122 BCE) before the Eight Dukes in Ge Hong's *Traditions of Divine Transcendents* (Smith 1992, 489 n. 45; Campany 2002, 236).

王母曰：

「女能賤榮樂卑，躭虛味道，自復佳耳。然女情恣，體慾淫亂過甚。殺伐非法，奢侈其性。恣則裂身之車，淫爲破年之斧。殺則響對，奢則心爛，慾則神隕。聚穢命斷。以子蕞爾之身，而宅滅形之殘。盈尺之材，攻以百刃之害。欲此解脫三尸，全身永久，難可得也。有似無翅之鷽，願鼓翼天池，朝生之蟲，而樂春秋者哉。

　　若能蕩此衆亂，撥穢易韻，保神炁於絳府，閉淫官而開悟，靜奢侈於寂室，愛衆生而不危，守茲道戒，思乎靈味，務施惠和，練惜精氣，棄却浮麗，令百競速游。女行若斯之事，將豈無彷彿也？如其不爾，無爲抱石而濟長津矣。」

　　帝跪受聖戒。請事斯語：

「養身之要，旣聞之矣。然體非玉石，而無主於恒。炁非四時，而常生於内。正當率御出入，呼吸中適，和液得循，形神靡錯。炁旣隨冝，則魂魄不滯。若使理合其分，炁甄其適，則形可不枯，宅可不廢。

27　See *Traditions of Lord Su*, p. 69 above.
28　A reference to suicide (Sima Qian 1997, 2490).

The Queen Mother of the West replied,

"If you could have brushed off glory and delighted in being humble, you could have lingered in the Void, tasted the Dao, and returned to goodness with ease. But instead, you have indulged your passions and given up your body to excessive licentiousness. Your executions and military campaigns are unjust, and you squander your inborn nature. To indulge yourself is like being dismembered by chariots, and being licentious is like an ax that chops away your years. These executions will come back to haunt you, squandering your inborn nature will cause your mind to rot, and passions will cause your spirit to falter. These impurities will accumulate and cut your life short. Thus, your wretched body is home to defects caused by this self-destruction. It is as if a blade that can fell a seven-hundred-foot tree is cutting through a board barely a foot long. Hence, it will be nearly impossible to keep your body whole by expelling the Three Corpses.[27] You would be like a bird trying to fly to the heavenly lakes without wings, or like a bug who wants to experience all the seasons yet can only live for a single day.

"If only you could cast away these many disorders by getting rid of such impurities and changing your tune, or protect the divine qi within your Scarlet Repository, or shut the door to the palace of licentiousness and achieve enlightenment, or calm excesses in a quiet chamber, or love all sentient beings and do them no harm, or uphold the Daoist precepts while focusing your mind on numinous delights, or serve others with mercy and gentleness while you work on preserving your refined qi, or abandon the ways of the world and thereby quickly set the hundred rivalries within you free. If you could do these things, would this not achieve all you want? But if you do not do these things, it will be as if you are fording a wide river while clutching a stone."[28]

The emperor knelt down and received these sacred precepts. He continued asking about these matters, saying,

"I have already heard about essential ways to nourish oneself. Nevertheless, my body is not like rock or jade, but is always changing. My qi are not regular like the four seasons, but constantly arise within. From here on out, I must regulate the movement of qi, breathe in a steady fashion, and harmonize my fluids as they move along so that my body and spirit will never falter.[viii] If my qi could follow the appropriate channels, my cloud-souls and white-souls would not be impeded. And if I could properly separate these souls and appropriately differentiate my qi, I could prevent my entire being from shriveling up and my bodily dwelling from rotting.

昔受道書，具以施業之矣，遂不獲眞驗，未爲巨益。使精神疲於往來，津液勞於出入。歲減其始，月虧其昔。形亦漸凋，神亦廢落。

是徹不得所奉於口訣，開闔塞於明堂爾。不審服御可以永久者，吐納可以延年者。乞賜長生之術，暫悟於行尸之身。若蒙聖誥於即日，臣伏聽麗天之教矣。」

王母曰：「昔先師元始天王時及閒居，登於聚霄之臺。侍者天皇槫桑大帝君及九眞諸王、十方衆神仙官。爰延弟子丹房之內，說玄微之言。因問我何爲而欲索長存矣。吾因避席叩頭，請問長生之術。天王登見遺以要言，辭深旨幽。實天人之玄觀，上帝之奇祕。女今日願聞之乎？」

帝跪曰：「徹小醜賤生，枯骨之餘。敢以不肖之軀，而慕龍鳳之年？欲以朝花之質，希晦朔之期？雖樂遠流，莫知以濟。塗路堅塞，所要無寄。常恐一旦死於鑽仰之難，取笑於世俗之夫。豈圖今日遭遇光會。一覯聖姿而精神飛揚，恍惚大夢。如以涉世千年，救護死歸之日。乞願垂哀，誥賜徹元元。」

---

29 On Bright Hall, see *Traditions of the Director of Destinies* (Lord Mao), p. 119 above.

"I have already completed everything mentioned in these books on the Dao that I received long ago, but I have yet to capture anything truly efficacious and have benefited little from them. These techniques only cause my vital spirits to become tired as they go every which way, and my bodily fluids to be taxed by constant production. My remaining years continue to decrease, just like an ever-waning moon. My body gradually decays, as my soul withers away.

"Since I have not received your oral instructions, I have been unable to remove the obstructions blocking [my mind's] Bright Hall.[29] I am not sure what potions or sexual practices will really lead to a long life, and what breathing techniques will really extend one's years. I now beg you to bestow the arts of long life, so that I, a walking corpse, might reach enlightenment. If you reveal to me your divine pronouncements this day, I will listen with humility to this teaching of the glorious heavens."

The Queen Mother of the West said, "Long ago, my former master, the Celestial King of Primordial Commencement, would ascend a terrace in the clustered clouds in his spare time. In attendance was the Heavenly Sovereign, the Great Imperial Lord of Fusang, as well as the kings of the Nine Perfected and the various divine transcendent officials of the ten directions. My master would invite his disciples into his elixir chamber, where he spoke arcane and subtle words to them. On one such occasion, he asked me how I wanted to seek a long life. I got up from my seat and kowtowed, then asked to hear about the arts of longevity. The celestial king immediately imparted essential teachings containing words deep with profound meanings. Truly, these were sublime insights of a heavenly being and marvelous secrets of a High Emperor. Would you like to hear them now?"

The emperor knelt and said, "I am a wretch and a lowlife, nothing but a pile of dry bones. How could I dare to admire the long lives of dragons and phoenixes with such a worthless body? How could a flower that blooms and dies in one morning hope to live for a month? While I would enjoy drifting distantly across the Milky Way, I know of no way to cross it. The road before me is blocked, and I have nothing to rely on. I have a constant fear that I will one day die from the hardships of searching high and low, and will become the laughing stock of even the most vulgar men. I never imagined that I would have the pleasure of this bright assembly today. One look at your divine appearance sends my spirits soaring, as if I were living in a fleeting dream. It is as if I have lived a thousand years, but only found salvation on the day of my death. I beg you to take pity on me by revealing [your teachings] and giving them to me, a mere common man."

王母曰:「將告女要言。我曾聞天王曰:

夫欲長生者,宜先取諸身。但

堅守三一
保爾旅族
金瑛夾草
廣山黃木
昌城玉藥
夜山火玉

逮及
鳳林鳴酢
西瑤瓊酒
中華紫蜜
北陵綠皁
太上之藥
風實雲子

30 In Supreme Purity literature, Daoist adepts are imagined traveling in an entourage with the gods of the Three Ones and their attendants, here called a traveling tribe. But we find no connection in any of these texts to this specific term.
31 For this and the following terms, see "A List of Uncommon Medicines" (Smith 1992, 688).
32 A mountain in Suining 遂寧 County of Sichuan Province (Schipper 1965, 82 n. 8).
33 The name of a prefecture in the early medieval era in a region very near Mt. Guang (Schipper 1965, 83 n. 1).
34 Many drugs in the Daoist pharmacopeia include stones or plants (such as foxfire) prized for their luminescence. After an adept consumes these substances, their light-giving properties were thought to cause the adept glow or give him the ability to see at night. The location of Mt. Ye is unclear.

The Queen Mother of the West said, "I will now tell you the essential teachings. I once heard the Celestial King say,

For those who wish to attain a long life, it is best to seek it first within yourself. You only need to

> Keep vigilant and guard your Three Ones
> To preserve your body gods[30]
> With bundled grasses of a golden luster,[31]
> Yellowwood from Mt. Guang,[32]
> Jade stamens of Chang City,[33]
> And fire jade from Mt. Ye.[34]
>
> Next acquire
> Vinegar made from the splashing of Feng Grove,[35]
> Rose-gem wine from Xiyao Lake,[36]
> Purple honey of Zhonghua,[37]
> And the green abundance of the northern uplands.
> These are the drugs of gods most high:
> Windy grains and cloudy seeds,[38]

---

35 The meaning of this line is unclear. The commentary to the text indicates that the character 酢 should be read *cu* (vinegar), as opposed to *zuo* (a toast by a guest or a libation offered in sacrifice). Feng Grove was the name of a mountain in Gansu Province during the early medieval era (Zang Lihe 1972, 1140).
36 In *DZ* 1016, 1.7a, this is an alternative name for Jasper Lake (Yaochi 瑤池), the Queen Mother's residence in the Kunlun Mountains.
37 While in later times, "Zhonghua" refers to the central plains of China, here it might be the name of a constellation. See Fang Xuanling 1997, 292.
38 *Yunzi* (cloudy seeds) refers to small white rocks, and the name was borrowed to describe a kind of white rice that Daoist adepts would eat. Ge Hong claims that this rice could be used in the alchemical production of mica, literally "mother of the clouds" (yunmu 雲母). Ge Hong 1996, 80.

玉津金漿

月精萬壽

碧海琅菜

蓬萊文醜

濁河七榮

動山高柳

北采玄都之綺華

仰漱雲山之朱蜜

夜河天骨

昆吾漆沫

空洞靈瓜

四劫一實

宜陵麟膽

炎山夜日

東掇扶桑之丹椹

俯探長河之文藻

素虬童子

九色鳳腦

太真虹芝

天漠巨草

南宮火碧

39 Jade spittle can refer to the spiritually potent fluids inside the body, most often saliva and semen. See Pettit and Chang 2020, 164, 201–202. Yang Xi uses the term "golden nectar" to refer to a medicine that bestows long life. See *DZ* 1016, 2.19a; Smith 2013, 140.
40 On lunar essences, see *Traditions of Lord Pei*, p. 45 above.
41 A synonym for the Gray-Blue Sea (canghai 滄海), imagined as the sea east of China that ultimately led to Fusang. See Smith 1990, 106.
42 Penglai is one of the three islands where various kinds of divine beings lived (Sima Qian 1997, 455).
43 There are several locations called Mt. Yun, but here the name may refer to a peak in Hunan Province. See Zang Lihe 1972, 967; Schipper 1965, 84 n. 7.

Jade Spittle and Golden Nectar,[39]
Lunar essences that give a myriad years of life,[40]
Gem herbs growing afar in the Bi Sea,[41]
Refined blotches from Penglai Island,[42]
The seven flowers appearing in a muddy river,
Towering willows that move mountains,

Exquisite blossoms of Mysterious Metropolis picked in the north,
Vermillion honey from Mt. Yun to rinse one's mouth,[43]
Heavenly bones in the Ye River,
Lacquer drops of Kunwu,[44]
A divine calabash of Mt. Kongdong[45]
That seeds once every four kalpas,
Bile of kirin from Mellow Knoll,[46]
Night sun of Mt. Yan.

Cinnabar mulberries of Fusang picked in the east,
Layered wrack of the Chang River found beneath the water,[47]
Offspring of white *qiu*-dragons,
Phoenix brains in nine colors,
Rainbow mushrooms of Grand Perfection,
Giant herbs of the Milky Way,
Blazing jade of the Southern Palace,

---

44 In the *Classic of Mountains and Seas*, "Kunwu" refers to a mountain, a monster, and a region. In the early Han dynasty, it was also the name of a royal park near Mt. Zhongnan 鍾南山, south of the capital of Chang'an. See Knechtges 1987, 114 n. 9. It is unclear to which of these possibilities the term applies here.
45 Likely a variant of Mt. Kondong 崆峒山 near Pingliang 平涼, Gansu Province.
46 "Mellow Knoll" possibly refers to Yiling 宜陵 commandery. See Zang Lihe 1972, 456.
47 An early medieval name for the Milky Way (Knechtges 1996, 37).

西鄉扶老
三梁龍華
生子大道
有得食之
後天而老

此太上之所服。非中仙之所保。其次藥有：

八光太和
斑龍黑胎
文虎白沫
出于西丘
七玄飛節
九孔連珠
雲漿玉酒
玄圃瓊胰
鍾山白膠
王屋青敷
閬風石髓
黑河珊瑚

48 On three-brim crowns for Daoist gods, see Pettit and Chang 2020 145–146.
49 The Eight Lights are cosmic lights found in an adept's body (Schipper 1965, 85 n. 6).
50 A "threaded pearl" may be a variation of *liu zhu* 流珠, another term for mercury (Ge Hong 1996, 287).

> A staff of bamboo from the western regions,
> A being with dragon blossom crowns of three brims[48]
> That will give birth to a newborn in the Great Dao.
> One who consumes any of these aforementioned things
> Will only grow old in age in the latter heavens.

These are the kinds of things that the gods most high consume. They are not something that a middle transcendent would ever keep. The next level of medicines includes,

> Grand harmony of the Eight Lights,[49]
> A black embryo of a spotted dragon,
> White saliva of a striped tiger
> From Xi Hills,
> Flying staves of the Seven Mysteries,
> A threaded pearl of the Nine Orifices,[50]
> Cloud liquor and jade wine,
> Rose-gem paste of the Mysterious Bower,[51]
> White resin of Mt. Zhong,[52]
> Azure leaves of the jade chamber,[ix]
> Stalactites from Mt. Langfeng,[53]
> Coral of the Hei River.

---

51 On the Mysterious Bower (Xuanpu), see the *Inner Tradition of Lord Wang*, p. 96 above.
52 Perhaps an alternate name for Mt. Kunlun. See Major et al. 2010, 90 n. 16.
53 A peak in the Kunlun Mountains. See Schipper 1965, 86 n. 9.

蒙山白鳳之肺
靈丘蒼鸞之血
東英朱菜
九節交結
太微嘉禾
瓊華腦實
流淵鯨眼
赤河絳璧
北汲太玄之酪
中握二儀之脉
雲漬蘪艾
昆丘神雀
廣夜芝草
流淵青狄
真陵雷精
玄都平蓋
左食神元
右飲玄瀨
上屈蘭園之金精
下摘圓丘之紫柰
鸞水靈蛤
八陔赤薤
萬載一生
流光九隊

54 "Nine Nodes" may refer to a variety of *Psychotria* (jiujiemu 九節木), a plant that sometimes has psychotropic effects.
55 "Brainy seeds" may refer to stony brains (shinao 石腦), a rock that Yang Xi describes as having tiny stripes and a soft texture. See *DZ* 1016, 13.7b–8a.
56 On the Two Mechanisms, see *Traditions of Lord Pei*, p. 31 above.

Lungs of a white phoenix from Dodder Mountain,
Blood of the azure simurgh of Numinous Hill,
Vermillion herbs of the Eastern Blossom,
Links between the Nine Nodes,[54]
Fine grains of Grand Tenuity,
Rose-gem flower of brainy seeds,[55]
Eyes of a whale from the swirling abyss,
A scarlet jade disk of the Red River,
Fermented milk of the Great Mystery drawn from the north,
Arteries of the Two Mechanisms grasped in the center.[56]
Tufts of artemisia from the river of clouds,
Divine sparrows of Kun Hill,
Numinous mushrooms of the vast night,
Azure grains of the swirling abyss,
Thundering essence of Mt. Zhenling,[57]
Flattened canopy of the Mysterious Metropolis,
Essences of the divine primordial consumed on the left,
Water from the mystic rapids drunk on the right,[x]
Golden essence picked from the top of the orchid garden,[xi]
Purple plums plucked from the foot of Round Hill,[58]
Numinous oysters from the phoenix waters,
Red scallops of the Eight Regions,[59]
And born once every ten thousand years,
The nine divisions of flowing light.

---

57 See Yuan Ke 1995, 178.
58 According to Guo Pu 郭璞 (276–324), this is the name of a mountain where wondrous plants grow (Lu Qinli 1998, 866).
59 Synonymous with the eight regions of the earth (Schipper 1965, 87 n. 11).

有得食之，後天而逝。此天帝之所服，下仙之所逮。其次藥有：

九丹金液
紫華紅英
太清九轉
五雲之漿
玄霜絳雪
騰躍三黃
東瀛白香
炎洲飛生

八石十芝
西流石膽
威僖九光
東滄青錢
高丘餘糧
積石瓊田
太虛還丹
盛次金蘭
長光綠草
雲童飛干
子得服之
白日升天

60 In the *Inner Chapters of the Master Embracing Simplicity* (Ge Hong 1996, 203), the "Five Clouds" refers to five types of mica. See *DZ* 1032, 75.3a–b.
61 According to *Records of the Multitude of Transcendents of the Three Caverns* (*Sandong qunxian lu* 三洞群仙錄 *DZ* 1248, 1.19a), these are orpiment, sulfur oxide, and gold.
62 A land of transcendent beings in the Eastern Sea.

One day after consuming these, you will leave the world. These are what the Heavenly Emperor consumes and what lower transcendents must acquire. The next tier of medicine includes,

> Golden Liquor of the Ninefold Elixir,
> Purple flowers and red blossoms,
> The nine-cycle elixir of Grand Purity,
> A brew made from the Five Clouds,[60]
> Dark frost and crimson snow,
> The Three Yellows[61] that bound and prance,
> White incense from Yingzhou[62] of the east,
> The flying beings of Yanzhou.[63]

> The eight minerals and ten mushrooms,
> Petrified gall in the Western Currents,
> Nine rays of Formidable Joy,[64]
> Azure coins in the Blue-Green Seas of the east,
> A surplus of rations from the High Hills,
> Stones from rose-gem fields of Piled Rocks,[65, xii]
> A recycled elixir of Grand Vacuity,
> Golden orchids of the Splendid Place,[66]
> Green grasses of the Everlasting Radiance,
> A flying buckler of the cloudy lads.
> If you can consume these,
> You will ascend to the heavens in broad daylight.

---

63 A southern land where transcendent beings live.
64 Schipper (1965, 88 n. 6) cites the *Inner Chapters of the Master Embracing Simplicity* (Ge Hong 1996, 83) to explain *weixi* as a plant that grants invulnerability.
65 A mountain in Qinghai rumored to grow herbs of longevity. See Zang Lihe 1972, 1232; Schipper 1965, 88 n. 8.
66 Given the structure of this stanza, this must be a place, likely mythical. It is otherwise unknown.

此飛仙之所服，地仙之所見也。其下藥有：

松栢之膏
山薑沈精
芻草澤瀉
枸杞茯苓
菖蒲門冬
巨勝黃菁
雲飛赤版
桃膠朱英
椒麻續斷
萎蕤黃連

如此下藥，略舉其端。草類繁多，名有數千，子得服之，可以延年。雖不長享無期，上升青天，亦能身生光澤，還髮童顏，役使羣鬼，得爲地仙。要且錄此有階，漸尋遠勝也。是以天官遠妙，靈藥別品。靈無奇挺，真仙有域。今不可謂。

呼吸六炁，安在一身。灌溉三宮，近出阿庭。淺薄其術，棄而不爲，其大戇者也。夫呼吸御精，保明神炁；足以精不脫則永久，炁長存則不死。旣得其和，其壽不已。

又復不用藥物之煩費，營索之劬勞者也。百姓日用，故上品謂之自然者矣。但不得游乎十天，飛

These are the drugs that a flying transcendent being would take, and that a terrestrial transcendent being might encounter. The lowest tier of medicine includes,

> Sap from pines and cypresses,
> The immersed essence of mountain ginger,
> Cut hay, alisma,
> Wolfberry, poria,
> Calamus, mondo grass,
> Sesame, yellow bamboo,
> Cloudy flight, gastrodia,
> Peach sap, vermillion blossoms,[67]
> Peppercorn, teasel,
> Solomon's seal, goldthread.

As for this lower class of drugs, I have listed only a few. There are an endless variety of herbs with countless names, and consuming any of them will extend your lifespan. Although you might not live forever, you will ascend into the azure heavens as a terrestrial transcendent whose body will emit a lustrous glow with the hair and complexion of a child, and who can command all kinds of demons. I have given you the essential information about these classes so that you can gradually work toward success. You must do this because the celestial offices are distantly marvelous, and numinous drugs are rare objects. The numinous nothingness has extraordinary qualities, and there are different domains for perfected and transcendent beings. But I say no more about these at this time.

You must circulate the six qi by breathing in and out, and conserve them inside your entire body. This will enable you to irrigate your Three Palaces, as well as to enter and exit the Talus Court. Your belittling or disregarding these techniques, or abandoning them midway, would make you a great fool. Harnessing your essential energy through breathing and constantly illuminating your divine qi will keep your essences intact to live forever and preserve your qi to stave off death. Whoever can find such harmony will have life everlasting.

Moreover, there is no need to use expensive drugs and put great effort into acquiring them. Commoners use these drugs every day and consider the highest grade as something that spontaneously appears. But no drug will enable you to roam the ten heavens or soar beyond

---

67 One of the foods of transcendents (Ge Hong 1996, 52).

我八外。自得縱身於四域之内，亦駐策衆靈焉。

夫始欲脩之，先營其炁，太上真經所謂行益易之道。益者益精；易者易形。能益能易，名上仙籍。不益不易，不離死厄。行益易者，謂常思靈寶也。靈者神也，寶者精也。

子但受精握固，閉炁吞液。炁化血，血化精，精化液，液化骨。行之不倦，神精充溢。爲之一年易炁，二年易血，三年易脉，四年易宍，五年易髓，六年易筋，七年易骨，八年易髮，九年易形變化。易形變化則道成，道成則位爲仙人。

吐納六炁，口中甘香。欲食靈芝，存得其味，微息挹吞，從心所適。炁者水也，無所不成。至柔之物，通致神精矣。

此元始天王丹房之中微言所說。今敕侍笈玉女李慶孫書出以相付子。善錄而循焉。」

於是王母言粗畢。嘯命靈官，使駕龍嚴車。欲去，帝

the eight ends of the earth. At most, you can only move freely within the four continents and command the various spirits therein.

When you embark on a path of self-cultivation, first nourish your qi, a process that the most high perfected scriptures call practicing the Dao of Abundant Changes. "Abundance" means an abundance of essence;[68] "changes" refers to changes to your form. The names of those who create abundance and change form will appear on the transcendent registers. But those who do not have abundance and who do not change form will forever be mired by misfortune. Those who practice the Dao of Abundant Changes are referred to as adepts who constantly meditate on the numinous treasure. "Numinous" means divine, and "treasure" means essence.

You need only to retain your essences with a firm grip, as you keep in the qi by swallowing your saliva. Qi alters blood, blood alters essence, essence alters saliva, and saliva alters bone. If you do this tirelessly, your divine essence will increase manyfold. If you do this for one year, your qi will change; in two years your blood will change; in three years your arteries will change; in four years your flesh will change; in five years your marrow will change; in six years your tendons will change; in seven years your bones will change; in eight years your hair will change; and in nine years your entire form will have undergone a complete metamorphosis. Whoever can undergo such a metamorphosis will have brought the Dao to completion, and thus will be ranked as a transcendent being.

When one inhales and exhales the six qi, your mouth will have a sweet and aromatic taste. When it is time to eat the numinous mushrooms, you can visualize their flavors in your mind and swallow them down with subtle breaths as you lead them wherever you wish. Qi is like water, for it can go anywhere. It is the gentlest of all things yet can penetrate to one's divine essences.

"These are the subtle words spoken by the Celestial King of Primordial Commencement in his cinnabar chamber. Now I will order the jade maiden who oversees the bookbag, Li Qingsun, to put these words into writing and give them to you. Learn them well, and follow them closely."

With this, the Queen Mother of the West appeared to have finished speaking. She whistled an order to her numinous officers to hitch the dragons and prepare the chariots. Just as she was about to go, the emperor

---

68 Likely meaning semen, as translated by Smith (1992, 497) and Schipper (1965, 91).

叩頭,請留殷勤。王母廼止。

王母廼遣侍女郭密香與上元夫人相問,云:

王九光母敬謝,但不相見四千餘年。天事勞我,致以愆面。劉徹好道,適來視之。徹了了似可成進。然形慢神穢,腦血淫漏,五藏不淳,關胃彭勃,骨無津液,浮反外內,宂多精少,瞳子不夷,三尸狡亂,玄白失時。

語之至道,殆恐非仙才。吾久在人間,實謂臭濁。然時復可游,望以寫細念。庸主對坐,悒悒不樂。夫人肯暫來否?若能屈駕,當停相須?

帝不知上元夫人何神人也。又見侍女下殿,俄失所在。須臾,郭侍女返。上元夫人又遣侍女答相問,云:

阿環再拜,上問起居。遠隔絳河,擾以官事,遂替顏色。近五千年,仰戀光潤,情係無違。密香至奉信。承降尊於劉徹處。聞

69 "Nine Lights" is used in many ancient texts to refer to various rays of colorful light. In Daoist texts, the term can also refer to the nine stars of the Dipper, two of which can be detected only by trained adepts. See Schafer 1981–1983, 332 n. 102.
70 According to Schipper (1965, 92 n. 5), the passages are the head (passage of heaven), feet (passage of earth), and hands (passage of man).

kowtowed and begged with all of his heart that she remain. So the Queen Mother of the West stayed.

The Queen Mother of the West next dispatched her servant girl, Guo Mixiang, to deliver a message to the Lady of the Upper Prime that read,

> The Queen Mother of the West of the Nine Lights offers her sincerest apologies, for we have not seen one another for over four thousand years.[69] The affairs of the heavens keep me so busy that my face has withered. I have come here to visit Liu Che, since he is fond of the Dao. Che is smart and seems like one who could make great progress. But his body is sluggish and his spirit sullied, the blood flowing in his brain overflows with licentiousness, his five viscera are impure, his passages and stomach are upset,[70] his bones lack fluids, he blithely confuses the superficial and essential, he is overweight and lacks seminal essences, his pupils are agitated, his three corpses run wild, and the timing of his black and white meditation will be off.[71]
>
> I have spoken to him about the ultimate Dao, yet I fear that he does not have the talent to be a transcendent being. I have been in the human world for a long time, and the place truly is dirty and stinks. But from time to time I travel here hoping to escape the trifling details of my duties. I now find myself sitting before this mediocre ruler who is despondent and can find no joy. Will you be willing to come without delay, my lady? Might you be kind enough to come visit and stay a while?

The emperor did not know this goddess called the Lady of the Upper Prime. He then saw the attendant girl leave the basilica and suddenly vanish.

Before long, the attendant girl Guo returned. The Lady of the Upper Prime had also dispatched a servant girl to deliver a message, which read,

> I bow twice before you and humbly ask about your present situation. I have been so busy with official duties since we were separated on distant ends of the Crimson River that my beauty too has deteriorated. For nearly five thousand years, I have longed to see your lustrous glow, and my affections for you have never wavered. Mixiang arrived with your message. I will gladly accept the offer to come down to you at Liu Che's palace. When I heard

---

71 In *DZ* 1016, 10.2a–b, Yang Xi describes black and white meditation as a meditative technique where one lies supine each morning to visualize black qi in the brain and white qi in the heart. The technique is thought to cause one to feel as though a fire is enveloping the body, and as though one can survive long periods without breathing. If done successfully, an adept's youthful appearance will return.

命之際,登當顛倒。先被大帝君勅使詣玄洲,校定天元。正爾暫往,如是當還。還便束帶,須臾少留。

帝因問上元夫人由。王母曰:「是三天上元之官,統領十方玉女之名錄者也。」

當二時許,上元夫人至。來時亦聞雲中簫鼓之聲。既至,從官文武千餘人皆女子。年同十八九許,形容明逸。多服青衣,光彩耀日。真靈官也。夫人可廿餘。天姿清輝,靈眸絕朗。着赤霜之袍,雲彩亂色。非錦非繡,不可名字。頭作三角髻,餘髮散垂之,至腰。戴九靈夜光之冠,帶六出火玉之珮,垂鳳文琳華之綬,腰流黃揮精之劍。上殿向王母拜。

王母坐而止之。呼同坐北向。夫人設廚,廚之精珍,與王母所設者相似。王母勅帝曰:「此真元之母,尊貴之神。女當起拜。」帝問寒溫,還坐。

夫人笑曰:「五濁之人,躭湎榮利,嗜味淫色,固其常也。

---

72 The "heavenly origin calendar" refers to the calendrical movement of the seasons (Sima Qian 1997, 1256).
73 For more on the Three Heavens' correlation with the high divine beings of the Supreme Purity pantheon, see Kohn 2011, 841.

your order, I wanted to drop everything I was doing. But I had previously been given an imperial order by the great imperial lord to pay a visit to the Mysterious Continent and revise the heavenly origin calendar.[72] So I must first head there for a little while and then return here. Upon my return, I will change into something more comfortable to go join you for a little while.

The emperor asked about the Lady of the Upper Prime. The Queen Mother of the West said, "She is an Upper Prime official of the Three Heavens overseeing the register of names for jade maidens everywhere."[73]

About two hours later, the Lady of the Upper Prime arrived. Sounds of flutes and drums could be heard in the clouds as she approached. When she appeared, a retinue of over one thousand civil and military aides, all young women, accompanied her. They were all about eighteen or nineteen years old, with a youthful glow, clad in azure clothes with brilliant patterns shining like the sun. They were truly numinous officers. The Lady looked a little over twenty years old. Her heavenly beauty was pure and radiant, with numinous eyes that shone bright. She wore a red frost robe embroidered with clouds in a profusion of colors. Her robe is hard to describe because it was neither brocade nor embroidery. Part of her hair was pulled up in a triangular chignon, while the rest hung down freely to her waist. She donned the Nocturnal Light of the Nine Numina crown, hung pendants of six-pointed snowflakes made of fire jade on her belt, dangled ribbons of phoenix patterns and glistening flowers, and wore the Dispersing Spirits with Brimstone sword at her hip. She ascended to the top of the basilica and bowed before the Queen Mother of the West.

The Queen Mother of the West remained seated and motioned for her to stop bowing. She instructed the Lady to sit with her facing north. The Lady laid out a feast of exquisite delicacies similar to the one that the Queen Mother of the West had brought. The Queen Mother of the West admonished the emperor saying, "This is the Mother of the Perfected Prime, a divine being who deserves honor and reverence. You should stand up and bow to her." The emperor asked if she was comfortable, and then returned to his seat.

The Lady laughed and said, "It is normal for people mired in the Five Defilements to be awash in glory and wealth, and addicted to lust and sex.[74]

---

74 The term "Five Defilements" was first coined by Buddhists (see Xingyundashi 2003, 1201c–1203b) to refer to personal afflictions, mistaken views, and social decay. The early Tang compilation *Discussion of the Daoist Classics* (*Daodian lun* 道典論, DZ 1130, 3.9b) has a lengthy explanation of its use in Daoism, but it is likely that here the defilements refer simply to the five negative qualities attached to Emperor Wu immediately below (such as his violence and licentiousness). See Schipper 1965, 94 n. 7.

且徹以天子之貴，其亂目者，倍於常人焉。而復於華麗之
墟，振根願無爲之事，良有志也。

　　王母曰：「所謂有心哉？」

　　上元夫人謂帝曰：

「女好道乎？聞數招方士，祭山嶽，祠靈神，禱河川，亦爲
勤矣。而不獲者，寔有由也。女胎性暴，胎性奢，胎性淫，
胎性酷，胎性賊。五者恒舍於榮衛之中、五藏之内。雖鋒鋩
良針，固難愈矣。

　　暴則使炁奔而神攻，是故神擾而炁竭。淫則使精漏而魂
疲，是故精竭而魂銷。奢則使真離而魂穢，是故本游而靈
髡。酷則使喪仁而自攻，是故失仁而服亂。賊則使心鬭而口
乾，是故內戰而外絶。五者皆是截身之刀鋸，剖命之斧鉞。
雖復疲好於長生，而不能遣兹五難。亦何爲損性而自勞乎？

　　然猶是得此小益，以自知往爾。若從今已捨爾五性，反
諸柔善？明務察下，慈務矜怨。惠務濟窮，賑務施勞。念務
存孤，惜務及身。

75　"Temptations" is literally "things that disrupt his vision."
76　"Mind" (gen 根, literally root/origin) is a common term in Buddhist and Daoist texts used to refer to the intellectual faculties of sentient beings.

But because Che holds the exalted position of emperor, he faces many more temptations than a normal person.[75] Yet for someone living among the ruins of beauty and decadence, he shows great ambition in rousing the mind and aspiring to practice nonaction."[76]

The Queen Mother of the West said, "Is this not what they call 'having a mind'?"[77]

The Lady of the Upper Prime said to the emperor,

"You love the Dao, do you not? I have heard about your great efforts in summoning masters of esoterica, sacrificing at the Sacred Peaks, enshrining the numinous spirits, and supplicating the river gods. But there is a reason why you have yet to benefit from this. From birth,[78] you have been violent, indulgent, licentious, cruel, and villainous. These five qualities are continually circulating in your body's qi and blood, and infusing your five viscera. Even the most advanced acupuncturist would find it difficult to heal you.

"Violence causes your qi to disperse and your spirit to be attacked, bewildering your spirit and exhausting your qi. Licentiousness causes your seminal essence to leak out and tires your cloud-souls, exhausting your essence and depleting your cloud-souls. Indulgence causes perfected beings to depart and sullies your cloud-souls, shifting your foundation and spoiling your numina. Cruelty leads to abandoning humaneness and opens one up to attacks, losing humaneness and inciting rebellion. Villainy leads to discord in your heart and parches your mouth, causing conflict within and cutting you off from others. These five qualities are all like knives or saws that sever your body, or like axes or halberds that chop years off your life. Although you immerse yourself in the arts of longevity time and again, you will never be able to cast aside the Five Difficulties. What will you do other than harm yourself and toil away?

"Nevertheless, you benefit slightly if you can be more aware of what you have done wrong. So, would it not be best to abandon these five characteristics from this point on, and return to being gentle and good? May you strive to inspect your subjects intelligently, and pity the oppressed with kindness. May you strive to save the poor with benevolence, and provide for workers with relief. May you strive to comfort orphans with care, and

---

77 See the Introduction, p. xxi.
78 Or "embryonic nature" (taixing 胎性).

恒爲陰德，救濟死厄。亘久孜孜，不泄精液。

於是閉諸淫，養爾神。放諸奢，從至儉。勤齋戒，節飲食。絶五穀，去臭腥。鳴天鼓，飲玉漿，蕩華池，叩金梁。按而行之，當有異爾。

今阿母迂天尊之重，下降於螻蛄之窟，霄虚之靈，而詣孤鳥之俎。且阿母至戒妙唱玄發。驗其敬勗節度。明脩所奉比及百年，阿母必能致女於玄都之墟，迎女於昆闕之中。位以仙官，游邁十方。吾言之畢矣，子屬之哉。若不能爾，無所言矣。」

帝下席跪謝曰：「臣受性兇頑，生長亂濁。面牆不啓，無由開達。然貪生畏死，奉靈敬神。今日受教，此廼天也。輒戢聖令，以爲身範。是小醜之臣，當獲生活，唯垂哀護，願賜元元。」

夫人使帝還坐。王母謂夫人曰：「卿之戒言，言甚急切，更使未解之人畏於至意。」

夫人曰：「若其志道，將以身投餓虎。忘軀破滅，蹈火履水。固於

---

79 For more on secret virtue, see *Traditions of Lord Pei*, p. 11, n. 29 above.

give yourself to their service. May you forever perform acts of secret virtue by saving those on the brink of death.[79] May you always show enthusiasm and eagerness while retaining your seminal essences.

"Therefore, stop your licentious ways, and nourish your spirit. Cast off your indulgent lifestyle, and lead a frugal life. Be zealous about fasting and the precepts, and show restraint in what you eat and drink. Cut out the five grains, and stop eating rancid flesh. Sound the heavenly drum, drink jade liquor, bathe in floriate pools, and knock the golden beam.[80] If you follow this and put it into practice, you will surely have all the help you need.

"Now Amah has rerouted the carriages of heavenly worthies to come down into a cicada's hole, as if the numina of the celestial void came before a single bird on the sacrificial table. Moreover, Amah has secretly given you the highest precepts in a sublime song. Prove that you will respectfully abide by these directives. If you can wisely cultivate what you have received for one hundred years, Amah will surely bring you to the hills of the Mysterious Metropolis and welcome you to enter the gate towers of Mt. Kunlun. You will be made a transcendent official and will travel to all corners of the world. This is all I have to say; please heed it well. If you cannot do this, then my words will have meant nothing."

The emperor got down from his seat, knelt, and expressed his gratitude, "Your subject is vicious and uncouth by nature, and I have grown into a wild and filthy man. I face a wall that I cannot pass, for I have no means to break through it. Thus, I cling to life and fear death by making offerings to numina and revering spirits. To have received these teachings here is truly a gift from heaven. I will immediately take up your saintly directives and use them as a model for my life. If your miserable servant can attain long life, it is due only to your compassionate care and goodwill."

The Lady asked the emperor to return to his seat. The Queen Mother of the West then said to the Lady, "Your words are most urgent and incisive, and should make one who hasn't understood be fearful with regard to such far-reaching ideas."

"If he really aspires to realize the Dao," the Lady said, "he will throw himself before starving tigers. He will step through fire and walk on water completely oblivious to the destruction of his body. If only he has a mind

---

80 In the *Inner Chapters of the Master Embracing Simplicity* (Ge Hong 1996, 111), this is a place in the body where one holds in numinous fluids (lingye 靈液), namely, spittle. Here it is likely the lower part of the tongue that the adept is knocking against the throat.

一志，必無憂也。若其無忠志，則心疑真信。嫌惑之徒，勿畏急言。急言之發，欲成其志耳。阿母既有念，必當賜以尸解之方耳。」

王母曰：「此子勤心已久，而不遇良師。遂欲毀其正志，當疑天下必無仙人。是故發我閬宮，暫舍塵濁。既欲堅其仙志，又欲令向化不惑也。今日相見，令人念之。至於尸解下方，吾甚不惜。復三年吾必欲賜以成丹半劑，石象散一具。與之，則徹不得復停。當今匈奴未彌，邊陲有事。何必令其倉卒，捨天下之尊而便入林岫也？但當問篤向之志必卒何如。如其回改吾方數來。」

王母因撫帝背曰：「女用上元夫人至言，必得長生，可不勗勉？」

帝跪曰：「徹書之金簡，以身模之焉。」帝又見王母巾笈中有卷子小書，盛以紫錦之囊。帝問：「此書是仙靈之方邪？不審其目，可得瞻眄。」

王母出以示之曰：「此《五嶽真形圖》也。昨青城諸仙就我求，請當過以付之。迺三天太上所出，文秘禁極重。豈女穢質所宜佩乎？今且與汝

---

81 For a thorough discussion of simulated corpses, see Campany 2014, 39–43.
82 Likely connected to Mt. Langfeng 閬風, one of the fantastic peaks of the Kunlun Mountains. It is mentioned by Yang Xi in *DZ* 1016, 5.15a and 1.17a. See also Smith 2020, 68 n. 182; Smith 2013, 70 n. 203.

focused on a single purpose, he will have no anxieties at all. But if he lacks faithful intentions, he will always harbor doubts about what is true and trustworthy. This despicable and deluded disciple should not fear my urgent words. I hoped that such urgent words might help him achieve his goals. That is all. If Amah is so inclined, perhaps she will bestow a method for escaping via a simulated corpse."[81]

The Queen Mother of the West said, "This disciple has been diligent for a long time, but has yet to encounter a good master. Because of this, he was about to give up his sincere ambition and had started to doubt that there were any transcendent beings in the world. This is why I set forth from my palace on Mt. Lang[82] and came here to this dusty and sullied world for a little while. I hoped to strengthen his ambition toward transcendence, and further hoped to clear up his misunderstandings about bodily transformations. Seeing him today, I feel pity for him. But I do not like the inferior method of corpse deliverance. I would rather give him a dose of a completed elixir mixed with a full measure of petrified image powder three years from now. If I give that to Che, he will never again give up. But right now, the Xiongnu have yet to be quelled, and there are many matters Che must deal with on the frontier. Why should we ask him to hurry this process along and give up his esteemed position in this world to go live deep in mountain forests? All that we need to do today is to consider whether he is sincere enough to carry out his intentions to the end. If he can change his ways, we can always come back."

The Queen Mother of the West then patted the emperor on the back, saying, "Do you think you will be diligent and carry out the lofty words of the Lady of the Upper Prime so that you can achieve long life?"

The emperor knelt, saying, "I will engrave these words on golden slips and use them to guide my life." Then the emperor noticed that the Queen Mother of the West's bookbag contained some fascicles bound together in a small book and kept in a purple brocade pouch. The emperor asked, "Doesn't this book contain recipes of transcendent numina? I cannot make out the title, may I dare ask to take a peek?"

The Queen Mother of the West took the text out and showed it to him, saying, "This is *Charts of the True Forms of the Five Sacred Peaks*. There was a group of transcendent beings from the Azure City Mountain[83] who requested this from me yesterday and asked if I could stop by and give it to them. It was revealed by the Most High Lord of the Dao of Three Heavens, and the text has many strict prohibitions. How could someone as bad as you be fit to carry this text around? For now, I will give you the *Living*

---

83 In present-day Sichuan Province. See Zang Lihe 1992, 570; Smith 1992, 505 n. 97.

《靈光生經》,可以通神勸志也。」

帝下地叩頭,固請不已。王母曰:

「昔上皇清虛元年,三天太上道君下觀六合。瞻河海之短長,察丘嶽之高卑。命立天柱,安于地理。植五嶽而擬諸鎮輔。貴昆靈以舍靈仙,尊蓬丘以館真人。安水神乎極陰之源,栖太帝乎榑桑之墟。

於是方丈之阜,爲理命之室,滄浪海島,養九老之堂。祖、瀛、玄、炎、長、元、流、生、鳳麟、聚窟,各爲洲名。並在滄流大海玄津之中。水則碧黑俱流,波則振蕩羣精。諸仙玉女,聚於滄溟。其名難測,其實分明。

廼因山源之規矩,睹河嶽之盤曲。陵回阜轉,山高壠長,周旋委蛇,形似書字。是故因象制名,定實之號。畫形祕於玄臺,而出爲靈真之信。諸仙佩之,皆如傳章。道士執之,經行山川,百神羣靈,尊奉親迎。

---

84 On the Six Harmonies, see *Traditions of Lord Su*, p. 73 above.
85 The term *ji yin* may mean the extreme north (Schipper 1965, 100 n. 3).

Scripture of Numinous Radiance, which will allow you to connect with the spirit world and will motivate you."

The emperor got down on the ground and kowtowed, remaining firm in his request. The Queen Mother of the West said,

"Long ago, in the first year of the Qingxu era of the Upper Sovereign, the Most High Lord of the Dao of Three Heavens came down and looked out over the Six Harmonies.[84] He gazed across the lengths of rivers and oceans, and investigated the heights of hills and peaks. He ordered that the Heavenly Pillar be raised, which set in place the contours of the land.[xiii] He determined the points of the five Sacred Peaks and drew up a plan for how to buttress them. He ennobled the holy Mt. Kunlun by housing numinous transcendents, and exalted the hills of Penglai by lodging perfected beings. He secured the water gods in the springs of ultimate yin,[85] and perched the Grand Emperor atop the highlands of Fusang.

"After this, he built a chamber for those who determine lifespans on Fangzhang Isle and made a hall to nourish the Nine Elders on the ocean isles of Gray-Blue Billows.[86] He named the isles Zu, Ying, Xuan, Yan, Chang, Yuan, Liu, Sheng, Fenglin, and Juku. These isles were placed in the Dark Channel in the great sea of gray-blue waves. The waters flowing between them were cyan and black, and the waves surged with one wave of spirits after another. All kinds of transcendents and jade maidens assembled in the gray-blue mist. Their names were difficult to decipher, but their bodies were clearly visible.

"Then he followed the shapes of mountain springs, and observed the curves of rivers and Sacred Peaks. The twisting hills, rolling mounds, rising mountains, and lengthy ridge paths coiled and circled like snakes, in shapes resembling written characters. Accordingly, he based the names of these places on these shapes, determining their true epithets. He drew these forms and secretly stored them in the Mysterious Terrace and brought them out to confirm the pledges of numinous perfected. All transcendent beings wear these shapes at their waist as an insignia of their post. If a gentleman of the Dao has them while crossing mountain streams, he will be revered and warmly welcomed by all gods and spirits.

---

86 For more on the blissful isle called Fangzhang, see Pettit 2013a, 302 n. 61. In ancient times, Gray-Blue Billows was the name of a tributary of the Han River 漢水. See Zang Lihe 1992, 1032.

女雖不正，然數訪山澤叩求之志，不忘于道。欣子有心，今以相與。當深奉慎，如事君父。泄示凡夫，必致禍考也。」

上元夫人語帝曰：「阿母今以瓊笈妙蘊，發紫臺之文，賜女八會之書。《五嶽真形》，可謂至珍且貴，上帝之玄觀矣。子自非受命合神，弗見此文。今雖得其《真形》，觀其妙理，而無：

五帝六甲左右靈飛之符
太陰六丁通真遁虛玉女之籙
太陽六戊招神天光策精之書
左乙混沌東蒙之文
右庚素收攝殺之律
壬癸六遁隱地八術
丙丁入火九赤班符
六辛入金致黃水月華之法
六巳石精金光藏影化形之方

87 According to the late-seventh-century treatise *The Order of Succession of the Daoist Scripture Legacy* (*Daomen jingfa xiangcheng cixu* 道門經法相承次序, *DZ* 1128, 1.4a), these are the eight days of each year associated with the three primes and five virtues (wude 五德). It is likely that "a book of the Eight Assemblies" refers to one of the books that gods use when they meet on the Eight Nodal Days.
88 The Six Jia were protective deities that could be summoned to help an adept. See Pettit and Chang, 2020, 311 n. 2. The talismans associated with them predate Supreme Purity writers; the texts are mentioned in Celestial Masters texts and by Ge Hong. See Robinet 1984, 1.12–13, 24–25; Schipper and Verellen 2004, 174–175.

"While it may not be right to give you these charts, you have visited mountains and lakes many times to make humble requests, and have never lost sight of the Dao. I am delighted that you have a mind, so I now give these charts to you. Be sure to treat them with the utmost respect, just as you would your lord or father. If you ever divulge them to ordinary people, you will bring misfortune upon your ancestors."

The Lady of the Upper Prime spoke to the emperor, saying, "From her miraculous collection in her rose-gem bookbag, Amah has now given you a Purple Terrace text, a book of the Eight Assemblies.[87] The *True Forms of the Five Sacred Peaks* is widely known as a most treasured and precious text of the Upper Emperor's Mysterious Belvedere. But you should not even see this text unless you have received an order to join with the spirits. Although you have now acquired the *True Forms* and have gazed upon their mysterious patterns, you still lack the following:

Five Emperors and Six Jia Talismans of Left and Right Numinous Flight Maidens[88]
Grand Yin and Six Ding Register of Jade Maidens Who Are Concealed in the Void and Communicate with the Perfected[89]
Grand Yang and Six Wu Book to Summon Spirits, Emit Celestial Brilliance, and Stimulate the Essences
Left Yi Writ of Chaotic Eastern Shroud
Right Geng Statute of Rounding Up and Exterminating in the White Reaping
Ren and Gui Methods for the Eight Arts of Six Concealments and a Hiding Place[90]
Bing and Ding Talismans of Nine Red Spotted Dragons to Enter Fire[91]
Six Xin Procedures to Enter Metal and Acquire the Lunar Blossom of Yellow Water
Six Si Methods for Concealing Shadows and Transforming One's Body with Lithic Essence and Golden Light

---

89 For more on the Six Ding, see *Traditions of Lord Su*, p. 73 above. This title resonates closely with the content of *DZ* 581, 5a–b, where the author speaks in detail about the power of the talismans to help an adept make his body invisible (yinshen 隱身).
90 Below (p. 200), a "method" (fang 方) is added. *Ren* and *gui* are the signs associated with summer. For more on the eight arts an adept can use to conceal himself, see Robinet 1984, 2.141–144; Schipper and Verellen 2004, 157–158.
91 On this scripture, see *Nine Red Spotted Talismans of the Five Emperors' Inward Contemplation* (*Taishang jiuchi banfu wudi neizhen jing* 太上九赤班符五帝內真經, *DZ* 1329).

子午卯酉八稟十決六靈威儀
丑辰未戌地真素訣長生紫書三五順行
寅申巳亥紫度炎光內視中方

凡闕此《十二事》者，何以召山靈，朝地神，總攝萬精，驅策百鬼，來虎豹，役蚊龍乎？子所謂適知其一，未見其他也。」

帝下席叩頭曰：「徹下土濁民，不識清真。今日聞道，是生命會遇聖母。今當賜與《真形》，脩以度世。夫人今告徹，應須五帝六甲、六丁、六戊致靈之術。既蒙啟發，弘益無量。唯原告誨，濟臣飢渴。得使已枯之木，蒙靈陽之潤，焦炎之草，幸甘雨之漑。不敢多陳，願賜指授。」

上元夫人曰：「我無此文也。昔曾扶廣山見青真小童。有此金書祕字云：『求道益命千端萬緒。皆須《五帝六甲靈飛》之術，六丁六壬名字之號，得以請命延筭，長生久視。驅策眾靈，役使百

---

92 See Li Fengmao 1986b, 64–65.
93 Below, different combinations of these texts are referred to. Nonetheless, we have translated each instance using the term the *Twelve Texts*.

> Zi, Wu, Mao, and You Awesome Ceremonies for Addressing the Six
> Numina through the Eight Petitions and Ten Instructions
> Chou, Chen, Wei, and Xu Immaculate Instructions of the Terrestrial
> Perfected, the Three and Five Effortless Practice from the Purple
> Book of Long Life[92]
> Yin, Shen, Si, and Hai Central Method for Inner Vision of the Purple
> Rules of Blazing Light

"If you lack these *Twelve Texts*,[93] how could you possibly summon the numina of the mountains, have an audience with the gods of the earth, command the myriad spirits, wield power over the hundred ghosts, beckon tigers and leopards, or put water-dragons and dragons under your service? We might call you one who is content to know one aspect without having seen everything."

The emperor got down from his seat, kowtowed, and said, "I am but a muddled person of this lowly world who cannot recognize the pure and perfected. By fate I have met the Sacred Mother and have heard this Dao today. She is now prepared to give me the *True Forms* so that I might use it to be saved from this world. But now, Lady, you have told me that I should learn techniques such as those in the *Twelve Texts*. If you bestow these and enlighten me, I will reap limitless benefits. I only wish you would teach me more to abate this servant's hunger and thirst. In this way, a desiccated tree will be moistened with numinous yang, and scorched grasses will be irrigated with sweet rain. I dare not say anything else, but I hope that you might further instruct me."

The Lady of the Upper Prime said, "I do not possess these texts. But once, long ago, I was at Mt. Fuguang, where I met the Young Lad of Azure Perfection. He had a golden book written in esoteric characters that read, 'There is an endless variety of ways to seek the Dao and add years to one's lifespan. But every adept needs the techniques of the *Five Emperors and Six Jia Talismans of Numinous Flight* and the Six Ding and Six Ren[94] names to request years added to their allotment and a long life of eternal youth. He will also be able to command the various numina, and make the hundred

---

94 Although the Six Ding and Six Ren appear here to be specific deities, in the *Inner Chapters of the Master Embracing Simplicity* (Ge Hong 1996, 292) they seem to be alchemical ingredients. If you combine Six Ding, Six Ren, and Superior Earth 六丁六壬上土 in a pill according to the method of Wu Chengzi 務成子法, you will be able to turn invisible. See Ōno Yuji 2006, 43; Como 2015, 28.

神者也。其無《六甲》要事，唯守《真形》者於通靈之來必無階矣。』女有心可念故相告篇目耳。幸復廣加搜訪焉。」帝固請不已叩頭流血。

上元夫人曰：「吾無此文。所以相示《十二事》者，欲令女廣尋博求，以參《真形》之用耳。」

王母廼告上元夫人曰：
「夫《真形》寶文，靈官所貴。此子守求不已，誓以必得，故虧科禁，特以與之。然《五帝六甲》、《通真》、《招神》，此術眇邈，必當須精潔至誠。殆非流濁所宜施行，吾今既賜徹以《真形》，夫人今當授以致靈之途矣。

吾嘗憶昔日與夫人共登玄壟朔野及曜真之山，眹王子童。王子童廼就吾請求《太上隱書》，吾以三元祕言，不可傳泄於中仙。夫人時亦有言見，守助子童之言志矣。吾既難違來意，不獨執惜。至於今日之事，有以相似。後造朱火丹陵，食靈瓜其味甚好。憶此未久，而已七千歲矣。夫人既已告徹篇目《十二事》畢，必當匠而成之。何緣令人主啓顙請乞，叩頭流血邪？」

上元夫人曰：「阿環不苟惜，向不持來耳，此是太虛羣文真人赤童所出。傳之既自有男女之限禁。又宜授得道者，恐徹下才，未應用此爾。」

spirits do his bidding. But if one lacks the *Twelve Texts* and only has the *True Forms*, he will certainly lack the ability to commune with the numina.' I have told you only the titles of these texts because you have a mind and are receptive. With luck, you will find them all after an extensive search." But the emperor kept repeatedly requesting them as he kowtowed until blood ran down his face.

The Lady of the Upper Prime said, "I do not have these texts with me. I told you only about the *Twelve Texts* so that you might look for them near and far, and use them together with the *True Forms*."

The Queen Mother of the West then told the Lady of the Upper Prime, "The precious text of *True Forms* is esteemed by numinous officials. Since this disciple keeps asking for them and has sworn to do anything to acquire them, let us put aside the rules and restrictions to make an exception for him. The *Twelve Texts* are deep and profound, and they require a pure mind and sincere intentions. While it really is not right for such a sullied person to use these texts, I am now giving Che the *True Forms*, and you should transmit to him a way for summoning the numina.

"I still remember in the old days when you and I climbed into the northern wasteland of the Dark Hills until we reached the Radiant Perfection Mountains, where we saw Wang Zitong. Wang requested that we give him the *Hidden Book of the Most High*, but I felt that the esoteric words about the Three Primes should not be transmitted or divulged to a middle transcendent being. At that time, you, Lady, expressed the idea that we should tell Zitong these things in order to bolster his resolve. It was hard to leave without giving him what he wanted, and I did not want to be the ungenerous one. It is easy to see the similarities between then and now. After that, we journeyed to the cinnabar hills of the Vermillion Fire and ate numinous mouthwatering melons. And although it feels like yesterday, seven thousand years have passed since then. Now, Lady, you have already told Che the titles of the *Twelve Texts*, so let us finish what we started. Why make the lord of humanity beg and kowtow to the point that his face flows with blood?"

The Lady of the Upper Prime said, "I am pained with regret that I have no way to bring the *Twelve Texts* with me, for all scriptures of the Grand Void are released by the perfected being Red Lad. Only certain people can receive transmission of these texts. Moreover, these texts should only be given to people who have realized the Dao, and I fear that Che is an inferior talent not worthy enough to use them."

王母色不平，廼曰：
「若天禁漏泄，犯違《明科》。傳必其人，授必知真者。何緣夫人向下才而說《靈飛》之篇目乎？妄言則漏，妄說則泄。說而不傳，是謂『衒天道』。此禁豈輕於傳也？別勑三官司，直推夫人之輕泄也。吾之《五嶽真形文》，廼太上天皇所出，其文寶妙，而爲天仙之信。豈復應下授之於劉徹也邪？

　　直以孜孜之心，數請川嶽，勤脩齋戒，以求神仙之應。志在度世，不遭明師，故吾等有以下眄之耳。至於教仙之術，不復限惜而弗傳。夫人但有致靈真之事，足以卻不信之狂夫耳？吾意在是矣。

　　然此子性氣淫暴，服精不純，何能得成真仙浮空參差十方乎？勤而行之，適足以不死耳。《明科》所云：『非長生難也，聞道難。非聞道難也，行之難。非行之難也，終之難。良匠能與人規矩，不能使人必巧。明師能授人妙術，不能使人

The Queen Mother of the West, showing dissatisfaction, said,

"If heaven has forbidden divulging and leaking a text, then doing so violates the *Bright Code*. If scriptures are to be transmitted to humans, they should be given only to people who know about perfection. Why do you, my Lady, speak of the titles of the *Twelve Texts* to a person of inferior talent? To mention them carelessly is to divulge, and to speak carelessly is to leak. But to speak about them without providing them is called 'flaunting the Heavenly Dao.' How is violating this taboo against divulging and leaking really a lesser offense than simply transmitting the texts? What's more, I might even notify the Three Officials, who will investigate your offense without delay. My *Writs of the True Forms of the Five Sacred Peaks* were revealed by the Heavenly Sovereign most high, and these treasured and marvelous words serve as a pledge for heavenly transcendents. So how is it not appropriate to transmit these texts to Liu Che?

"With his steadfast mind, Che has supplicated many times at rivers and Sacred Peaks, and has kept fasts and precepts to become a divine transcendent. He wants to be saved from this world even though he lacks an enlightened master, and this is why we have come to pay him a visit. So, as far as teaching the arts of transcendence goes, we can no longer be stingy and refuse to transmit them. But, my Lady, do you not possess the *Twelve Texts* to summon numinous perfected that would satisfy the most foolish nonbeliever?[xiv] These are my thoughts.[xv]

"Though this disciple is a licentious and cruel person who partakes in all that is impure, how else can he become a perfected or transcendent being who can drift into emptiness from every direction? Striving to put these scriptures into practice will help one stave off death. And as it says in the *Bright Code*,[95] 'It is not long life that is hard; rather, it is hard to hear about the Dao. It is not hearing about the Dao that is hard; rather, it is hard to put it into practice. It is not putting it into practice that is hard; rather, it is bringing it to completion. A good carpenter can give a person his compass and square, but cannot guarantee that the person will be skilled. An enlightened master can transmit miraculous techniques, but cannot

---

95 See Pettit and Chang 2020, 112–120, for more information on possible references for this term.

必爲。』何足其隱之也?夫人不嘗憶問爲長桑公子請吾,求八光揮疾藥玉樹方乎?」

上元夫人有慙色。跪謝曰:

「阿環昔初學道於廣都之丘建木。丹誠術數未成之時,倒景君、無常先生,此二人蓋太清玄和天之靈官也,見授《六甲左右靈飛方十二事》。初授之日,二君告阿環曰:『初學道者聽四十年一傳。得道者四百年一傳。得仙者四千年一傳。得真者四萬年一傳。得昇太上者四十萬年一傳。女受傳女,男受傳男。《太上科禁》,已表於《昭生之符》矣。』

阿環受書已來,凡傳六十八女子。賢大女郎抱蘭,即阿環之弟子也。阿環所授者固不可以授男也。伏見扶廣山青真小童,往授太微中元君五帝《六甲靈飛》、《遁虛》、《天光左右策精》等方,凡《十二事》。與阿環所受者同文,一無異也。青真男官也,未聞復有所授。此子先是阿環學入火弟子。今正勑取,以授徹也。

96 For more on this figure, see *Records of the Historian* (Sima Qian 1997, 2785).

guarantee the person will put them into practice.' Given this, why would you hide these texts from him? And do not forget that you, Lady, once requested that I give Master Changsang[96] a Jade Tree recipe for a drug to dispel illness with the eight lights."

The Lady of the Upper Prime looked ashamed. She knelt down and apologized, saying,

"Long ago, I first started studying the Dao at Jianmu in the hills of Guangdu.[97] Before I had finished my exhaustive attempts to master the esoteric arts and divination, the Lord of Inverted Phosphors and the Master of Ephemera, who were numinous officials of the Grand Purity's Sublime Harmony Palace, transmitted the *Twelve Texts* to me. The day they gave them to me, they told me, 'Those who have just started studying this Dao are permitted to transmit the *Twelve Texts* once every forty years. Those who have attained this Dao may transmit them once every four hundred years. Those who have attained transcendence may transmit them once every four thousand years. Those who have attained perfection may transmit them once every forty thousand years. Those who have ascended to the Most High may transmit them once every four hundred thousand years. Women should receive transmission from women, and men from men. The Coded Taboos of the Most High are expressed in the *Talisman of Glorious Life*.'

"Since I, Ahuan, received the texts, I have transmitted them to sixty-eight other women. Even esteemed noblewomen such as Baolan count among my disciples. But I am not allowed to transmit these texts to men. Once I saw the Lesser Lad of Azure Perfection from Mt. Fuguang visit the Central Primal Lord of Grand Tenuity, one of the Five Emperors, and receive the *Twelve Texts*. These are exactly the same as my texts, without a single difference. The Lesser Lad of Azure Perfection is a male official, and I have not heard that he has transmitted this text to anyone else. This lad was once my disciple, whom I taught how to enter fire. We should order him to bring the texts and transmit them to Che.

---

97 Also written Duguang 都廣 in the *Classic of Mountains and Seas* (Yuan Ke 1995, 445). Jianmu is a heavenly pillar at Duguang in Han lore (Zhang Shuangdi 1997, 136; Major et al. 2010, 157).

先所以告徹篇目者，意是愍其有心，將欲堅其專氣。今且廣求，他日與之，亦欲以男授男。承科而行，既勤而獲。令知天真之珍貴，非徒苟執銜泄天道矣。本情如此。阿環主臣，願不皋焉。

　　阿母，《真形》之妙，靈人傳信。天仙寶貴，封之金臺。佩入紫微，廼經行而前。衛門大虎，却伏抱關。出過太清，則振身瑤房。左遨滄海，長揖東蒙。右接常陽，下盼板桐。汎彼八海，則乘蚪從龍。游此名山，則衆真奉迎。動有雲輪羽蓋。靜可長存永安。至術洪矣！

　　初不傳地官，阿母今廼授於淫濁之尸，賜於枯骨之身。可謂太不宜矣。況阿環有六甲下術：

唯
驅策百靈
致日月之華精
藏匿形影
化生萬物
出入水火
唾叱杳冥
徹視反聽
收束千精

"I first told Che about this catalog of titles because I wanted to act charitably to one with a mind, in the hope that it would help him focus on his qi. From here, he can broaden his search, and I hope he will receive these texts some other time from a man. If he diligently adheres to the Code in his practice, he will obtain these texts. Letting him know about the precious treasures of the celestial perfected is not the same thing as flaunting and divulging the celestial Dao. These were my real intentions. Your humble servant hopes that you do not hold this against me.

"Amah, the wonders of the *True Forms* are the insignia that numinous beings receive when they pledge. Celestial transcendents treasure these texts and seal them away in the Golden Terrace. They wear them on their belt when entering Purple Tenuity, and thus they can pass through and onward. Great tigers guard the entrance and stand down when they reach the gate. When these beings go out beyond Grand Purity, their bodies are lifted into the Jasper Room.[98] To the east, they travel to the Gray-Blue Sea, where they make a deep bow to the Eastern Shroud. To the west, they reach Mt. Changyang, and look out over Mt. Bantong.[xvi] Floating across the Eight Seas, they ride *dou*-dragons following other dragons.[xvii] Roaming among the famed peaks, they are warmly welcomed by all the perfected. They move on carriages with cloudy wheels and feathered canopies. They rest in states of long meditation and eternal peace. Great indeed are these ultimate techniques!

"Originally, the *True Forms* was not transmitted to earthly officials, but now that you have transmitted it to this licentious filthy corpse, Amah, you grant it to a body of dried bones. This is inappropriate. Furthermore, the minor techniques of the *Twelve Texts* that I have,

> Verily they can
> Drive forward the hundred numina,
> Procure the blossoming essences of the sun and moon,
> Conceal and hide one's form and shadow,
> Transform and produce all things in the world,
> Pass through water and fire,
> Exhale into distant darkness,
> See in the distance and listen inwardly,
> Gather and wield the thousand essences,

---

98 A dwelling place of transcendent beings (Ge Hong 1996, 189).

乘虎豹以驅馳
采月華以長生
隱淪八地
回倒辰星
久視輕身
與天相傾耳

安得及太上之靈書，八會之奇文乎？
用之眇邈，可以游景靈之宮
紛紛飈飈，登流霞之堂
臣五嶽之主
挹藥醴之觴
駕九龍以虛騰
落紫鴻而玄翔邪」

　　王母笑曰：「先失自可恕乎？」
　　上元夫人即命侍女紀離容徑到扶廣山。勅青真小童出《六甲左右靈飛致神之方十二事》，來以授徹也。須臾侍女還，奉八色玉笈鳳文之蘊。玄光明曜，真華煒煥。云

青真小童問訊：
「弟子阿昌言向奉詣絳河，攝南真七元君，檢校羣龍猛獸之數事。畢，過門受教承阿母相邀詣劉徹家。不意天靈至尊廼復下降於臭濁中也。不審起居如何。侍女紀離容

---

99 Likely Mercury. See *Traditions of Lord Pei*, p. 23 above; Schafer 1977a, 213–214.

Ride tigers and leopards to gallop onward,
Pick lunar blossoms to gain a long life,
Hide and disappear in the Eight Directions,
Return back to the Chronographic Star,[99]
Live endlessly with a light body,
And be esteemed just like the heavens.

Should he really be given the most high numinous books, these miraculous texts of the Eight Assemblies?
Should he really use its miraculous powers to roam to the Palace of Phosphor Numen,
Or to ascend to the Hall of Drifting Aurorae on an ever-flowing wind?
Should he serve the lords of the Five Sacred Peaks,
Or pour a cup of sweet stamen wine?
Should he gallop through the void driving nine dragons,
Or glide down on a purple swan and mysteriously take flight?"

The Queen Mother of the West laughed and said, "Surely those with past mistakes can forgive others, no?"

The Lady of the Upper Prime then ordered her attendant girl, Ji Lirong, to leave for Mt. Fuguang. There she would deliver an edict to the Lesser Lad of Azure Perfection, who was to bring the *Twelve Texts* and give them to Che. Before long, the attendant girl returned and presented an eight-colored jade bookbag containing a collection of phoenix writs. A mysterious light dazzled brightly, and perfected flowers shimmered and shone. She said,

"The Lesser Lad of Azure Perfection sends the following message:

Your disciple Achang informs you that I was ordered to travel to the Scarlet River,[100] to assist the Seventh Primal Lord of Southern Perfection by taking inventory of the number of his dragons and fearsome beasts. Afterward, once I had passed through my gate, I was told that Amah had invited me to Liu Che's house. I did not expect that the most respected celestial numina would ever descend once again down to that rank and sullied world. I found it hard to understand what led you down there. Your attendant girl Ji Lirong

---

100 Smith (1992, 515 n. 120) says that "Scarlet River" denotes the southern sky.

至云:『尊欲得金書祕字《六甲靈飛左右策精之文十二事》。』

輒封一通付。徹雖有心求慕,實非仙才。詎宜以此術傳泄於行尸乎?阿昌近在帝處,見有上言者甚衆云:『山鬼哭於藜林,孤魂號於絶域。興師旅而族有功。忘賞勞而刑士卒。縱橫白骨,奢擾黔首。淫酷自恣。』罪已彰於太上,怨已見於天氣。囂言互聞,必不得度世也。真尊見勅不敢違耳。」

王母笑曰:

「言此子者誠多愆,帝亦不必推也。夫好道慕仙者,精誠志念,齋戒思愆,輒除過一月。剋己反善,奉敬真神,存真守一,行此一月,輒除過一年。

徹念道累年,齋亦勤積。屢禱名山真靈,願求度脱。校計功過,殆以相掩。但自今已去,勤脩至誠,奉上元夫人之言,不宜復奢淫暴虐。使萬兆勞殘,怨魄窮鬼有破掘之訴。流血之尸,忘功賞之辭耳。」

於是上元夫人離席起立。手執八色玉笈鳳文之蘊,

arrived and said, 'The esteemed Amah needs a copy of the golden books of secret characters of the *Twelve Texts*.'

I quickly sealed them up to give to him. Although Che has the mind of one who searches for what he adores, truly he does not have the ability to reach transcendence. Is it really appropriate to transmit and divulge these techniques to a walking corpse? Recently, I was present at the [Celestial] Emperor's residence when I heard many memorials stating, 'Mountain ghosts cry out from thickets and groves, lone cloud-souls cry out from faraway lands. He mobilized troops to exterminate families of the meritorious. He forgets to reward hard work and punishes his troops with mutilation. White bones are scattered everywhere, as he excessively harasses commoners. He is licentious and cruel and does whatever he pleases.' His transgressions are obvious to the most high gods, and complaints against him can be heard from heaven. People everywhere are bad-mouthing him, so it seems certain that he will not be saved from this world. But I dare not disobey an edict from you, Perfected Worthy."

The Queen Mother of the West laughed, saying,

"All that has been said about this disciple's wicked acts are true, but the [Celestial] Emperor will not necessarily reject him. Whoever loves the Dao and yearns for transcendence, has sincere intentions, fasts, and keeps the precepts while contemplating their wickedness, can absolve one month's worth of wrongdoings. If, over the course of one month, he restrains himself, returns to goodness, honors the perfected spirits, visualizes the perfected by guarding the One, then he can absolve a year's worth of wrongdoings.

"Che has contemplated the Dao for many years while remaining diligent about fasting.[xviii] He has repeatedly beseeched the perfected numina of famous mountains in hopes of finding salvation. If he was to calculate the number of his good deeds and wrongdoings, he would find that they nearly cancel each other out. But going forward, if he diligently cultivates himself with utmost sincerity and honor according to the words of the Lady of the Upper Prime, it is unlikely that he will resume his licentious, cruel, and violent ways again. Nor will his subjects be overwhelmed by corvée labor in places where cloud-souls and impoverished ghosts file grievances because their graves have been disturbed. Nor will bloody corpses give testimony that their meritorious actions have been forgotten."

The Lady of Upper Prime then left her seat and stood up. She took out an eight-colored jade bookbag containing a collection of phoenix writs,

仰天向帝，而祝曰：

  九天浩洞
  太上曜靈
  神照玄寂
  清虛朗明
  登虛者妙
  守氣者生
  至念道臻
  寂感真誠
  役神形辱
  安精年榮
  授徹靈飛
  及此六丁
  左右招神
  天光策精
  可以步虛
  可以隱形
  長生久視
  還白留青
  我傳有四萬之紀
  授徹傳在四十之齡
  違犯泄漏
  必沉於幽冥
  必慎其禍
  敢告劉生

then looked to the heavens toward the [Celestial] Emperor and made the following incantation:

> Nine Heavens vast and infinite,
> Shining and numinous Most High.
> Spirits shine in mysterious stillness;
> The Pure Void gleams and glows.
> The one who ascends to the Void is sublime,
> And the one who guards his qi shall live long.
> In deep concentration he attains the Dao,
> And silences his emotions so as to have true integrity.
> Belaboring his spirits will cause his body to degrade,
> But quieting his essences makes his years flourish.
> Now I transmit the *Talismans of Numinous Flight* to Che,
> Along with the *Six Ding Register*,
> The *Left Writ* and *Right Statute*, and *Book to Summon Spirits*,
> And *Emit a Celestial Brilliance and Stimulate Essences*.
> He will be able to traverse the Void.
> He will be able to hide his bodily form.
> He will have long life and eternal youth.
> His hair will turn black, and he'll stay forever young.
> While I can transmit these texts every forty thousand years,
> After receiving them, Che can transmit them every forty years.
> If he violates the injunctions against divulging them,
> He will certainly be plunged into the netherworld.[xix]
> He must remain cautious about these misfortunes,
> I dare pronounce this warning to Disciple Liu.

爾師主是青童小君。太上中黃道君之師,真元始天王入室弟子也。姓延陵,名陽,字庇華。形有嬰孩之貌,故仙官以青真小童之號。其爲器也:

環朗洞照
聖周萬變
玄鏡幽鑒
才爲真儔
游于扶廣
權此始運
宮館玄圃
治仙職分
子存師君
從爾所願
不存所授
命必傾隕

Your master is the Lesser Lord Azure Lad. He is the teacher of the Middle Yellow Lord of the Dao Most High, and is the intimate disciple of the Heavenly King of Perfected Primordial Incipience. His surname is Yanling, his name is Yang, and he is styled Bihua. His body has the appearance of an infant, which is why the transcendent officials call him the Lesser Lad of Azure Perfection. He is capable of many things:

> He shines everywhere with a penetrating brilliance.
> His saintliness encompasses the myriad transformations.
> He is like a subtle reflection in a dark mirror,
> His achievements as a perfected are unsurpassed.
> He travels off to Mt. Fuguang,
> Where he governs the start of the cycle.
> He makes his palace in the Mysterious Bower,
> Where he oversees the assignments of transcendents.
> If the disciple cherishes his master and lord,
> All will be according to your wishes.
> But if you do not cherish what you have received,
> Your lifespan will certainly be cut short.

上元夫人祝畢，乃一一手指所施用節度示帝。

第一篇有《五帝六甲左右靈飛之符》
第二篇有《六丁通真遁虛玉女之籙》
第三篇有《太陽六戊招神天光策精之書》
第四篇有《左乙混沌東蒙之文》
第五篇有《右庚素收攝殺之律》
第六篇有《壬癸六遁隱地八術之方》
第七篇有《丙丁入火九赤班文之符》
第八篇有《六辛入金致黃水月華之法》
第九篇有《六巳石精金光藏影化形之方》
第十篇有《子午卯酉八稟十訣六靈威儀》
第十一篇有《辰戌丑未地真曲素之訣長生紫書三五順行》
第十二篇有《寅申己亥紫度炎光內視中方》

　　凡《十二事》都畢，因復告帝曰：

　夫五帝者方面之天精
　六甲六位之通靈

After the Lady of the Upper Prime finished her incantation, she took out the texts one by one, showed them to the emperor and explained how to use them.

> The first text was the *Five Emperors and Six Jia Talismans of Left and Right Numinous Flight Maidens*.
> The second text was the *Grand Yin and Six Ding Register of Jade Maidens Who Are Concealed in the Void and Communicate with the Perfected*.
> The third text was the *Grand Yang and Six Wu Book to Summon Spirits, Emit Celestial Brilliance, and Stimulate the Essences*.
> The fourth text was the *Left Yi Writ of Chaotic Eastern Shroud*.
> The fifth was the *Right Geng Statute of Rounding Up and Exterminating in the White Reaping*.
> The sixth text was the *Ren and Gui Methods for the Eight Arts of Six Concealments and a Hiding Place*.
> The seventh text was the *Bing and Ding Talismans of Nine Red Spotted Dragons to Enter Fire*.
> The eighth text was the *Six Xin Procedures to Enter Metal and Acquire the Lunar Blossom of Yellow Water*.
> The ninth text was the *Six Si Methods for Concealing Shadows and Transforming One's Body with Lithic Essence and Golden Light*.
> The tenth text was the *Zi, Wu, Mao, and You Awesome Ceremonies for Addressing the Six Numina through the Eight Petitions and Ten Instructions*.
> The eleventh text was the *Chen, Xu, Chou, and Wei Immaculate Instructions of the Terrestrial Perfected, the Three and Five Effortless Practice from the Purple Book of Long Life*.
> The twelfth text was the *Yin, Shen, Si, and Hai Central Method for Inner Vision of the Purple Rules of Blazing Light*.

When the Lady had finished speaking about the *Twelve Texts*, she then revealed the following incantations to the emperor:

> The Five Emperors are the celestial essences of all directions,
> The Six Jia are the numina linked to the six positions.

太陰有潛空之妙
遁靈履機之神
秋含春挺
千真之生
動則寂應成波
靜則川陵緬平
所以毫末不移
浩嶽可傾
赫哉太陽之招神
策萬靈而驅馳
六戊飛而神暢
天光因景以揚暉
西鄉激電而砰磕
東桑空震以成雷
蓋陽靈之日
丙赫實九天之元威

左乙混沌
萬物始通
陽微其升
蒼暉應龍
輕雲揚景
颸胎潛風
神眇集於有宅
真感應而必鍾
萬春廻始
是爲東蒙

The Grand Yin contains the marvel of hiding in the void,
With concealed numinous spirit maidens who follow the pivot.
From gathering in autumn to emerging in spring,
These give life to the thousand perfected beings.
When moving, their silence and response churn out great waves.
When still, the rivers and hills are rolled out flat before them.
Thus, without even moving the tip of a single hair,
One can topple massive peaks.
Glorious indeed is *Grand Yang Book to Summon Spirits*,
For it stimulates the myriad numina and hastens them along.
Its Six Wu soar, and their spirits are carefree;
Its Celestial Brilliance shines forth from their phosphors.
Flashes of lightning over the western lands turn into thunderclaps,
A quake in the skies over the eastern mulberries becomes thunder.
This is brighter than the sun of yang numina.
With fire flashing, truly this is the primal power of the Nine
    Heavens.

With the *Left Yi Writ of Chaos*,[xx]
The myriad phenomena start to spread out.
Subtle hints of yang begin to rise.
A silver radiance responds to dragons.
Light clouds lift up with phosphors.
A tempestuous embryo is hidden in the wind.
Gods miraculously convene where there is a residence.
The perfected will respond and surely assemble here.[101]
The myriad springtimes start again and again.
This is what is called the Eastern Shroud.

---

101 For the pervasive role of this concept of spiritual beings responding in Chinese religious thought, see Scharf 2005.

右庚素秋
歛散聚炁
攝萬神而我役
白虎動以彭勃
少女起而通眞
延九天之眄視
金精地靈
來爲身衛
鹹彼邪惡
故稱攝殺之律

壬癸六遁
沉淪無根
藏蔽萬鋒
移行丘山
隱地匿影
崩流塞川
八術六奇
萬勝常全
佩我六遁
久視長存

丙丁入火
凌煙雲漠
九赤龍書
翳蔚朗煥
爾用斑符致千靈以朝謁
廼由丙神廻丹火以衝散
炎光上術
妙乎異觀

With the *Right Geng Statute of White Autumn*,
One gathers what has scattered by amassing qi.
One masters the myriad spirits to make them one's own servants,
Like a white tiger who moves with a vigorous pounce.
The young maiden rises to communicate with perfected beings,
As she draws sidelong glances from the Nine Heavens.
Metallic essences and terrestrial numina
Come forth to guard my body.
They chop off the heads of evil and vile forces.
This is why it is called the *Statute of Rounding Up and Exterminating*.

The *Ren and Gui Methods of Six Concealments*
Lets one sink down to what has no root.
One can take cover from a myriad sharp blades,
And move the hills and mountains.
A hiding place will conceal one's shadow,
Landslides flow down and block up rivers.
With these six marvels of the Eight Arts,
Ten thousand victories will come without fail.
Wearing the *Six Concealments* on one's waist
Makes one eternally young and makes one live forever.

The *Bing and Ding Talismans for Entering Fire*
Rises above the haze of the Milky Way.
This *Nine Red Spotted Dragon* Book
Obscures everything with its brilliant light.
You can use the *Spotted Talismans* to beckon the thousand numina
    for an audience,
And then use the Bing Spirits to recycle the cinnabar fire and
    quickly disperse them.
These superior arts of fiery radiance
Are marvelous and unique to behold.

六辛入金
飛害銷磨
致日精得陽光之珠
求月魄獲黃水之華
能致八石之靈菌
能引扶桑之丹霞
酣雲漿於丹庭
騰碧川於玄河
其用少矣
有益蓋多
佩此六辛
必造我家

六巳石精
金液流光
變化萬端
千載孰當
佩我六巳
易形游行
長生畢天
無復始終
元哉巳書
甚要難衝

The *Six Xin Procedures to Enter Metal*
Obliterates all unexpected calamities.
Acquire the solar essences to obtain the pearl of yang radiance,
And seek the lunar energy to capture the Blossom of Yellow Water.
One can conjure up the numinous fungus of the Eight Stones
And draw in the cinnabar auroras from the tree of Fusang.
Quaff the cloudy nectar of the Cinnabar Court,
And leap across a cyan stream into the Mysterious River.
Such small doses
Will have benefits too many to count.
By wearing the *Six Xin* at your waist,
You will certainly arrive at my house.

The *Six Si Methods of Lithic Essence*
Are a golden fluid of swirling light.
It leads to transformation in ten thousand ways,
And stands unopposed for a thousand years.
By wearing my *Six Si Methods* at the waist,
You can change form to roam freely
And have a long life equal to Heaven,
Never again to be born or die.
Primordial indeed are the *Six Si* writings.
They are vitally important and hard to undertake.

子午卯酉
大神四界
方面峙鎮
八稟十訣
降靈之來
必由齋祭
萬事取成於精慎
千神求通於此術
知我名字
天人可致

丑辰未戌
地真之符
游行五嶽
當用紫書
曲素訣辭
可以凌虛
三五順行
與靈同車

寅申巳亥
可禳飛灾
紫度炎光
內視反聽

「神辭通達六甲，收攝地司。游天踐地與真不疑。夫此《十二事》者，上帝封於玄景之臺，子其祕慎之焉。」

Zi, Wu, Mao, and You
Are the great spirits of the Four Realms.[102]
They stabilize all four directions
With the Eight Petitions and the Ten Instructions.
The arrival of the descending numina
Will surely happen on account of fasting and the rites.
One can succeed in a myriad affairs while in deep contemplation.
One can request an audience with a thousand spirits via these arts.
Knowing the personal names of gods
Will cause these celestial beings to come.

Chou, Chen, Wei, and Xu
Are the Talismans of the Terrestrial Perfected.
To roam freely among the Five Sacred Peaks,
One must use the *Purple Book*.
Explanations of Spells from the Meanderings and Immaculates
Will enable one to pass into the void of the heavens.
With the Effortless Procedure of the Three and Five,
One can share a carriage with numina.

The Yin, Shen, Si, and Hai Central Method
Can avert disasters flying down from heaven.
With the Purple Rules of Blazing Light
And Inner Vision, we reflectively listen.

"Once these divine words reach the Six Jia, you will assume control of terrestrial officials. You will never doubt that you can roam the heavens and ramble across the earth with perfected beings. As for these *Twelve Texts*, because the high emperors have sealed them within the Mysterious Phosphor Terrace, you must be cautious with their secrets."

---

102   According to *DZ* 1128, 3.5b, a synonym for the Four Reaches (sida 四達) of space.

王母曰：

「此皆太靈羣文，並三天太上所譔。或三皇天真所造校定。或九天父母真人赤童所出。此輩書符藏之於紫陵之臺，隱以靈壇之房，封以華琳之函，蘊以蘭簡之帛，約以北羅之素，印以太帝之璽。

諸名真貴靈，下遊山川。看林岫以眇視，察有心之學夫。或告之以道德。或傳之以天符。諸學道未成者，受此書文，聽四十年授一人。如無其人，八十年可頓授二人。得道者，四百年授一人。無其人，八百年併授二人。得仙者，四千年授一人。如無其人，八千年可頓授二人。得真者，四萬年授一人。如無其人，八萬年頓授二人。昇太上者，四十萬年授一人。

傳非其人，是爲『洩天道』。可授而不傳，是爲『閉天寶』。不計限而妄授者，是爲『輕天老』。受而不敬，是爲『慢天藻』。洩閉輕慢四者，取死之刀斧，延禍之車乘也。」

---

103 A parent-official (fumu guan 父母官) is a common term for a local official (Schipper 1965, 188 n. 4; Smith 1992, 522 n. 132).

The Queen Mother of the West said,

"This collection of writings of the grand numina were collated by the most high gods in the Three Heavens. Some were edited and corrected by the heavenly perfected of the Three Sovereigns. Some were released by the Red Lad, the Perfected Being of the Parent[103] of the Nine Heavens. Such books and talismans are stored in a terrace in the Purple Tumulus, hidden in a room with a numinous altar, sealed in a coffer of patterned jade, wrapped in silks of Lanjian, bound in raw silk of Gujarat,[104] and stamped with the seal of the Grand Emperor.

"Every famous perfected and cherished numen descends to roam across the mountains and rivers. They look out over the tree-lined peaks and inspect those adepts who have a mind. Sometimes they instruct adepts about the Dao and its virtues. Other times the perfected transmit celestial talismans. Once a person whose study of the Dao is not yet complete receives this text, he may transmit it to one person every forty years. If there is no such person, he may transmit it to two people simultaneously every eighty years. Those who have attained the Dao can transmit it to one person every four hundred years. If there is no such person, they can transmit it to two people simultaneously every eight hundred years. Those who have attained transcendence can transmit it to one person every four thousand years. If there is no such person, they can transmit it to two people simultaneously every eight thousand years. Those who have attained perfection can transmit it to one person every forty thousand years. If there is no such person, they can transmit it to two people simultaneously every eighty thousand years. Those who have ascended to heaven most high can transmit it to one person every four hundred thousand years.

"Transmitting it to an unworthy person is called 'divulging the celestial Dao.' To not transmit it to a worthy person is called 'obstructing the heavenly treasure.' To disregard these restrictions and carelessly transmit it is called 'belittling the celestial venerable.' To lack respect for what one has received is called 'disrespecting the writings of heaven.' These four things—divulging, obstructing, belittling, and disrespecting—will lead to a death by knives and axes, for one will ride atop the carriage of misfortune.

---

104 In Buddhist texts, "Beiluo" refers to Gujarat, India (Xingyundashi 2003, 2162a–b). Medieval Daoism authors often borrowed Indian place names for their mysterious and exotic qualities (Zürcher 1980, 107).

泄之者身死道路，受上形而骸裂。閉則目盲耳聾於來生，命凋枉而卒没。輕則鍾禍於父母，詣玄都而考罰。慢則暴終而墮惡道，生棄疾於後世。復有愈兹罪者，則宗斷而族滅。

同道謂之『天親』，同心謂之『地愛』。爲道者當相親授：

共均榮辱
營守真一
珍惜精液
恭養和氣
氣全神歸
必齋靈會
如其不爾
天降爾癘

此皆道之科禁。今故相誡，不可不慎。然此法宜傳，但當以年限齊之爾。若便有其人，不必須限詑而授之也。汝欲授五嶽真形者，董仲舒似其人也。欲行《六甲靈飛左右之符》者，可傳李少君。此二人得道者也。」

王母又命侍女宋靈賓更取一《圖》與帝。靈賓探懷中得一卷，盛以雲錦之囊。

105 Evil destiny, literally an evil path, is an idea adapted from Buddhism referring to the three unfortunate reincarnations that befall sentient beings—animals, hungry ghosts, and beings in hell. Xingyundashi 2003, 4950b–c. For *qiji* 棄疾 as calamities, see *Zuo Tradition*, "Duke Ai" 7 (Durrant et al. 2016, 1872).

"Whoever divulges these texts will walk the path of death, and will be drawn and quartered, the highest punishment.[xxi] Whoever obstructs these texts will be born deaf and blind in the next life, and his lifespan will shrivel away until he sinks into oblivion. Misfortune will rain down on the parents of anyone who belittles the texts, and he will be summoned to the Mystic Metropolis for interrogation and punishment. Whoever disrespects the texts will meet a violent end and succumb to an evil destiny, and he will suffer calamities in future lives.[105] Any adept who repeats these transgressions will cause a rupture in his family line, and his clan will be exterminated.

"Those who follow the same Dao are called 'celestial kin,' and those who are of the same mind are called 'terrestrial friends.'[106] All those who practice this Dao should transmit these texts to one another as they:

> Equally share honor and disgrace,
> While keeping watch over the Perfected One,
> And cherish their seminal fluids,
> While respectfully nourishing harmonious qi.
> With qi whole and spirits restored,
> One must fast before this numinous meeting.[xxii]
> If this is not done,
> Heavenly beings will send down illness.

"These are all the regulations and prohibitions of the Dao. So I warn you now that you must be extremely cautious. It is fine to transmit these texts as long as you follow these guidelines and observe yearly limits. If someone is worthy, you do not necessarily need to wait until the end of the time period to transmit a text to him. If you want to transmit the *True Forms of the Five Sacred Peaks*, you should consider Dong Zhongshu. If you want to circulate the *Twelve Texts*, you should transmit them to Li Shaojun. These two men have already realized the Dao."

The Queen Mother of the West then commanded her attendant girl, Song Lingbin, to give a copy of *Charts of the True Forms* to the emperor. Lingbin pulled from her robe a fascicle kept within a cloudy brocade pouch.

---

106 Schipper (1965, 120 n. 1) notes that celestial kin and terrestrial friends are terms used by adepts when they receive transmission of the Five Talismans in *DZ 388*, 3.7a.

形書精明，俱如向巾器中者。

　　王母起立，手以付帝，又祝曰：

　　天高地卑
　　五嶽鎮形
　　元津激朶
　　滄澤玄精
　　天回九道
　　六和長平
　　太上八會
　　飛天之成
　　真僊節信
　　由茲通靈
　　泄墜滅腐
　　寶歸長生
　　徹其慎之
　　敢告劉生

　　祝畢，授帝。帝拜稽首。

王母曰：「夫始學道符者，宜別祭五嶽諸仙真靈。潔齋而佩之。今亦以六甲雜事。須用節度。相與可明。依案之也。若女遂尅明正身，反惡修善，復三年七月，更來告女要道也。」

　　須臾殿南朱雀窗中忽有一人來窺看仙官。帝驚問：「何人？」

　　王母曰：

「女不識此人邪？是女侍郎東方朔，是我鄰家小兒也。性多滑稽，曾三來偷此桃。此子昔爲太上使，令到方丈助三天司命收錄仙家。朔到方丈，

The calligraphy was exquisite and distinct, and appeared just like the one from the bookbag.

The Queen Mother of the West stood up and presented the texts to the emperor as she made this incantation:

> From the heights of heaven to the depths of earth,
> The Five Sacred Peaks safeguard all forms.
> Overflowing Qi of the Primordial Ford.
> Mysterious essence of the Blue-Green Marsh.
> The Ninefold Dao encircling the heavens.
> The Six Harmonies of everlasting peace.
> The Eight Assemblies most high
> Of those who have flown to the heavens.
> With this insignia of initiation as a perfected transcendent,
> You will be able to make contact with the numina.
> Divulge them and you will fall into destruction and decay;
> Be true to them and your return will be long life.
> Che, be careful with these texts
> That I have dared to reveal to you, my disciple Liu.

When she finished this incantation, she gave them to the emperor. The emperor knelt down and kowtowed.

The Queen Mother of the West said, "One who has just started studying these Daoist talismans should make a special sacrifice to all the transcendent and perfected numina of the Five Peaks. Purify yourself through fasting, and wear them at your waist. Today you have also acquired the *Twelve Texts*. Be sure to follow the rules for their use. One text will help you understand another. Follow them closely. If, hereafter, you can conquer your mind and rectify your body while turning away from evil and cultivating the good, I will come back three years from now in the seventh lunar month to reveal to you the essential Dao."

A moment later, a man appeared in the Vermillion Sparrow Window on the southern side of the basilica, spying on the transcendent officials. The emperor was startled and asked, "Who is that?"

The Queen Mother of the West asked,

"Do you really not know? It is your servant, Dongfang Shuo, the youngest son of one of my neighbors. A mischievous child by nature, he stole my peaches three times. Long ago, this lad, an emissary of the most high gods, was sent on a mission to Fangzhang Isle to help the directors of destinies in the Three Heavens collect records on the transcendent families. But when he arrived at Fangzhang Isle, the only kind of work he did was to play in the mountains and rivers. He never worked together to harmonize with

但務山水游戲。了不共營和氣，擅弄雷電，激波揚風。風雨失時，陰陽錯迕。致令蛟鯨陸行，山崩境壞。海水暴竭，黃鳥宿淵。妨農芸田，沉湎玉酒。失部御之和，虧奉命之科。

　　於是九源丈人廼言之於太上，太上遂謫斥，使在人間。去太清之朝，令處梟濁之鄉。近金華山二仙人及九疑君比爲陳乞，以行原之。」

　　於是帝廼知朔非世俗之徒也。

　　時酒酣周宴，言請粗畢。上元夫人自彈雲林之璈，鳴絃駭調。清音靈朗，玄風四發。廼歌《步玄之曲》。辭曰：

昔涉玄真道
騰步登太霞
負笈造天關
借問太上家
忽過紫微垣
真人列如麻
渌景清飈起
雲蓋映朱葩
蘭宮敞琳闕
碧空啓璃沙
丹臺結空構
暐暐生光華
飛鳳踶薈峙
燭龍倚委蛇
玉胎來絳芝
九色紛相拏

others, but would brazenly make thunderstorms appear, stirring up waves and bringing on gale winds. The seasons went off-kilter, and yin and yang went awry. Even today, water dragons and whales move over the land, and mountains have collapsed and obscured borders. The ocean waters boiled away, and yellow birds made nests in chasms. He impeded farmers tilling the land, and wallowed in jade liquor. He disrupted harmony between the officials and administrators, and violated the protocols demanded by his appointment.

"At this point the elders of the Nine Fonts filed a report about Shuo to the Most High Lord of the Dao, who banished him to the human world. After leaving the court of Grand Purity, he was ordered to live in this putrid and defiled country. Recently, two transcendent beings at Mt. Jinhua and the Lord of Mt. Jiuyi have filed an appeal asking for clemency."

Because of this report, the emperor knew that Shuo was not an ordinary man of this world.

At this point, wine was brought out to conclude the banquet, for their conversation was nearing an end. The Lady of the Upper Prime played a tune on the jade zither from the Cloudy Forest, and the resounding strings lifted the melody upward. These pure tones were bright like the numina, and blew out in all directions like a mystic wind. After this, she sang the song *Pacing the Mystery*. The lyrics went,

> Long ago I started down the path of mysterious Perfection,
> And galloped up to the Grand Aurora Palace.
> With a bookbag on my back, I arrived at the gates of heaven,
> Where I made inquiries in the houses of the most high.
> I quickly passed through the realm of Purple Tenuity,
> Where perfected beings were lined up like stalks of hemp.
> A pellucid gale blew across a crystal-clear vista,
> As vermillion blossoms shone in the cloud canopy.
> The Orchid Palace opened out to gate towers of pale jade,
> And the cyan void spread over orange-jade sand.
> The cinnabar terrace was built with an invisible frame,
> And the radiant blossoms growing there shimmered.
> Soaring phoenixes perched on the edge of its towering eaves,
> As a torch dragon pressed in like a coiling snake.
> A jade embryo produced a scarlet mushroom,
> Whose nine hues intertwined with one another.

挹景練仙骸
萬劫方童牙
誰言壽有終
扶桑不爲查

王母又命侍女田四飛答歌曰：

晨登太霞宮
挹此八玉蘭
夕入玄元闕
采藥掇琅玕
濯足匏瓜河
織女立津盤
吐納挹景雲
味之當一餐
紫微何濟濟
璃輪復朱丹
朝發汗漫府
暮宿句陳垣
去去道不同
且各體所安
二儀設猶存
奚疑億萬椿
莫與世人說
行尸言此難

107　See Li Fengmao 1986a, 32.
108　"Gourd River" perhaps refers to the Milky Way (Smith 1992, 527 n. 148).
109　For this as a region, see *Inner Chapters of the Master Embracing Simplicity* (Ge Hong 1996, 2).
110　A constellation near Polaris (Smith 1992, 527 n. 150).

Drawing in phosphors, I refined my transcendent bones,
And after ten thousand kalpas, I regained my baby teeth.
Whoever says that long life has an end
Has never laid eyes upon Fusang.

The Queen Mother of the West then ordered her attendant girl, Tian Sifei,[107] to sing in reply:

At dawn, I ascended to the Palace of Grand Auroras,
Where I plucked orchids of eight-colored jade.
In the evening, I entered the Mysterious Prime Watchtower,
Where I picked stamens from the gems I have gathered.
I washed my feet as I floated down Gourd River,[108]
And like the Weaver Maiden, I stood at the far other end of the shore.
Breathing in and out as I took hold of phosphors and clouds,
I savored them as if they were a meal.
Oh, how grand and glorious is Purple Tenuity,
With its sun-dog wheels and vermillion cinnabar.
In the morning, I set out for the bureaus of the Boundless Office;[109]
In the evening, I slept on the ramparts of Gouchen.[110]
I traveled far on paths that were never the same,
And yet in each place, I could find rest.
The Two Mechanisms[111] are displayed and both in existence,
Who could doubt that the Cedrela trees[112] live billions of years?
Do not speak of this to anyone in this human world,
For even a walking corpse would say it is impossible.

---

111 See *Traditions of Lord Pei*, p. 31 above.
112 A mythical tree mentioned in *Zhuangzi* that lives for thousands of years. See Schafer 1981–1983, 331 n. 96.

歌畢,因告武帝仙官從者姓名,及冠帶執佩物名,所以得知而紀焉。至明旦,王母別去,上元夫人謂帝曰:「夫李少君者,專念精進,理妙微密。必得道矣。其似未有《六甲靈飛》之文,女當可以示之。」

帝曰:「諾。」於是夫人與王母同乘而去。臨發,人馬龍虎,威儀如初來時。雲氣勃蔚,盡爲香氣。極望西南,良久廼絕。

於是帝既見王母及上元夫人,廼信天下有神仙之事。亦有欲去世計數矣,而淫色、恣性、殺伐不休。兆人怨於勞役,死者怨於無辜。

其年作甘泉宮通天臺,長安蜚廉館。朝鮮王攻遼東都尉,廼募天下死罪擊朝鮮。八月甘泉宮內生芝草九莖。詔曰:「甘泉宮中產芝九莖聯葉。上帝博臨,不異下房。賜朕弘休,其大赦天下,賜雲陽都百戶牛酒。」作《芝房》之歌。

113　The Han name for a kingdom on the Korean peninsula situated near present-day Pyongyang. Here the author may be referring to two expeditions in 109 BCE that established four commanderies on the northern end of the Liaodong peninsula. See Twitchett and Loewe 1995, 446–451.

Once the song was finished, they told Emperor Wu all the names of the transcendent officials and their attendants, as well as the names of all their crowns, sashes, and other objects, so that he would know these things and have a record. At daybreak the Queen Mother of the West was departing, and the Lady of the Upper Prime told the emperor, "Li Shaojun is focused and zealous, circumspect and subtle. Surely, he has already realized the Dao. And yet he still seems to lack the *Twelve Texts*, so you should show them to him."

The emperor said, "I promise to do this." And at that, the Lady and the Queen Mother of the West mounted the same carriage and left together. When they took off, the entourage of men, horses, dragons, and tigers was just as impressive as when they arrived. Puffs of cloudy qi billowed out, spreading fragrance everywhere. The emperor watched far into the distance as the group approached the southwest horizon and finally disappeared.

Because the emperor had seen the Queen Mother of the West and the Lady of the Upper Prime, he firmly believed that divine beings existed in the world. He was even making plans to depart from this world, but he could never quell his carnal desires, indulgent nature, and murderous campaigns. Commoners were aggrieved by corvée labor, while the dead were aggrieved by their unjust executions.

That same year [109 BCE], the emperor completed the construction of the Tongtian Terrace in the Ganquan Palace and the Feilian Lodge in Chang'an. The King of Chosŏn attacked the Liaodong commandery,[113] and those guilty of capital offenses were conscripted for a counterattack. In the eighth month of that year, a nine-stemmed mushroom grew in the Ganquan Palace. His edict read, "A nine-stemmed plant with linked leaves has appeared inside the Ganquan Palace. The High Emperor looks down over all and does not neglect the lowly houses of this earth. He has bestowed upon us great fortune, so let there be a general amnesty in our empire, and may every hundred households in Yunyang City be given meat and wine."[114] He then composed a song called "Mushroom Room."[115]

---

114 Yunyang is the location of a summer palace used by the emperor (Dubs 1954, 90 n. 27.4).
115 This entire story of the miraculously sprouting mushrooms is taken nearly verbatim from the *History of the Former Han* (Dubs 1954, 90).

至元封三年春，作角觝戲三百人。至元封四年，又行幸雍祠五畤。至元封五年，行内守，至於盛唐祠虞舜。于九疑登灊山、天柱山。春三月還至泰山增封。甲子祠高祖于明堂，以配上帝，因朝諸侯王。元封六年，行幸回中作首山宮。三月行幸河東，祠后土。

　　又先以元封二年七月七日，西王母、上元夫人下降於武帝，王母授帝《五嶽真形圖》《靈光生經》。上元夫人授《六甲靈飛、招真、十二事》。

　　王母及上元夫人見帝之日，多所稱說，或延年之訣、致神靈之法、或乘虛之數、步玄之術。諸要妙辭，帝迺自撰爲一卷。及所授《真形經書》、《六甲靈飛之事》，帝迺盛以黃金之箱，封以白玉之函，珊瑚爲軸紫錦爲幬囊。安着栢梁臺上，數自齋戒。整衣服，親詣朝拜，燒香盥漱。然後執省之焉。

　　帝自受書已來，出入六年，意吉自暢，高韻自許，云以爲神真見降，必當度世。強悍氣力，不脩至誠。迺興起臺館，勞弊百姓。坑殺降卒，遠征夷狄。路盈怨嘆，流血皋城。每事不從王母之深言，上元夫人之妙誡。王母遂不復來也。

116　See Dubs 1954, 129–131, for an explanation of these games, as well as various parallel passages below.
117　Emperor Shun, successor to Emperor Yao 堯 and the last of the so called Three Sovereigns and Five Emperors, the legendary rulers of China.
118　Located in present day Henan (Zang Lihe 1972, 675).
119　The soil deity, whose cult became part of state ritual during the Han period (Birrell 1999, 260).

In the spring of the third year of the Yuanfeng era [108 BCE], the emperor staged competitive games with three hundred participants.[116] The following year, he led a tour to Yong and made sacrifices for the Five Lords. In the next year, he led a defensive maneuver, and he traveled to Shengtang, where he made sacrifices to Yu and Shun.[117] He went to Mt. Jiuyi, and then ascended Mt. Qian and Mt. Tianzhu. That spring in the third month, he returned to Mt. Tai and repeated the imperial sacrifice. On the *jiazi* day, he made sacrifices to Gaozu in the Bright Hall and made him equal to the High Emperor, and then he held court with the feudal lords and princes. In the sixth year of the Yuanfeng era [105 BCE], he led a tour to Huizhong and built a palace at Mt. Shou.[118] In the third month, he led a tour of the Yellow River Delta and sacrificed to the Earth Sovereign.[119]

Previously, when the Queen Mother of the West and Lady of the Upper Prime appeared before the emperor on the seventh night of the seventh month in the second year of the Yuanfeng era [109 BCE], the Queen Mother of the West bestowed the *Charts of the True Forms of the Five Sacred Peaks* and the *Living Scripture of Numinous Radiance*. The Lady of the Upper Prime gave him the *Twelve Texts*.

When the Queen Mother of the West and the Lady appeared before the emperor, they spoke about many things, including other formulas for extending life, rituals to summon divine numina, calculations necessary to ride through the void, and techniques to pace the mystery. The emperor compiled their essential and subtle words into one scroll. He stored this scroll, along with the *True Forms Scripture* and the *Twelve Texts* he had received, by putting them in a golden cabinet, binding them in a white jade coffer, and placing them on a dowel made of coral and in a bag of purple brocade. He deposited all the texts at the top of the Boliang Terrace, and frequently held fasts and maintained the precepts there. He donned proper attire as if he were personally calling on the gods, burned incense, washed his hands, and rinsed his mouth. Only then would he study the texts closely.

In the six years that had passed after the emperor received the texts, he gave free rein to his desires and became increasingly pompous, saying that he surely would be saved, since the divine perfected had appeared before him. He became brutal and violent, and no longer cultivated the ultimate precepts. He then erected more lodges and living quarters, imposing a great burden on the common people. He buried prisoners of war alive and went on expeditions to fight the barbarian tribes. The streets were full of people heaving sighs of resentment, as blood flowed down the fields and city walls. At each turn, the emperor did not follow the Queen Mother of the West's profound words and the Lady of the Upper Prime's sublime injunctions. Subsequently, the Queen Mother of the West never again came back to visit him.

到太初元年十一月乙酉，天火燒栢梁臺。於是《真形圖》者凡四卷，共函燒失。王母嘗以武帝不能從訓，故以火災之耳。但帝先承王母言，以元封三年七月齋戒，以《五嶽真形圖》授董仲舒登受。帝又承上元夫人言，以元封四年七月齋戒，以《五帝六甲靈飛十二事》授李少君登寫受。此書得傳行於世者，先傳此二君以存矣。

帝既失書，悔不行德，自知道喪。其後東方朔一旦乘雲龍飛去。同時衆人見從西北上，再仰望。大霧覆之，不知所在。帝愈懊惱，其年禪蒿里，祠后土。東臨渤海，望祠蓬萊。仰天自誓，重要靈應，而終無感。

春還，受計於甘泉。二月，起建章宮。夏五月正曆，以正月爲歲首。色尚黃，數用五。定官名，協律呂。此本王母意也。

至太初二年三月，行幸河東，祠后土。以太初三年正月行幸，東巡海上。夏四月還，脩封泰山。以太初四年起明光宮，改號天漢。元年正月，行幸河東，祠后土。至天漢二年春，行幸東海，還幸回中。三月行幸泰山脩封祠明堂。

---

120 The land of the dead, where nothing grows (Kroll 2015, 153).
121 When the emperor received the yearly accounts of the commanderies and kingdoms (Dubs 1954, 98).

On the *yiyou* day in the eleventh month of the first year in the Taichu era [104 BCE], a fire rained down from heaven upon the Boliang Terrace. As a result, all four fascicles containing the *Charts of the True Forms* were incinerated. The Queen Mother of the West had ordered this conflagration because Emperor Wu did not follow her orders. But prior to this, the emperor had followed the Queen Mother of the West's instructions by observing the fast and precepts in the seventh month of the third year in the Yuanfeng era and bestowing the *Charts of the True Forms of the Five Sacred Peaks* to Dong Zhongshu. The emperor had also followed the words of the Lady of the Upper Prime by observing the fast and precepts in the seventh lunar month of the fourth year of the Yuanfeng era and bestowing the *Twelve Texts* to Li Shaojun. These two texts are being transmitted today because they were first transmitted to these two men, who safeguarded them.

After the emperor lost the books, he regretted not conducting himself properly, and he knew that his chances to attain the Dao had been lost forever. Soon thereafter, at dawn, Dongfang Shuo mounted a dragon and flew off into the clouds. At the time, throngs of people gathered and looked at the northwest skies as he ascended. Then a dense fog enveloped him, and no one knew where he went. The emperor became increasingly vexed and regretful, and that year arranged for an imperial sacrifice at Haoli,[120] and also sacrificed to Houtu. He led his entourage to the Bohai Sea, and gazed off to the Penglai Isles to make sacrifices. While gazing up to the heavens, he made pledges, and repeatedly tried to make the numina respond, but in the end they were unmoved.

The next spring, he held an annual review at the Ganquan Palace.[121] The following month, he started work on the Jianzhang Palace. In the fifth month of that year, he reformed the calendar to ensure that the first moon was on the first of the year. The new imperial color was now yellow, and the era number was made five. He determined the names of official titles and calibrated the tones of the seasonal pitchpipes. These were originally the Queen Mother of the West's ideas.

In the third month of the second year of the Taichu era, he toured Hedong, where he sacrificed to Houtu. In the first month of the next year, he led an imperial tour and an eastern inspection along the shore. In the fourth lunar month of that same year, he returned to conduct imperial sacrifices atop Mt. Tai. In the following year, he built the Mingguang Palace, and then changed the era name to Tianhan. In the first lunar month of the first year of Tianhan, he led another expedition to Hedong, where he sacrificed once again to Houtu. In the spring of the second year of the Tianhan era, he led a tour of Donghai and favored Huizhong with a visit. In the third lunar month, he traveled to Mt. Tai, where he performed the Feng ritual to heaven and made sacrifices in the Bright Hall.

至太始三年五月，行幸東海山，稱萬歲。冬賜行所道戶錢五千餘，鰥寡孤獨者，人帛一匹。

太始四年三月，行幸泰山，祠西王母，求靈應。

征和四年春，行幸東萊，臨大海。清齋，祀王母、上元夫人，求應亦不得。還行幸泰山，脩封。庚寅祀于明堂，改號後元。元年正月，行幸甘泉宮，效泰畤。秋七月地震湧泉。二年春，朝諸侯王於甘泉宮，賜宗室。二月，帝疾，行幸盩厔五柞宮。丁卯帝崩，入殯未央前殿。

三月，葬茂陵。山陵之夕，帝棺自動，而有聲聞宮外。如此數過。又有芳香之氣，異常陵畢。於是墳埏間，大霧門壞。霧經一月許日。

帝塚中先有一玉箱、一玉杖。此二物是帝所蓄用者，忽出在世間。人見其誌，告之有司。有司詰辭：「買者乃商人也。從關外來詣鄘市。見一人於北車卷賣此二物，責素三十匹，錢九萬，即售之。度實不知賣箱杖主名。昨來洛市，

---

122 See a parallel passage in *History of the Former Han* (Dubs 1954, 117–118).
123 A county in Shanxi Province, now written as Zhouzhi 周至 (Zang Lihe 1972, 1286).

In the fifth month of the third year of Taishi era [94 BCE], he led an expedition to the mountains of Donghai, where chants of "Long live the emperor!" were heard. In winter, he gave a gift of five thousand in cash to households along the roads he traveled, and gave one bolt of silk each to widowers, widows, orphans, and the childless.

In the third month of the fourth year of the Taishi era, he went to Mt. Tai again, and this time made sacrifices to the Queen Mother of the West and begged her to respond.

In the spring of the fourth year of the Zhenghe era [89 BCE], the emperor led an expedition to Donglai, where he gazed out over the sea. He held a pure fast and made offerings to the Queen Mother of the West and the Lady of the Upper Prime, but received no response to his requests. On his return, he led an imperial tour to Mt. Tai again and conducted the Feng sacrifice. On the following *gengyin* day, he made sacrifices in the Bright Hall and changed his era title to Houyuan. In the first month of the inaugural year of this era, he led an imperial tour of the Ganquan Palace and made suburban sacrifices toward Mt. Tai.[122] In fall, during the seventh month, there was an earthquake that made the springs gush forth. During spring of the following year [88 BCE], he held court with the feudal lords and princes in the Ganquan Palace, bestowing gifts upon members of the imperial clan. In the second month of that year, the emperor fell ill, but he still led an imperial tour to the Wuzuo Palace in Zhouzhi.[123] On the next *dingmao* day, the emperor passed away. He was laid in state in the antechamber of the Weiyang Palace.

In the third month, he was interred in Maoling.[124] That evening, the emperor's coffin started shaking in the tomb, and those outside the mausoleum heard noises. This happened many times. There was also a fragrant qi that unexpectedly wafted across the burial grounds. After this, a dense fog rolled up the graveyard paths, and the gate to his tomb was smashed. This fog lingered a little longer than a month.

The emperor's tomb contained a jade box and jade staff. These two objects, which the emperor had personally used, suddenly surfaced in the marketplace. When someone discovered the imperial markings on the objects, they reported this to an official. The deposition taken from the seller stated, "I, the seller, am a merchant. When I was in foreign lands, I passed through the Mei City marketplace. There I saw a man in Beiche Alleyway selling these two items for thirty bolts of plain silk and ninety thousand in cash, and I bought them right away. I truly do not know the name of the person who sold this box and staff. I arrived at the marketplace in Luoyang

---

124 The imperial tomb. See Dubs 1954, 119.

因見詰此二物。事實如辭」。有司以聞，二物簿入官，遣商人勿問。

帝未崩時，先詔以雜書四十餘卷，常所讀玩者，使隨身斂於棺內。至延康二年，河東功曹李友入上黨抱犢山採藥。於巖室中得所葬之書，盛以金箱。書卷後題東觀臣姓名，記書月日。

武帝時侍臣，有典書郎冉登。見書及箱，流涕曰：「此是孝武皇帝殯殮時物也。臣時料以著棺中，不知何緣得出耳。」宣帝大愴然驚愕，以書又付武帝廟中。其茂陵安完如故，而書箱玉杖忽出地外。又物尚鮮盛，無點污也。見之者，亦甚惑，不能名之矣。

按《九郁龍真經》云：「得仙之下者，皆先死，過太陰中，練尸骸。度地戶，然後廼得尸解去耳。」

按武帝箱、杖、雜書，先並隨身入槨，廼從無間忽然顯出。貨杖於市，書見山室。自非神變幽妙，孰有如此者乎？明武帝之死，尚未可知應運靈化。

又王莽篡位。到地皇二年，莽使通祭漢家諸陵，言符瑞之意。使者到茂陵，聞地中大噫咤而長嘆者。四使者悚怖，以聞莽。莽曰：「武帝當恨吾祠祭之晚耳」。又特更祭以太牢。

125　A Great Sacrifice is an ancient offering to ancestors made by rulers. See Bodde 1975, 224.

yesterday and am now being questioned about these two items. These events happened exactly as I have described them." The officials recorded his account verbatim, confiscated the two items, and the merchant was released without further interrogation.

Before the emperor died, he issued a decree that more than forty fascicles of various texts that he had often read for pleasure were to be buried with him in his coffin. In the second year of the Yankang era [64 BCE], Li You, a local labor official at the Hedong commandery, went to Mt. Baodu in Shangdang to gather medicinal herbs. There, in a cave on the cliffside, he found all of the emperor's texts stored in a golden box. All of the texts had handwritten notes of the names of all the palace officials, as well as a record of all the important dates of Emperor Wu's reign.

A library clerk named Ran Deng was one of Emperor Wu's courtiers. When he saw these texts and their box, he broke down in tears saying, "These are the things placed alongside the August Filial Martial Emperor when he was interred. I was the one who arranged for these items to be put in his coffin at that time, but I have no idea how they could have gotten out." Emperor Xuan [r. 91–48 BCE] was greatly saddened and distressed by these events, and had the books installed in Emperor Wu's imperial temple. The tomb appeared as before, and yet the books, box, and jade staff had somehow been taken out. Moreover, all these objects were in immaculate condition without the slightest blemish. All who saw them were very perplexed by this and unable to explain it.

According to the *Perfected Scripture of the Dragons of the Nine Adornments*, "Those who attain the inferior arts of transcendence must die, go to the realm of Grand Yin, and then refine their corpse. After this, they will pass back through the doorway to Earth, where they will be able to escape via a simulated corpse."

Emperor Wu's box, staff, and various texts were first interred with his body, but they reemerged in no time at all. The staff and box were sold in the market, and the texts were discovered in a mountain cave. If this is not a miracle of spirit transformation, how else can it be explained? Although Emperor Wu clearly died, no one knows whether he was truly destined for such a numinous transformation.

Later, Wang Mang usurped the throne. In the second year of the Dihuang era [15 CE], Mang sent envoys to arrange for sacrifices at the Han family's imperial tumuli, and said he hoped this might cause an auspicious sign to appear. When the envoys reached Wu's tomb, they heard wails of lament and long grieving sighs. The four envoys were horrified and scared by this, and reported it to Mang. Mang replied, "This happened only because Emperor Wu begrudges me for being late with my sacrifice." After this, Wang arranged for a Great Sacrifice to be made.[125]

所葬書目

《老子經》二卷
《太上紫文》十三卷
《靈蹻經》六卷
《太素中胎經》六卷
《天柱經》九卷
《六龍步玄文》七卷
《馬皇受真術》四卷。

These are the titles buried with Emperor Wu:

Scripture of Laozi, two scrolls
Most High Purple Writs, thirteen scrolls
Scripture of Numinous Bravery, six scrolls
Scripture of the Central Embryo of Grand Simplicity, six scrolls
Scripture of the Heavenly Pillar, nine scrolls
Writ of the Six Dragons Pacing the Mystery, seven scrolls
Perfected Techniques Received by Mahuang, four scrolls

Text-Critical Endnotes

i. Reading *qi* 齊 as *zhai* 齋.
ii. *Extensive Records of the Taiping Era* (Li Fang 2003, 13) reads *shi* 侍 as *zaice* 在側.
iii. Reading *xuan* 懸 for *xian* 縣.
iv. Reading *cheng* 乘 for *cheng* 桀.
v. In other versions, this is written as "canopied carriages" (*xuanche* 軒車), which are flanked by "celestial horses" (*tianma* 天馬) (Schipper 1965, 71; Smith 1992, 483).
vi. Reading *huang* 簧 as *heng* 鐄.
vii. Reading *chun* 椿 as *chuan* 踳.
viii. Reading *zheng* 正 for *zheng* 政.
ix. Schipper (1965, 86) reads *yu* 玉 as *wang* 王.
x. Reading *lang* 閬 as *yin* 飲, based on *DZ* 1138, 53.4b.
xi. Reading *yuan* 圓 as *yuan* 園, based on *DZ* 1138, 53.4b. That version also reads rose-gem (*qiong* 瓊) for golden (*jin* 金).
xii. Reading Jing 精 as Ji 積, based on *DZ* 1032, 114.11b and 115.11b.
xiii. Reading *ming* 名 as *ming* 命.
xiv. Alternative versions of the text read, "I also want to let those in despair know that between heaven and earth there exist these wonderful, true things quite sufficient to refute unbelieving madmen" 知天地間有此靈真之事，足以卻不信之狂夫耳 (Schipper 1965, 106; Smith 1992, 511–512).
xv. *Extensive Records of the Taiping Era* reads *shi* 是 as *ci* 此 (Li Fang 2003, 20).
xvi. Reading Bantong 版桐 as Bantong 板桐, one of the three peaks of Mt. Kunlun (Ge Hong 1996, 198).
xvii. Reading *dou* 蚪 as *jiu* 蚪.
xviii. Reading *qi* 齊 as *zhai* 齋.
xix. In *DZ* 1032, 80.14a, this couplet is the first and last line of the following two couplets: If he violates the injunctions against divulging them, misfortunes will certainly cause his family to topple. If he goes against the celestial

perfected, he will certainly be plunged into the netherworld. 違犯泄漏，禍必族傾。反是天真，必沉幽冥。

xx. Reading *dong* 洞 as a scribal error for *dun* 沌.
xxi. Reading *shang* 上 for *tu* 土, based on fascicle 3 of *Extensive Records of the Taiping Era* (Li Fang 2003, 22).
xxii. Reading *qi* 齊 as *zhai* 齋.

Appendix: List of Titles from the *Daoist Canon of the Zhengtong Era*

Based on Schipper and Verellen 2004, 1392–1440

DZ 7   *Dadong yujing* 大洞玉經 [Great Cavern's Jade Scripture]

DZ 87   *Yuanshi wuliang duren shangpin miaojing sizhu* 元始無量度人上品妙經四註 [The Four Commentaries on the Miraculous Scripture of the Highest Form of the Primordial Commencement's Immeasurable Powers of Salvation]

DZ 167   *Dongxuan lingbao zhenling weiye tu* 洞玄靈寶真靈位業圖 [Cavernous Mystery Numinous Treasure Table of the Ranks and Functions in the Pantheon]

DZ 179   *Taiwei lingshu ziwen xianji zhenji shangjing* 太微靈書紫文仙忌真記上經 [Upper Scripture of the Grand Tenuity's Purple Writs and the Perfected Record of the Transcendent Taboos]

DZ 184   *Taizhen yudi siji mingke jing* 太真玉帝四極明科經 [Sworn Code of the Four Bournes of the Grand Perfected Jade Emperor]

DZ 219   *Lingbao wuliang duren shangjing dafa* 靈寶無量度人上經大法 [Numinous Treasure Great Rites of the Book of Universal Salvation]

DZ 292   *Han Wudi neizhuan* 漢武帝內傳 [Inner Tradition of Han Emperor Wu]

DZ 298   *Lishi zhenxian tidao tongjian houji* 歷世真仙體道通鑑後集 [Continuation of the Comprehensive Mirror of the Transcendents Who Embodied the Dao through the Ages]

DZ 302   *Zhoushi mingtong ji* 周氏冥通記 [Mr. Zhou's Records of His Communications with the Invisible World]

DZ 303   *Ziyang zhenren neizhuan* 紫陽真人內傳 [Inner Tradition of the Perfected Purple Yang]

DZ 304   *Maoshan zhi* 茅山志 [Monograph on Mt. Mao]

DZ 324   *Shangqing wuchang biantong wanhua yuming jing* 上清五常變通萬化鬱冥經 [Supreme Purity Airy and Mysterious Scripture on the Universal Metamorphosis and Ten Thousand Transformations of the Five Permanent Ones]

DZ 331   *Taishang huangting neijing yujing* 太上黃庭內景玉經 [Most High Jade Classic of the Yellow Court's Inner Phosphors]

DZ 354　*Shangqing sanyuan yujian sanyuan bujing* 上清三元玉檢三元布經 [Supreme Purity Three Primes' Jade Rule and the Three Female Primes' Promulgated Scripture]

DZ 388　*Taishang lingbao wufuxu* 太上靈寶五符序 [Most High Prolegomena to the Five Numinous-Treasure Talismans]

DZ 394　*Shangqing taiyi jinque yuxi jinzhen ji* 上清太一金闕玉璽金真紀 [Supreme Purity Golden Transcendent Annals of the Jade Seal of the Supreme One's Golden Porte]

DZ 421　*Dengzhen yinjue* 登真隱訣 [Secret Instructions for the Ascent to Perfection]

DZ 435　*Taishang yuchen yuyi jielin ben riyue tu* 太上玉晨鬱儀結璘奔日月圖 [Illustrations of the Flight of Most High Jade Dawn to the Sun and the Moon of Streaming Regalia and Knotted Spangles]

DZ 581　*Lingbao liuding bifa* 靈寶六丁祕法 [Numinous Treasure Secret Procedure Concerning the Six Ding]

DZ 598　*Shizhou ji* 十洲記 [Record of the Ten Continents]

DZ 599　*Dongtian fudi yuedu mingshan ji* 洞天福地嶽瀆名山記 [Record of Cavern-Heavens, Auspicious Sites, Holy Mountains, and Conduits, as Well as of Famous Mountains]

DZ 781　*Xuanpin lu* 玄品錄 [Record of Occultists]

DZ 783　*Yongcheng jixian lu* 墉城集仙錄 [Records of the Assembled Transcendents of the Fortified Walled City]

DZ 876　*Taishang wuxing qiyuan kongchang jue* 太上五星七元空常訣 [Most High Instructions of the Five Planets, the Seven Original Ones, and Kong-Chang]

DZ 1016　*Zhen'gao* 真誥 [Declarations of the Perfected]

DZ 1032　*Yunji qiqian* 雲笈七籤 [Seven Slips from a Cloudy Bookbag]

DZ 1128　*Daomen jingfa xiangcheng cixu* 道門經法相承次序 [The Order of Succession of the Daoist Scripture Legacy]

DZ 1130　*Daodian lun* 道典論 [Discussion of the Daoist Classics]

DZ 1138　*Wushang biyao* 無上祕要 [Essence of Supreme Secrets]

DZ 1139　*Sandong zhunang* 三洞珠囊 [Pearlbag of the Three Caverns]

DZ 1168　*Taishang Laojun zhongjing* 太上老君中經 [Lord Lao Most High's Book of the Center]

DZ 1248　*Sandong qunxian lu* 三洞群仙錄 [Records of the Multitude of Transcendents of the Three Caverns]

DZ 1281　*Wuyue zhenxing xulun* 五嶽真形序論 [Introductory Treatises to the True Forms of the Five Sacred Peaks]

APPENDIX

DZ 1294 *Shangqing huangshu guoduyi* 上清黃書過度儀 [Supreme Purity Yellow Book's Ritual of Passage]

DZ 1312 *Taishang dadao yuqing jing* 太上大道玉清經 [Scripture of Jade Purity of the Great Dao Most High]

DZ 1314 *Dongzhen taishang suling dongyuan dayou miaojing* 洞真太上素靈洞元大有妙經 [Cavernous Perfection Most High Wondrous Scripture of the Immaculate Numen Celestial Palace and Penetrating Mystery of the Great Existence Heaven]

DZ 1315 *Dongzhen shangqing qingyao zishu jin'gen zhongjing* 洞真上清青要紫書金根眾經 [Cavernous Perfection Supreme Purity Purple Book of the Green Waist with the Combined Scriptures of the Golden Root]

DZ 1317 *Dongzhen shangqing kaitian santu qixing yidu jing* 洞真上清開天三圖七星移度經 [Cavernous Perfection Supreme Purity Scripture on Dipper Transfer with Three Limits for Opening Heaven]

DZ 1329 *Taishang jiuchi banfu wudi neizhen jing* 太上九赤班符五帝內真經 [Nine Red Spotted Talismans of the Five Emperors' Inward Contemplation]

DZ 1330 *Dongzhen taiyi dijun taidan yinshu dongzhen xuanjing* 洞真太一帝君太丹隱書洞真玄經 [Cavernous Perfection Supreme One Imperial Lord's Grand Elixir Hidden Book from the Mysterious Scripture of Cavernous Perfection]

DZ 1343 *Dongzhen huangshu* 洞真黃書 [Cavernous Perfection Yellow Book]

DZ 1377 *Shangqing taishang jiuzhen zhongjing jiangsheng shendan jue* 上清太上九真中經降生神丹訣 [Supreme Purity Most High Divine Elixir Instructions of Incarnation from the Central Scripture of the Nine Perfected]

DZ 1389 *Shangqing gaosheng taishang dadao jun dongzhen jinyuan bajing yulu* 上清高聖太上大道君洞真金元八景玉錄 [Supreme Purity Most High Cavernous Perfection Golden Prime Eight Phosphors Jade Record of the High Sage Lord of the Great Dao]

Bibliography

Editions

Our translations of Yang Xi's inner traditions and the *Inner Tradition of Han Emperor Wu* rely upon texts in the following editions:

A: Li Yongcheng 李永晟, ed. 2012. *Yunji qiqian* 雲笈七籤 [Seven Slips from a Cloudy Bookbag]. 5 vols. Zhonghua shuju.
B: Sanjiaben 三家本. 1988. *Zhengtong Daozang* 正統道藏 [Daoist Canon of the Zhengtong Era]. Wenwu chubanshe; Shanghai shudian; Tianjin guji chubanshe.
C: Wang Yunwu 王雲五, ed., 1935. *Congshu jicheng* 叢書集成 [Compendium of Collected Works]. Shangwu yinshuguan.
D: Zhang Jiyu 張繼禹, ed. 2004. *Zhonghua daozang* 中華道藏 [Daoist Canon of China]. 49 vols. Huaxia chubanshe.

Traditions of Lord Pei, the Perfected Being of Pure Numinosity: (A) 2263–2287; (B) 105.1a–26b; (D) 29.808c–818a.
Traditions of Lord Su, Upper Chamberlain of the Mysterious Continent: (A) 2244–2247; (B) 104.1a–4b; (D) 29.801c–802b.
Inner Tradition of Lord Wang, Perfected Being of Pure Vacuity: (A) 2288–2294; (B) 106.1a–8a; (D) 29.818b–820c.
Inner Tradition of the Lady of the Southern Sacred Peak, Primal Lord of Purple Vacuity: (A) 53–56; (B) 4.6a–10a; (D) 29.51a–52a.
Traditions of the Perfected Director of Destinies, Grand Prime Perfected Being and Upper Chamberlain of the Eastern Sacred Peak: (A) 2254–2262; (B) 104.10b–20a; (D) 29.804c–808b.
Inner Tradition of Han Emperor Wu: (B) 292, 1a–31a; (C) 3436–3453; (D) 46.160a–171c.

Translations

Berkowitz, Alan J. 1996. "Records of Occultists." In *Religions of China in Practice*, edited by Donald S. Lopez, 446–470. Princeton University Press.
Cahill, Suzanne. 1993. "Mao Ying." In *Transcendence and Divine Passion: The Queen Mother of the West in Medieval China*, 183–189. Stanford University Press.
Campany, Robert Ford. 2002. *To Live as Long as Heaven and Earth: A Translation and Study of Ge Hong's Traditions of Divine Transcendents*. University of California Press.

Pettit, J. E. E., and Chao-jan Chang. 2020. *A Library of Clouds: The Scripture of the Immaculate Numen and the Rewriting of Daoist Texts*. University of Hawai'i Press.

Pettit, J. E. E., and Matthew Wells. 2020. "The Revelation of Hagiographies in Early Daoism: A Case Study of the Traditions of Lord Pei." *Asia Major*, 3rd Series 33 (2): 1–24.

Raz, Gil. 2008. "The Way of the Yellow and the Red: Re-examining the Sexual Initiation Rite of Celestial Master Daoism." *Nan Nü: Men, Women, and Gender in Early and Imperial China* 10 (1): 86–120.

Schipper, Kristofer Marinus. 1965. *L'Empereur Wou des Han dans la légende taoïste: Han Wou-Ti nei-tchouan* [Emperor Wu of the Han in Daoist Legend: Han Wudi neizhuan]. Publications de l'École française d'Extrême-Orient.

Smith, Thomas E. 1992. "Ritual and the Shaping of Narrative: The Legend of the Han Emperor Wu." PhD diss., University of Michigan.

Secondary Scholarship

Campany, Robert Ford. 2009. *Making Transcendents: Ascetics and Social Memory in Early Medieval China*. University of Hawai'i Press.

Chang Chao-jan 張超然. 2008. "Xipu jiaofa ji qi zhenghe: Dong Jin Nanchao Daojiao Shangqingpai de jichu yanjiu" 系譜教法及其整合：東晉南朝道教上清派的基礎研究 [The Integration of Pedagogy and Genealogy: Eastern Jin and Southern Dynasties Shangqing Daoism]. PhD diss., Cheng-chi University.

Chang Chao-jan 張超然. 2012. "Chuanshou yu jiaocai: *Qingling zhenren Peijun zhuan* zhong de wuling fa" 傳授與教材：《清靈真人裴君傳》中的五靈法 [Teaching and Teaching Materials: The Five Spirit Method in the *Legend of Lord Pei, the Pure Numen Perfected Being*], *Huaren zongjiao yanjiu* 1: 109–134.

Chen Zhaozhen 陳兆禎. 1980. "*Han Wu gushi, Han Wu neizhuan, Han Wu mingdongji* yanjiu" 漢武故事漢武內傳漢武冥洞記研究 [Research on the *Story of Han Emperor Wu*, *Inner Tradition of Han Emperor Wu*, and *Han Emperor Wu Cavern Record*]. MA thesis, Furen University.

Esposito, Monica. 2004. "Sun-Worship in China: The Roots of Shangqing Taoist Practices of Light." *Cahiers d'Extrême-Asie* 14: 345–402.

Gao Lifen 高莉芬. 2020. "Busi yu changsheng: *Han Wudi neizhuan* zhong de Xiwangmu ji qi xiandao changsheng shu" 不死與長生：《漢武帝內傳》中的西王母及其仙道長生術 [Immortality and Long Life: Queen Mother of the West and the Transcendent Arts of Longevity in the *Inner Tradition of Han Emperor Wu*]. *Shida xuebao* 師大學報 65 (2): 1–25.

Kamitsuka Yoshiko 神塚淑子. 1999. *Rikuchō Dōkyō shisō no kenkyū* 六朝道教思想の研究 [Research in Six Dynasties Daoism]. Sōbunsha.

Kominami Ichirō 小南一郎. 1975. "*Kan Butei naiden* no seiritsu" 漢武帝內傳の成立 [The Creation of the *Inner Tradition of Han Emperor Wu*]. *Tōhō gakuhō* 東方学報 48: 183–227.

Kominami Ichirō 小南一郎. 1981. "*Kan Butei naidan* no seiritsu" 漢武帝內傳の成立 [The Creation of the *Inner Tradition of Han Emperor Wu*]. *Tōhō gakuhō* 東方学報 153: 423–546.

Kroll, Paul W. 1981. "Review of *Biographie d'un taoïste légendaire: Tcheou Tseu-yang*, by Manfred Porkert." *Chinese Literature: Essays, Articles, Reviews* 3 (1): 163–167.

Li Fengmao 李豐楙. 1982. "*Han Wu niezhuan* de zhucheng ji qi liuchuan" 漢武內傳的著成及其流傳 [The Authorship and Transmission of the *Inner Tradition of Han Emperor Wu*]. *Youshi xuezhi* 幼師學誌 17 (2): 21–55.

Li Fengmao 李豐楙. 1986a. "*Han Wu neizhuan* yanjiu" 漢武內傳研究 [Research on the *Inner Tradition of Han Emperor Wu*]. In *Liuchao Sui Tang xiandao lei xiaoshuo yanjiu* 六朝隋唐仙道類小說研究, 21–122. Taiwan xuesheng shuju.

Liu Yuan-ju 劉苑如. 2000. "Liuchao zhiguai Han Wu xilie de 'xiaoshuo' shi tan" 六朝志怪漢武系列的「小說」試探 [Six Dynasties Anomalous Tales and the Emperor Wu Stories]. *Zhongguo wenzhe zhuankan* 中國文哲專刊 17: 194–256.

Miller, James. 2008. *The Way of Highest Clarity: Nature, Vision, and Revelation in Medieval China*. Three Pines Press.

Porkert, Manfred. 1979. *Biographie d'un taoïste légendaire: Tcheou Tseu-yang* [Biography of a Legendary Daoist: Zhou Ziyang]. Collège de France, Institut des hautes études chinoises.

Robinet, Isabelle. 1981. "Review of *Biographie d'un taoïste légendaire: Tcheou Tseu-yang*, by Manfred Porkert." *T'oung Pao* 67 (1–2): 123–135.

Robinet, Isabelle. 1984. *La révélation du Shangqing dans l'histoire du Taoïsme* [The Revelation of Shangqing in the History of Daoism]. École française d'Extrême-Orient.

Smith, Thomas E. 2017. "Xu Mi's Network: A Different Perspective on Early Higher Clarity Daoism." *Journal of Daoist Studies* 10: 15–48.

Strickmann, Michel. 1977. "The Mao Shan Revelations: Taoism and the Aristocracy." *T'oung Pao* 63 (1): 1–64.

Xie Conghui (Hsieh Tsung-hui) 謝聰輝. 1999. "Xiuzhen yu jiangzhen: Liuchao Daojiao Shangqing jingpai xianzhuan yanjiu" 修真與降真：六朝道教上清經派仙傳研究 [Cultivation and Perfection: Research on the Hagiographies of the Daoist Lineage Supreme Purity in the Six Dynasties]. PhD diss., Taiwan shifan daxue.

Yoshioka Yoshitoyo 吉岡義豐. 1955. *Dōkyō kyōten shiron* 道教経典史論 [A History of Daoist Scriptures]. Dōkyō kankōkai.

Zhang Jinghua 張景華 and Qin Taichang 秦太昌. 2001. "Jin Wei Huacun xiudao Yangluoshan kao" 晉魏華存修道陽洛山考 [A Study of the Daoist Practice of Wei Huacun of the Jin Dynasty at Mt. Yangluo]. *Zhongguo daojiao* 中國道教 1: 40–43.

Works Cited

Andersen, Poul. 1990. "The Practice of Bugang." *Cahiers d'Extrême-Asie* 5: 15–53.

Andersen, Poul. 2019. *The Paradox of Being: Truth, Identity, and Images in Daoism.* Harvard-Yenching Institute.

Ban Gu 班固. 1997. *Hanshu* 漢書 [History of the Former Han]. Zhonghua shuju.

Birrell, Anne. 1999. *The Classic of Mountains and Seas*. Penguin Books.

Bodde, Derk. 1975. *Festivals in Classical China: New Year and Other Annual Observances during the Han Dynasty, 206 b.c.–a.d. 220*. Princeton University Press.

Bokenkamp, Stephen R. 1986. "The Ledger on the Rhapsody: Studies in the Art of the T'ang fu." PhD diss., University of California, Berkeley. 1986.

Bokenkamp, Stephen R. 1996. "Declarations of the Perfected." In *Religions of China in Practice*, edited by Donald S. Lopez, 166–179. Princeton University Press.

Bokenkamp, Stephen R. 1997. *Early Daoist Scriptures*. University of California Press.

Bokenkamp, Stephen R. 2007. *Ancestors and Anxiety: Daoism and the Birth of Rebirth in China*. University of California Press.

Boltz, Judith. 2011. "Da Jin Xuandu baozang." In *The Encyclopedia of Taoism*, edited by Fabrizio Pregadio, 292–293. Routledge.

Bray, Francesca. 2015. "Qinmin yaoshu." In *Early Medieval Chinese Texts: A Bibliographical Guide*, edited by Cynthia L. Chennault et al., 232–241. University of California Press.

Campany, Robert Ford. 2014. "The Sword Scripture: Recovering and Interpreting a Lost 4th-Century Daoist Method for Cheating Death." *Daoism: Religion, History, and Society* 6: 33–84.

Chang Chao-jan 張超然. 1998. "Liuchao Daojiao Shangqing jingpai cunsifa yanjiu" 六朝道教上清經派存思法研究 [Research on Supreme Purity Meditation Techniques in Six Dynasties Daoism]. MA thesis, National Chengchi University.

Chen Guying 陳鼓應, ed. 1994. *Zhuangzi* jinzhu jinyi 莊子今注今譯 [Modern Commentary and Translation of *Zhuangzi*]. Zhonghua shuju.

Chen Shou 陳壽. 1997. *Sanguo zhi* 三國志 [*Record of the Three Kingdoms*]. Zhonghua shuju.

Cheng Junying 程俊英 and Jiang Jianyuan 蔣見元, eds. 1999. *Shijing* zhuxi 詩經注析 [Analysis and Commentary to the *Classic of Poetry*]. Zhonghua shuju.

Como, Michael. 2015. "Daoist Deities in Ancient Japan: Household Deities, Jade Women, and Popular Religious Practice." In *Daoism in Japan: Chinese Traditions and Their Influence on Japanese Religious Culture*, edited by Jeffrey L. Richey, 24–36. Routledge.

Dubs, Homer, trans. 1954. *The History of the Former Han Dynasty*. Vol. 2. Waverly.

Durrant, Steven, David Schaberg, and Wai-yee Li, trans. 2016. *"Zuo Tradition" – "Zuozhuan": Commentary on the "Spring and Autumn Annals."* University of Washington Press.

Espesset, Grégoire. 2011. "Yang Xi." In *The Encyclopedia of Taoism*, edited by Fabrizio Pregadio, 1147–1148. Routledge.

Fahr, Paul. 2021. "On the Meaning of *shi* 事 in Han Historiography." *T'oung Pao* (107): 189–196.

Fang Xuanling 房玄齡, ed. 1997. *Jinshu* 晉書 [History of the Jin]. Zhonghua shuju.

Felt, D. Jonathan. 2021. *Structures of the Earth: Metageographies of Early Medieval China*. Harvard University Asia Center.

Ge Hong 葛洪. 1996. *"Baopuzi" neipian jiaoshi* 抱朴子內篇校釋 [The Inner Chapters of the *Master Embracing Simplicity*, with Commentary]. Zhonghua shuju.

Graham, A. C., trans. 1960. *The "Book of Lieh-Tzu": A Classic of Tao*. Columbia University Press.

Harper, Donald. 1998. *Early Chinese Medical Literature: The Mawangdui Medical Manuscripts*. Kegan Paul International.

Harper, Donald. 2017. *Books of Fate and Popular Culture in Early China: The Daybook Manuscripts of the Warring States, Qin, and Han*. Brill.

Hawkes, David. 1959. *The Songs of the South: An Ancient Chinese Anthology*. Oxford University Press.

Huang, Shih-shan Susan. 2012. *Picturing the True Form: Daoist Visual Culture in Traditional China*. Harvard University Asia Center.

Hucker, Charles O. 1985. *A Dictionary of Official Titles in Imperial China*. Stanford University Press.

Jin Kaicheng 金開誠, ed. 1999. *Qu Yuan ji jiaozhu* 屈原集校注 [Collated and Annotated Edition of Qu Yuan's Works]. Zhonghua shuju.

Kleeman, Terry. 2011. "San guan." In *The Encyclopedia of Taoism*, edited by Fabrizio Pregadio, 833–834. Routledge.

Kleeman, Terry. 2016. *Celestial Masters: History and Ritual in Early Daoist Communities*. Harvard University Asia Center.

Knechtges, David R. 1982. *Wen Xuan, or, Selections of Refined Literature*. Princeton University Press.

Knechtges, David R. 1987. *Wen Xuan, or, Selections of Refined Literature*. Vol. 2: *Rhapsodies on Sacrifices, Hunting, Travel, Sightseeing, Palaces and Halls, Rivers and Seas*. Princeton University Press.

Knechtges, David R. 1996. *Wen Xuan, or, Selections of Refined Literature*. Vol. 3: *Rhapsodies on Natural Phenomena, Birds and Animals, Aspirations and Feelings, Sorrowful Laments, Literature, Music, and Passions*. Princeton University Press.

Knoblock, John, and Jeffrey Riegel, trans. *The Annals of Lü Buwei: A Complete Translation and Study*. Stanford, CA: Stanford University Press, 2000.

Kohn, Livia. 1995. *Laughing at the Dao: Debates among Buddhists and Taoists in Medieval China*. Princeton University Press.

Kohn, Livia. 2011. "Sanqing." In *The Encyclopedia of Taoism*, edited by Fabrizio Pregadio, 840–844. Routledge.

Kroll, Paul W. 1984. "Li Po's 'Rhapsody on the Great P'eng Bird.'" *Journal of Chinese Religions* 12: 1–17.
Kroll, Paul W. 1996. "On 'Far Roaming.'" *Journal of the American Oriental Society* 116 (4): 653–669.
Kroll, Paul W. 1997. "Li Po's Purple Haze." *Taoist Resources* 7 (2): 21–37.
Kroll, Paul W. 2003. "The Divine Songs of the Lady of Purple Tenuity [Tzu-wei Fu-jen]." In *Studies in Early Medieval Chinese Literature and Cultural History: In Honor of Richard B. Mather and Donald Holzman*, edited by Paul W. Kroll and David R. Knechtges, 149–211. T'ang Studies Society.
Kroll, Paul W. 2015. *A Student's Dictionary of Classical and Medieval Chinese*. Brill.
Kubo Noritada 窪德忠. 1956. "Nihon ni denrai shita sanshi shinkō no ichi sokumen: sanshi kujohō o chūshin toshite" 日本に伝来した三尸信仰の一側面：三尸駆除法を中心として [One Facet of the Three Worms Belief in Japanese Legend: With an Emphasis on Methods for Expelling the Three Worms]. *Tōyō bunka kenkyūsho kiyō* 東洋文化研究所紀要 9 (3): 127–216.
Lagerwey, John. 1975. "A Translation of the Annals of Wu and Yüeh, Part I." PhD diss., Harvard University.
Lagerwey, John. 1981. *Wu-shang pi-yao: Somme taoïste du VIe siècle* [A Daoist Summa of the 6th Century]. École française d'Extrême-Orient.
"Laozi" jiaoshi 老子校釋 [Annotated and Collated *Laozi*]. 1996. Zhonghua shuju.
Li Daoping 李道平, ed. 1994. *"Zhou yi" jijie suanshu* 周易集解纂疏 [Collected Commentaries of the *Zhou Changes*]. Zhonghua shuju.
Li Daoyuan 酈道元. 2007. *"Shuijing" zhu* 水經注 [Commentary on the *Water Classic*]. Zhonghua shuju.
Li Fang 李昉. 1967. *Taiping yulan* 太平御覽 [Imperial Reader from the Taiping Era]. Taiwan shangwu yinshuguan.
Li Fang 李昉. 2003. *Taiping guangji* 太平廣記 [Extensive Records of the Taiping Era]. Zhonghua shuju.
Li Fengmao 李豐楙. 1986b. *Liuchao Sui Tang xiandao lei xiaoshuo yanjiu* 六朝隋唐仙道類小說研究 [Research on the Daoist Short Stories of the Six Dynasties, Sui, and Tang]. Taiwan xuesheng.
Li, Jianmin. 2008. "Etiology, the Medical Canon, and the Transformation of Medical Techniques before the Tang." In *Early Chinese Religion*, part 1: *Shang through Han (1250 bc–220 ad)*, edited by John Lagerwey and Marc Kalinowski, 1103–1150. Brill.
Li Yongcheng 李永晟, ed. 2012. *Yunji qiqian* 雲笈七籤 [Seven Slips from a Cloudy Bookbag]. 5 vols. Zhonghua shuju.
Liu, Tseng-kuei. 2008. "Taboos: An Aspect of Belief in the Qin and Han." In *Early Chinese Religion*, part 1: *Shang through Han (1250 bc–220 ad)*, edited by John Lagerwey and Marc Kalinowski, 881–948. Brill.
Liu Xu 劉昫. 1975. *Jiu Tang shu* 舊唐書 [Old History of the Tang]. Zhonghua shuju.

Loewe, Michael. 2000. *A Biographical Dictionary of the Qin, Former Han and Xin Periods (221 bc–ad 24)*. Brill.

Lu Qinli 逯欽立, ed. 1998. *Xian Qin, Han, Wei-Jin, Nanbeichao shi* 先秦漢魏晉南北朝詩 [Poetry of the Pre-Qin, Han, Wei-Jin, and Northern and Southern Dynasties Periods]. Zhonghua shuju.

Major, John, Sarah A. Queen, Andrew Meyer, and Harold Roth, trans. and eds. 2010. *The "Huainanzi": A Guide to the Theory and Practice of Government in Early Han China*. Columbia University Press.

Maspero, Henri, and Frank A. Kierman Jr., trans. 1981. *Taoism and Chinese Religion*. University of Massachusetts Press.

Mather, Richard B., trans. 2002. *A New Account of Tales of the World*. 2nd ed. University of Michigan Center for Chinese Studies.

Morohashi Tetsuji 諸橋轍次, ed. 1955–1960. *Dai kan-wa jiten* 大漢和辭典 [Comprehensive Chinese-Japanese Dictionary]. Taishūkan shoten.

Mugitani Kunio. 2011a. "Huoling" In *The Encyclopedia of Taoism*, edited by Fabrizio Pregadio, 532–533. Routledge.

Mugitani Kunio. 2011b. "Liujia and Liuding." In *The Encyclopedia of Taoism*, edited by Fabrizio Pregadio, 695–697. Routledge.

Needham, Joseph, and Wang Ling. 1959. *Science and Civilisation in China*, vol. 3: *Mathematics and the Sciences of the Heavens and the Earth*. Cambridge University Press.

Ōno Yuji 大野裕司. 2006. "Gyokunyo henbai kyokuho ni tsuite" 玉女反閉局法について [On the Protocols for 'Closing the Door' with Jade Women]. *Hokkaido-daigaku daigakuin bungaku kenkyū-ka* 北海道大学大学院文学研究科 (6): 35–53.

Ouyang Xiu 歐陽修. 1975. *Xin Tang shu* 新唐書 [New History of the Tang]. Zhonghua shuju.

Peng Dingqiu 彭定球. 1960. *Quan Tang shi* 全唐詩 [Complete Anthology of Tang Poetry]. Zhonghua shu ju.

Pettit, J. E. E. 2004. "Weaving Maid Goddess, a Lover of Men: Medieval Rhapsodies on the Seventh Night." MA thesis, University of Colorado.

Pettit, J. E. E. 2013a. "Learning from Maoshan: Temple Construction in Early Medieval China." PhD diss., Indiana University.

Pettit, J. E. E. 2013b. "The Reclamation of Maoshan." *Studies in Chinese Religions* 1: 79–104.

Pregadio, Fabrizio. 2004. "The Notion of 'Form' and the Ways of Liberation in Daoism." *Cahiers d'Extrême-Asie* 14: 95–130.

Pregadio, Fabrizio, ed. 2011. *The Encyclopedia of Taoism*. Routledge.

Qu Shouyuan 屈守元 and Chang Sichun 常思春, eds. 1996. *Han Yu quanji jiaozhu* 韓愈全集校注 [The Complete Works of Han Yu, Collated with Commentary]. Sichuan daxue chubanshe.

Qu Wanli 屈萬里 and Wang Yunwu 王雲五, eds. 2009. *Shangshu* jinzhu jinyi 尚書今注今譯 [*Classic of Documents*, Modern Annotation and Translation]. Taiwan shangwu yinshuguan.

Raz, Gil. 2004. "Creation of Tradition: The Five Talismans of the Numinous Treasure and the Formation of Early Daoism." PhD diss., Indiana University.

Raz, Gil. 2012a. "Imbibing the Universe: Methods of Ingesting the Five Sprouts." *Asian Medicine* 7: 65–100.

Raz, Gil. 2012b. *The Emergence of Daoism: Creation of Tradition*. Routledge.

Read, Bernard Emms. 1977. *Chinese Medicinal Plants from the "Pen ts'ao kang mu."* 1936. Reprint: Southern Materials Center.

Robinet, Isabelle. 1983. "*Le Ta-tung chen-ching*: Son authenticité et sa place dans les textes du Shang-ch'ing ching" [*Dadong zhenjing*: Its Authenticity and Its Place among the Texts of the Supreme Purity Scriptures]. In *Tantric and Taoist Studies in Honour of Rolf A. Stein*, edited by Michel Strickmann, 2: 394–433. Institut belge des hautes études chinoises.

Robinet, Isabelle. 1993. *Taoist Meditation: The Mao-Shan Tradition of Great Purity*. Translated from *Méditation taoïste*, 1979. State University of New York Press.

Robinet, Isabelle. 2011a. "Bajing." In *The Encyclopedia of Taoism*, edited by Fabrizio Pregadio, 210–211. Routledge.

Robinet, Isabelle. 2011b. "Basu jing." In *The Encyclopedia of Taoism*, edited by Fabrizio Pregadio, 219–220. Routledge.

Rogers, Michael. 1968. *The Chronicle of Fu Chien: A Case of Exemplar History*. University of California Press.

Schafer, Edward H. 1954. "Non-Translation and Functional Translation: Two Sinological Maladies." *Far Eastern Quarterly* 13 (3): 251–260.

Schafer, Edward H. 1977a. *Pacing the Void: T'ang Approaches to the Stars*. University of California Press.

Schafer, Edward H. 1977b. "The Restoration of the Shrine of Wei Hua-ts'un at Lin-ch'uan in the Eighth Century." *Journal of Oriental Studies* 15: 124–137.

Schafer, Edward H. 1978. "The Jade Woman of Greatest Mystery." *History of Religions* 17 (3–4): 387–398.

Schafer, Edward H. 1981–1983. "Wu Yün's Stanzas on 'Saunters in Sylphdom.'" *Monumenta Serica* 35: 309–345.

Schafer, Edward H. 1984. "Hallucinations and Epiphanies in T'ang Poetry." *Journal of the American Oriental Society* 104: 757–760.

Scharf, Robert. 2005. *Coming to Terms with Chinese Buddhism: A Reading of the "Treasure Store Treatise."* University of Hawai'i Press.

Schipper, Kristofer Marinus. 1975. Concordance du *Houng-t'ing king*: *Nei-king* et *Wai-king* [Concordance to the *Huangting jing*: *Neijing* and *Waijing*]. École française d'Extrême-Orient.

Schipper, Kristofer Marinus. 1993. *The Taoist Body*. Translated by Karen C. Duval. University of California Press.

Schipper, Kristofer, and Franciscus Verellen, eds. 2004. *The Taoist Canon: A Historical Companion to the Daozang.* University of Chicago Press.

Schlegel, Gustave. 1967. *Uranographie chinoise* [Chinese Uranography]. 2 vols. 1875. Reprint: Chengwen.

Shen Yue 沈約, ed. 1974. *Songshu* 宋書 [History of the Liu-Song]. Zhonghua shuju.

Sima Qian 司馬遷. 1997. *Shiji* 史記 [Records of the Historian]. Zhonghua shuju.

Smith, Thomas E. 1990 "Record of the Ten Continents." *Taoist Resources* 2 (2): 87–119.

Smith, Thomas E. 2011. "Qingtong." In *The Encyclopedia of Taoism*, edited by Fabrizio Pregadio, 803. Routledge.

Smith, Thomas E. 2013. *Declarations of the Perfected: Part One: Setting Scripts and Images into Motion.* Three Pines Press.

Smith, Thomas E. 2020. *Declarations of the Perfected: Part Two: Instructions on Shaping Destiny.* Three Pines Press.

Stanley-Baker, Michael. 2013. "Daoists and Doctors: The Role of Medicine in Six Dynasties Shangqing Daoism." PhD diss., University College of London.

Steavu, Dominic. 2009. "The Many Lives of Lord Wang of the Western Citadel: A Note on the Transmission of the Sanhuangwen 三皇文 (Writ of the Three Sovereigns)." *Journal of the International College for Postgraduate Buddhist Studies* 13: 109–162.

Stein, Rolf A. 1979. "Religious Taoism and Popular Religion from the Second to Seventh Centuries." In *Facets of Taoism: Essays in Chinese Religion*, edited by Holmes Welch and Anna Seidel, 53–81. Yale University Press.

Strickmann, Michel. 1979. "On the Alchemy of T'ao Hung-Ching." In *Facets of Taoism: Essays on Chinese Religion*, edited by Holmes Welch and Anna Seidel, 123–192. Yale University Press.

Strickmann, Michel. 1981. "Le Taoïsme du Mao chan: Chronique d'une révélation" [The Daoism of Mt. Mao: A Chronicle of a Revelation]. Collège de France, Institut des hautes études chinoises.

Tuzuki Akiko 都築晶子. 1995. "Rikuchō kōki ni okeru Dōkan no seiritsu" 六朝後期における道館の成立 [The Establishment of Daoist Lodges in the Six Dynasties]. In *Oda Yoshihisa hakushi kanreki jinen* 小田義久博士還暦記念 [Prof. Yoshihisa Oda's 60th Birthday Commemoration], 317–351. Ryūkoku daigaku.

Twitchett, Denis, and Michael Loewe, eds. 1995. *The Cambridge History of China*, vol. 1: *The Ch'in and Han Empires, 221 b.c.–a.d. 220.* Cambridge University Press.

Wang Chong 王充. 1996. *Lun heng* 論衡 [Balanced Discourses]. Zhonghua shuju.

Wang Gang 王崗 (Richard Wang). 2016. *Maoshan zhi* 茅山志 [Record of Mt. Mao]. Shanghai guji chubanshe.

Wang Ka 王卡. 1997. "*Huangshu* kaoyuan" 《黃書》考源 [A Study of the Origins of the *Yellow Book*]. *Shijie zongjiao yanjiu* 世界宗教研究 2: 69–77.

Wang Shuming 王叔岷, ed. 2007. *Liexianzhuan jiaojian* 列仙傳校箋 [Arrayed Traditions of Transcendents, Revised with Commentary]. Zhonghua shuju.

Wang Wenjin 王文錦, ed. 2001. *Li ji* 禮記 [Classic of Rites]. Zhonghua shuju.

Wang Yunwu 王雲五, ed. 1935. *Congshu jicheng* 叢書集成 [Compendium of Collected Works]. Shangwu yinshuguan.

Watson, Burton. 1968. *The Complete Works of Chuang Tzu*. Columbia University Press.

Wei Zheng 魏徵, ed. 1973. *Sui shu* 隋書 [History of the Sui]. Zhonghua shuju.

Welch, Holmes, and Anna Seidel, eds. 1979. *Facets of Taoism: Essays in Chinese Religion*. Yale University Press.

Xiao Tong 蕭統. 1983. *Wenxuan* fu kaoyi 文選附考異 [Critical Edition of *Selections of Literature*]. Yiwen yinshuguan.

Xingyundashi 星雲大師, ed. 2003. *Foguang da cidian* 佛光大辭典 [Buddha's Light Dictionary]. Foguang wenhua shiye youxian gongsi.

Xu Yuangao 徐元誥. 1998. *"Guoyu" jijie* 國語集解 [*Conversations of the States*, with Collected Commentaries]. 1998. Zhonghua shuju.

Xu Zhen'e 徐震堮, ed. 1989. *"Shishuo" xinyu jiaojian* 世說新語校箋 [A New Account of *Tales of the World*, Revised with Commentary]. Wenshizhe chubanshe.

Yoshikawa, Tadao 吉川忠夫. 1987. "Seishitsu kō" 静室考 [An Examination of Oratories]. *Tōhō gakuhō* 東方学報 59: 125–162.

Yoshikawa Tadao 吉川忠夫 and Mugitani Kunio 麥谷邦夫. 2000. *"Shinkō" kenkyū: Yakuchū hen* 「真誥」研究——譯注篇 [Annotated Translation of *Declarations of the Perfected*]. Kyōto daigaku Jinbun kagaku kenkyūjo.

Yuan Ke 袁珂. 1995. *"Shanhai jing" jiaozhu* 山海經校注 [*Classic of Mountains and Seas*, Collated and Annotated]. Liren shuju.

Zang Lihe 臧勵龢, ed. 1972. *Zhongguo gujin diming da cidian* 中國古今地名大辭典 [Dictionary of Modern and Ancient Chinese Placenames]. 1931. Reprint: Taiwan shangwu yinshuguan.

Zhang Shuangdi 張雙棣, ed. 1997. *"Huainanzi" jiaoshi* 淮南子校釋 [*Huainanzi*, Collated and Annotated]. Beijing daxue chubanshe.

Zhu Yueli 朱越利. 1998. "*Huangshu* kao" 《黃書》考 [An Examination of the Yellow Books]. *Zhongguo zhexue* 中國哲學 19: 167–188.

Zürcher, Erik. 1980. "Buddhist Influence on Early Taoism." *T'oung Pao* (66): 84–147.